THE REFERENCE SHELF

Vol. 18   No. 1

DUMBARTON OAKS

COMPILED BY
ROBERT E. SUMMERS

THE H. W. WILSON COMPANY
NEW YORK   1945

PREFACE

The Dumbarton Oaks Proposals are just six months old. The plan there outlined was admittedly tentative, and left many details to be added later. Yalta supplied several, and San Francisco is supposed to complete the picture. But the recency of the Proposals together with the generality of the plan set forth have served to keep both criticism and competent analysis to a minimum. Too little generally has been known about the Proposals to provide even a basis for argument.

There have been many criticisms, however, but they are based not upon the Proposals as such, but upon reputed inadequacies, upon points which the Proposals do not cover. That is the basis generally for the heavy volume of amendments which have been suggested from every conceivable source—various peace organizations, prominent individuals, and from various governments of the United Nations as well. The fact remains, however, that the criticisms thus implied are based largely upon conjecture and predictions as to what may be, not what is.

This volume attempts to limit criticism to the details of the Oaks plan itself, eliminating most of the criticism pertaining to points which will be covered at San Francisco. Every effort has been made to provide a comprehensive analysis of the background of international organization and the particular major problems which face nations as they attempt to establish such an organization at this time. Space did not permit much more than the barest analysis of the problem themselves, however. A more complete picture can be obtained through reference to the published materials of organizations which have devoted much study to the problems of international organization. Two such organizations are worthy of special mention: the Commission to Study the Organization of Peace, under the capable direction of Clark M. Eichelberger; and the Universities Committee on Post-war International Problems, representing college faculty study groups in more than forty major American universities.

For their kindness in permitting the reproduction of copyrighted materials which appear in these pages, the compiler is deeply indebted to the editors of the following periodicals:

American Business, the *American Mercury*, the *Annals of the American Academy of Political and Social Science*, the *Christian Science Monitor*, *Foreign Policy Reports*, *Fortune*, *International Conciliation*, *Life*, the *Nation*, the *New Republic*, the *New York Herald Tribune*, the *New York Times*, the *New York World-Telegram*, *Newsweek*, the *North American Newspaper Alliance*, *PM*, the *United Nations Review*, the *United States News*, *World Affairs*, and *World Federation Now*.

And to the following foundations and associations: American Academy of Political and Social Science, Carnegie Endowment for International Peace, the Commission to Study the Organization of Peace, the National Education Association, the National Catholic Welfare Conference, the National Opinion Research Council, the Universities Committee on Postwar International Problems, the Woodrow Wilson Foundation, and the World Wide Broadcasting Foundation.

R. E. Summers

April 20, 1945

CONTENTS

CONTENTS

CHAPTER I

THE BASIS OF INTERNATIONAL ORGANIZATION

Since the founding of this nation, the United States has been strongly isolationist. America's foreign policy stems from the single idea expressed by George Washington when he retired from the presidency with the admonition for this country to stay out of European affairs.

While his words have often been misinterpreted, his general meaning was clear. He realized, as did many other statesmen of the period, that politics in Europe was a fine art with which no homespun frontiersman could hope to cope. Benjamin Franklin, undoubtedly our ablest ambassador during the Revolutionary War, spent several years in a determined (and eventually successful) effort to win French support for the Colonial cause. He was willing, at last, to concede defeat, when success unexpectedly overwhelmed him.

Our experiences during this, our most crucial period, gave birth to the distrust of European political "horse-trading" which has characterized our public attitude ever since. Whenever our statesmen have chosen sides in one of the intermittent European feuds, it has meant that the United States usually came out the loser, with lowered prestige, and renewed determination to "mind our own business."

So, for nearly 160 years, our nation has consistently followed a policy of political isolation. At times, we have veered from this course, but the lapse was usually so brief or of so little political consequence that it cannot be considered a true departure from the general policy. Our foreign policy, in brief, has not prevented us from taking sides, or even kept us out of war. It has prevented us from making too many enemies abroad, and perhaps saved us from becoming too deeply involved in European affairs. But credit for the many decades of peace and security we have enjoyed cannot be given to our foreign policy. In a few instances, quite unintentionally, European power politics served to protect our neutrality. One notable instance is that which occurred during our Civil War. At that time a coalition of England and France could have taken over much of the American continent and firmly established the American Confederacy as a check-rein on the power of the United States on the American continent. In fact, there is an interesting parallel between the British foreign policy of that day and of our own just preceding World War II. Britain in 1861 offered the American Confederacy as much support, for all practical purposes, as the United States gave Britain in 1939. Everything, that is, except recognition as a nation. Unofficially, however, the Confederacy received economic support from the English, and received English-built warships (paralleling our own Lend-Lease transfer of over-age destroyers to England in this war). England scrupulously hewed to the line of legal isolationism, as did we until Pearl Harbor. But England was held in check by an imperialistic France. If the French threat had been removed from her back, if France and England had laid aside their firmly entrenched fears of each other (Napoleon, after all, had only been vanquished 45 years previously), England might well have risked war to aid the Confederacy. France did take advantage of our weakness as a nation and officially invaded Mexico, establishing a monarchy and laying plans for a possible reconquest of Texas, *if and when* the South won the war. Again, lack of unity prevented French designs. The danger of a powerful English fleet, a definite break in Anglo-French diplomatic relations over European internal affairs, forced Louis Napoleon to abandon his grand scheme of reconquest of the Americas (which, incidently, involved returning most of the independent nations of Latin America to Spain) and France and England returned to the European sphere for good.

The purpose, however, of this volume is not to judge European power politics. In the one instance quoted above, and in many others, the power politics which we deplore has operated in our interests. Many people now claim that we should thank England, whose powerful fleet and whose friendship with us has acted to check the powers of aggression in Europe from attacking the United States or other parts of the Western Hemisphere. I will say only this, whether power politics is good or evil is not the question. Perhaps England can be given most of the credit for our past security. But who has held England in line? Certainly during the Civil War, the England that wished to see the United States divided into two equal American powers was not prevented by motives of friendship. A strong France, even an aggressive France, was responsible for our ability to settle our domestic affairs without interference. And, as we see from the French invasion of Mexico, her opposition to Britain in this instance was not one based upon friendship toward the United States.

We must be realistic in our thinking about the nations of the world, particularly in planning our participation in a world organization for peace. We must forget the emotional aspects of the situation, and weigh the evidence. "Power politics," "spheres of influence," "bilateral treaties," "war as an instrument of policy," "buffer states," are only some of the phrases which are commonly used in reference to European (and even to our own) foreign policies. These expressions must be understood, and their implications as a factor for good or evil realized, now, before we actually set up a world organization.

In spite of all the neighborly expressions of goodwill and undying affection so freely issued by the governments of the United Nations, it must be remembered that no country, not even the United States, in the final test, serves any cause but that of self-interest. If that self-interest is served by power politics, by setting up a sphere of influence, or even by war, the nation will follow that policy and no other. It is only when national self-interest will apparently be enhanced that a national government will offer to cooperate with other nations. For that reason, the nations of the world today have indicated their desire for a world organization—not because they are necessarily friendly toward us or Britain or Russia (quite the contrary)—but because they feel that their best *protection*, their self-interest, lies in the setting up of such an organization.

But what are the issues involved here? For one thing, even though all of the United Nations are eager to participate in the organization of a new world order, all is not well at the council tables. The Big Three are under fire by the small nations for having settled too many problems affecting certain of the small nations, without consulting them (Poland, Greece and Italy). Eastern Europe feels itself menaced by the newly nationalist Russia, and bitterly criticized the results of the Yalta conference on the basis that it violates the Atlantic Charter which guaranteed the sovereignty of nations. Britain is critized for having apparently agreed with Stalin to split the pie of Europe into two equal segments, England to own one and Stalin the other, with the United States on the sidelines. This country receives a large share of European criticism for its very inactivity, its refusal to participate in the reorganization of Europe. Certainly, power politics are the order of the day, as General de Gaule emphasized with his refusal to serve as an "inviting power" at San Francisco because he felt that too many decisions had been made at Yalta affecting the peace of Europe, without debate by the parties concerned. In his estimation, any evils coming out of Yalta should never be attributed to French machination, and to accept the invitation to serve as a sponsor-power at San Francisco would, in effect, put France in the position of unreservedly approving the Yalta decisions. Indeed, criticism has been bitter, often justifiably so. If the situation is as black as it is pictured, it is no wonder that the small nations, and even the members of the Big Three, begin to take precautions individually, without waiting for the promised new order of things. There is fast developing a mad scramble by the nations of Europe, at least, to make treaties, economic pacts, monetary agreements, non-aggression pacts, pledges of eternal friendship—to pledge their good faith and hopes for peaceful cooperation now to relieve their fears as to what their neighbor might be thinking of doing later. In spite of the effective demonstration by Nazi Germany of the results of power politics, and the uselessness of "pieces of paper," there is still a desperate effort to renew all of the old familiar methods.

That is the first issue! The nations of the world are not in any true degree united. Although they are perhaps as ready as they ever will be to make concessions necessary to establish an organization for peace.

The second major issue involved is here in the United States. In 1939 and 1940, during the days of the "blitz," the halls of Congress rang with impassioned oratory opposing our aid to Britain and demanding strict neutrality in the letter of the law as followed for a century and a half by this nation. Public opinion supported the views thus expressed. We would not go to war. We would not meddle in Europe's domestic squabbles—or Asia's—or Africa's. *We* had three thousand miles of oceans between us and the German goose-steppers. Economists since the depression years had been harping on the same old subject— inter-dependence of nations. But, as usual, they were "theorists," "impractical dreamers", "brain trusters" and the like. War was very far away in 1939. Public opinion supported isolation, even though a large body of opinion was becoming increasingly critical of its dangers.

What was the result? Overnight (the night of December 7th), opinion reversed itself. The three thousand miles dwindled to the length of a city block. The "Yellow Peril" was practically in our backyard. Hitler's minions were a stone's throw from the White House. And not only did public opinion awaken to the changed world situation with regard to war, but to most of the many problems attendant upon war. Almost any suggestion as to cooperation in any sphere was widely approved. We suddenly made up our minds that the Russians had a lot in common with us, in spite of a different government. It was possible to get along with a country although perhaps you didn't like its plumbing. Latin Americans, usually thought of merely as country cousins, suddenly achieved a new status—brothers-in-arms. We realized, for the first time, just what it might mean for our own security if one of those quaint little countries south of the border should actually be unfriendly . . . and the glorious opportunity for Hitler's *unterseebooten* and *luftwaffe* the situation might provide. We discovered, in Latin America, for the first time, our own need for the friendship and assistance of every nation, regardless of how small.

The current sentiment favoring a world security organization stems definitely from the newly devoloped feeling of lack of security which Pearl Harbor engendered. This sentiment is most certainly commendable. Even if we recognize that it is synonomous with our self-interest—for our own security—it still provides the best opportunity in history for the setting up of an organization geared to accomplish something.

But this sentiment, this shift in public opinion to internationalism, can be exceedingly dangerous, both for us and the rest of the world. The danger lies upon the insecurity of its foundation. The American public has been far too long "out of this world," so to speak. We have not "meddled" in the affairs of Europe, but, therefore, we do not possess the degree of tolerance and understanding of the problems and fears of other nations, which is so necessary in building an effective instrument for world peace.

This fact is readily recognized abroad. Already, doubts as to the durability of American sentiment in favor of a peace organization have been expressed by leaders of several of the smaller European powers. They recall too vividly the days of the Peace Conference of 1919 and after when at the behest of Woodrow Wilson they jumped on a bandwagon to build a permanent "League of Nations." They particularly remember the sudden cooling of American sentiment, and point to the failure of the League to keep peace in the thirties as a direct result. They fear we may go back on our pledged word, even if we should join a new League. In the emotional stress of war, we cannot say definitely what our sentiment may be even one year from now, much less ten or twenty. We cannot imagine, however, ever breaking a pledge. Still, such events are possible, and it is exceedingly probable that once the war is over the American public will quickly tire of the bickering and squabbling of Europe and want to return mentally to the time-honored shell of isolationism once more. It is with this in mind that we think twice before we commit ourselves too enthusiastically to any program, particularly one that asks from us (although from the others as well) certain guarantees of force, of delegation of sovereignty, of economic and social adjustment—and particularly a program which, even in a limited sense, requires that we surrender our national rights to make our own decisions, such as whether we may have high tariffs or not, whether we can export certain commodities, whether we can interfere in a nation to protect our nationals there, whether we can independently declare war.

With these issues in mind before us, let us turn to the underlying problems affecting the establishment of world organization.

We know, simply, that a world organization is projected, that it seems like a good idea, so create it. But it isn't that simple. Besides the myriads of problems concerning individual nations which are continually cropping up, and which seemingly defy equitable decision, there are certain changed concepts, or changing trends in international affairs which should be recognized. In the following pages, these concepts have been defined, and as much as possible their relationship to international organization explained.

Naturally, the ideas here expressed on sovereignty, security, balance of power, etc., cannot possibly present the entire story. They should however supply a broad basis of understanding of the implications involved in that simple, all-inclusive phrase "organization for peace." Not only have our concepts about our own interests changed, but the concepts of people throughout the world have changed, about war, about peace, and particularly about the relationship of nations to each other. As newcomers to the field of power politics, we are "green" in even the barest essentials. We have a lot to learn, and accordingly cannot condemn any method of international operations such as "balance of power" or "spheres of influence" without seeking out its values and uses. What we learn and how effectively we learn it and use it, will determine our ability to compete effectively and in friendly spirit over the councils of the new United Nations Organization.

The battle for the peace is just beginning. Our statesmen must do their jobs well to protect our interests. Their ability to do so depends largely on our understanding of their problems and willingness to abide by their decisions.

THE NEW CONCEPT OF TOTAL WAR [1]

War in our time shares little but the name with the military conflicts in previous periods, including the nineteenth century.

[1] From "The Changing Nature of War," Albert Lauterbach, New School of Social Research. *Preliminary Report and Monographs.* Commission to Study the Organization of Peace. New York. p. 22-8. Reprinted by permission.

While warfare among primitive peoples involved a use of their entire resources, tiny as they were, later phases of social development confined war actions to comparatively small bodies of combatants and narrow sections of the national production. Although prolonged wars or major defeats occasionally resulted in such temporary effects as heavy taxation or disrupted transport, the manner of living outside the immediate theater of war was, as a rule, little affected.

Since the development of big industries, however, there has been an unmistakable trend toward extending the scope of military action by increasingly utilizing the tremendous new scientific possibilities of the modern world for systematic destruction. The World War, which had started in 1914 as a "partial" war on old patterns, ended with all belligerent countries attempting feverishly to make it "total." During the apparently peaceful twenties, a whole philosophy of "total warfare" was worked out by Ludendorff and others. . . .

Subsequently, various systems of totalitarian government were established on the lines of a total utilization of all national resources for definite political aims, the latter as a rule involving war and conquest. . . .

At the same time, military technique had undergone essential changes that adapted it to the technical level of our industrial society. Ever since the early large-scale employment of the machine gun in this century, the share of industry in the military equipment has been growing. Most of the new weapons, such as airplanes, tanks, and gas, are products of highly specialized factories. Infantry, cavalry, and artillery have been motorized and equipped with a high amount of automatic weapons. Mechanization has by no means replaced the mass armies with small bodies of specialists, as many people expected, and the actual trend has favored mechanized mass armies. In other words, destruction has been industrialized and "rationalized" up to the level of present-day technical and social organization. . . .

Most industries have become war-relevant in some respect. Peaceful cotton or rubber now belong to the outstanding items of the contraband lists, which tend increasingly to include any article going to or coming from an enemy country.

Gone are the times when war activities started after the outbreak of war and stopped after the truce. In and after 1914, an economic war organization had everywhere to be improvised. After the World War, and particularly in the thirties, all the Great Powers and many smaller countries took measures with a view to mobilizing their economy at a fast pace in case of war. While the military strength of a country had previously been measured according to her military manpower and armament, a new yardstick now arose: Raw material resources, output capacity for foodstuffs, size and location of heavy industries, number of skilled workers, and financial condition, all this together being called the "economic war potential."

During the Disarmament Conference, certain observers suggested that even under the optimistic assumption that all nations would destroy all stocks of arms existing at a given moment, world peace would still remain uncertain as long as the basic philosophy of certain governments favors war. For a while existing stocks of arms may be of importance in the initial phase of a war, the normal productive capacity of any industrialized nation is far more important; it would in itself give an opportunity to take up large-scale war production within a moderate space of time, if a possible economic war organization has been elaborated in advance. . . .

The Western powers, which had once started from the concept of "business as usual," elaborated in the thirties such emergency schemes as the British "shadow industries," the French Bill on the Organization of the Nation in Wartime, and the United States Industrial Mobilization Plan.

In any case, September, 1939, marked the transition from one phase of war to another, rather than from peace to war. For years, "peace" had only been a camouflage for a permanent state of war, in which alliances, methods and intensity of aggression, and resistance of the attacked, varied very widely. In certain cases, military conflicts were preceded by economic warfare for years. . . .

Growing expenditures, whether covered by taxation, loans, or increased money circulation, are only one sign of the restriction of private consmuption which is a dominating feature of military economy in the prewar, war, and postwar periods. In its initial phases, this may be hidden by certain temporary advantages resulting from a utilization of previously idle resources, such as unemployed manpower or capital. Later on, however, it becomes evident that the essence of military economy is both the biggest possible increase in national production and the greatest possible restriction of private consumption, thus leaving a maximum margin for accumulation and subsequent "consumption" of concrete, steel, shells, and torpedoes. . . .

Almost all the governments have embarked upon such measures in case of war or serious tension, but long-term preparations usually go even farther. Far beyond the general purpose of shortening the starting time of war economy, they often involve desperate efforts for self-sufficiency in essential raw materials and foodstuffs even where nature itself appears to forbid this. New industries are erected in, and old industries transferred to, regions which although far from the raw material bases as well as the markets, power plants, or transportation lines, are apparently safe from air attacks. Enormous stores of essential commodities are established without much regard to economic yardsticks such as cost of erection or maintenance of additional warehouses. Legislation to restrict profits from armament orders, or even all profits in wartime, is elaborated, though it is not always effective. . . .

Even far from the actual combat areas, there no longer exists such a thing as a noncombatant. Each individual is subject to all-embracing regulations of a centralized government, whose war preparations have, even in peacetime, more and more upset the competitive system and all previous conceptions of private ownership. Thousands of people, who declined planning or collectivization as peacetime principles, have readily accepted them for destructive aims.

Whoever conceives of war today as a number of preconceived military operations fairly in accord with peacetime-made schedules, lags far behind the actual development. War no longer, even primarily, a collision of limited military bodies in accordance with their long-term plans for such an event, but a mobilization of all the human and material resources of each nation for mutual mechanized destruction, which has largely displaced indi-

vidual gallantry or skill. Any discrimination between combatants and peaceful civilians is quickly fading, as is the distinction between objects of attack. A nation that wants to conquer
its enemy, and to prevent any prompt vengeance on the latter's
part, would, under the present psychological conditions, have to
destroy not only its armed forces but its industrial resources as
well, and to break permanently the whole morale of the enemy
population. In other words, a "total" victory can only mean a
physical extermination of substantial sectors of the enemy's population, and a destruction of all its essential industrial resources.
With each of the belligerents embarking on such a policy, the
result will be an indiscriminate and unrestricted mutual destruction.

While plans for military offensives may easily prove to be
vain in view of iron and concrete walls hundreds of miles deep,
no one can foretell which plants, buildings, or roads, may first
be hit by bombs, or which part of the industrial machinery may
first be worn out. In any case, the losses even in a "victorious"
war against a well-equipped enemy will be prohibitive. Of
course, a "total" war of a big industrialized nation against a
smaller and insufficiently equipped enemy may temporarily bring
quick success—as Poland's fate shows—or may even be "total"
only from the angle of the victim and not of the raider. In the
long run, however, even in this case a disastrous conflict between
great powers may develop.

A few months before the outbreak of the present war, and
perhaps a few months after, no one had any idea of even the
exact composition of the rival blocks of powers. This is but
one of the reasons why preconceived strategic plans are less
decisive of the actual course of a war than ever. What a
disastrous irony to consider a policy of conquest "realistic" under
the conditions of modern warfare! Even the last war, which all
belligerents expected to end within a few weeks, took more than
four years, and even in 1918 its final effects were just as little
foreseen by the victors as by the vanquished. Yet the present
war started again from the old Schlieffen ideas and the blockade,
while both sides in its early months were reluctant to embark
upon the unforeseeable path of total warfare. Our knowledge

of the factors which determine social development, insufficient even in peacetime, is reduced to a trifle in times of an industrialized war.

The conclusions for a new peace policy are evident. Peace in the present phase of social development involves more than a mere end to military operations, or even a destruction of existing stocks of arms, desirable as this would certainly be. Peace between industrialized nations in our days can only be based on a general understanding of the terrific implications of modern warfare. . . . In a world of unprecedented scientific possibilities, either for destruction or reconstruction, our task is to secure a determination of the great nations of the world to devote their economic policies in a future peace period to a steady increase of the standard of living rather than to preparations for the next war, and to abandon outmoded notions of sovereignty and political domination.

EFFORTS TO OUTLAW WAR [2]

War is a method, or a weapon, which may be used for various purposes, good or bad. Among these, it serves such functions as settling disputes, remedying wrongs, enforcing rights. No worse method of accomplishing these ends could be imagined, but human beings have as yet provided no accepted substitute; and until these human beings apply reason and intelligence to the problems of finding better means . . . war will continue to be used. A people will not forever submit to what they regard as injustice; and if there is no tribunal or legislature to which they can apply for the statement and maintenance of their rights, they will defend their own conception of those rights by the use of force. And so long as it is legitimate to use force for these purposes, and so long as each state is its own judge as to what its rights may be, so long may war be abused and employed for selfish aggrandizement. . . .

War was generally regarded, by philosophers, as immoral unless in self-defense or for the maintenance of rights; not all

[2] From "Aggression and War," by Clyde Eagleton, Professor of International Law, New York University. *Preliminary Report and Monographs.* Commission to Study the Organization of Peace. New York. p. 29-33. Reprinted by permission.

injuries required a resort to war, but in some cases war was not only a right but a duty. The difficulty which all these writers faced was the impossibility of securing an impartial judgment; and as nationalism developed, it was more than ever asserted that each state was the sole judge of its own rights. The international lawyer was, therefore, unable to fix the responsibility for a war, and abandoned as futile the distinction between just and unjust wars. War came to be regarded as a fact, like fire or earthquake, with which law could not deal.

Nevertheless, the concept of "just war" has never been abandoned in human thought. International lawyers were unable to say that war was illegal, but they did not admit that it was legal. Public opinion always inquired as to the reasons for which a war was fought, and vigorously took sides as to whether it was justified; statesmen found it necessary always to offer explanation for their wars, perhaps in the declaration of war itself, perhaps by propaganda. The great debate over responsibility for the World War illustrates this, as does current discussion. The pressure of public opinion, steadily increasing, has led to search for new criteria, and an effort was made to distinguish between the merits of the dispute itself, and the necessity for going to war over it. Arbitration was developed, and came to be regarded as a prerequisite to the use of force. The Bryan treaties sought to postpone resort to force until the merits of the dispute had been investigated. Certain areas, such as Belgium, were neutralized, thus limiting the use of war in these areas. The principle of responsibility for aggressive war was stated in Article 231 of the Treaty of Versailles, though in somewhat ex post facto manner. The difficulty in all this development was the lack of international judges or law to determine when war was justified and according to what criteria.

When the League of Nations was set up, substituting community judgment for that of the individual state, it became possible to advance. One of the purposes of the League was to "achieve international peace and security," through "the acceptance of obligations not to resort to war." It is to be noted that, under the Covenant of the League, the criteria for judgment as to whether a war was legal or illegal were not to be found in defense and aggression, in the military sense alone, for aggressive war (in the sense of first attack) might not always be illegitimate, and defensive war might be illegitimate. The Covenant, in this regard, was largely built upon the principle stated by Thucydides many centuries ago: "it is wicked to proceed against him as a wrongdoer who is ready to refer the dispute to an arbitrator." Articles 12-15 of the Covenant require submission of all disputes to pacific settlement, and go very far toward forbidding war when a solution has been offered; there are, however, a certain number of situations within which war remains legal. The sanctions of Article 16 can be used only against the state which resorts to war in disregard of Articles 12-15. Thus there are cases within which war would not be illegal, even though unjustifiable.

These gaps in the Covenant were known, and steady efforts were made to repair them; it was during this period that the word "aggressor" came into use. The Covenant employs this word only in Article 10, which does not have the backing of the sanctions of Article 16, and which fell into desuetude, though it is actually the most important principle of international government. "Aggression," according to the dictionary definition, means first or unprovoked attack; it has come to have a different, though as yet undetermined, connotation as a result of League discussions and popular usage. It has come to express an objective; it vaguely covers any war which ought to be made illegal.

By the Treaty of Mutual Assistance which was proposed in 1923, signatory states were to come jointly to the aid of a signatory which was the object of aggression; and aggressive war was declared to be an international crime. This necessitated a definition of aggression; and a committee was established to study this question. It reported that "no satisfactory definition of what constitutes an act of aggression could be drawn up"; and a committee of jurists, appointed to study the draft treaty, also objected to the word "aggression," and seemed rather to favor a statement in terms of a war licit or illicit under the terms of the Covenant. As a matter of fact, it is extraordinarily difficult to define aggression in such a way as to cover all cases of war which ought to be held illegal. Thus, under the terms of Article 13, a state is free to go to war against a state which refuses to accept an arbitral award; and the latter state is not free to fight back in self-defense.

In the following year, the Geneva Protocol was offered, the most intelligent effort ever made to strengthen the League of Nations. Meanwhile, an American committee had proposed what has probably been the most favored test of aggression: the state which employs force without resort to arbitration should be considered the aggressor. The Geneva Protocol set up certain automatic tests of aggression, largely carrying on this test. A state was presumed to be the aggressor which should resort to war without submission to pacific settlement under Articles 13-15, or without conforming to the award, or which might violate provisional arrangements made by the Council. Two difficulties arose, which need to be noted. In the first place, the definition of war in international law is uncertain; it might be better to use the broader term "use of force." And in the second place, the debate over aggression and defense raised a question as to whether these are proper criteria and whether the test should not rather be observance of obligations under the Covenant.

The Geneva Protocol, of course, failed of acceptance, and was replaced by the Locarno treaties, which distinguished between aggression and flagrant oppression, but left the meaning of aggression as uncertain as ever. The League continued the effort to find a definition. The Eighth Assembly declared that a war of aggression is an international crime. At the Disarmament Conference, the Soviet Government proposed a definition, which was incorporated into some nonaggression treaties, in terms which went far back toward the original definition of first attack. No definition, however, has ever been accepted; and Secretary Kellogg's interpretation of the Pact of Paris, recognizing to each state the right to determine what constitutes an act of self-defense, complicated the problem. At the same time, public opinion more vigorously than ever condemns aggression. . . .

The end which we seek is not a definition of aggression, but the elimination of violence between nations. It was not possible to think of such a possibility two decades ago, for the community of nations was not organized so as to perform the functions for which war had been used. It is not yet sufficiently well organized; but the experience of the League of Nations has given us enough light to find the main road again.

What we now have to do is to make the use of force the monopoly of the international government, and forbid its use by any state against another. If self-defense is required, its bona fide character must be judged by community tribunals, and not by the state which claims it. We are now able to have such a judge; and this changes the whole complexion of our thought, for it was the absence of the impartial judge which made impossible decision as to which state had improperly gone to war. We must have more, for war cannot be forbidden to a state unless the community is prepared to provide justice for that state. The organization of peace must, therefore, have the power to change existing legal or factual situations; and it must have the physical force with which to compel conformity with its decisions. When this is done, it will be possible to forbid the use of force by states. . . . The elimination of war must certainly be one of the objectives of the organization of peace, and to achieve it, the organization must be strong enough to substitute satisfactorily for the functions which have so long and so badly been performed by war.

DEFINITION OF SOVEREIGNTY [3]

Generally speaking, national sovereignty can be defined as the power of a state to take action equally binding upon all persons subject to its authority. The existence of this power is undoubted but its source has often been a subject of controversy. A view, generally accepted in democratic states, is that this power is derived from the people and that the government of the state is the agent of the people and exercises its powers within the limits and by the procedures determined by the fundamental law or constitution of the state, representing the popular will.

This national sovereignty, which in democracies rests in the last analysis in the people, has its internal and its external at-

[3] *Universities Committee on Post-war International Problems.* Problem XVI: "American Membership in a General International Organization: Constitutional Difficulties." July, 1944. p. 2-3. Reprinted by permission.

tributes. Internally, the sovereignty of the state, at least in a legal sense, is rather generally admitted to be absolute. The early writers on sovereignty were primarily concerned with the concept from this point of view. They were engaged in defending the sovereign state against rival contenders for authority, feudal or ecclesiastical, within the territorial limits of the state. The extent of a state's sovereignty in its external relations has become more recently a subject for discussion. Among those who have concerned themselves with the problem at least three different conceptions have won support:

a. National sovereignty may be regarded as a "concept of international law and hence as limited by the obligations which that law imposes upon members of the family of nations, including the obligation to observe their contractual engagements with one another." This theory of sovereignty has impressive historical support. That it was generally held by the founders of our nation is not open to question, and it has been invoked many times by the Department of State. It is consistent with the historical development of a supreme authority within the state and progressive subordination of such national authorities to certain rules of agreed-on conduct which we know as international law. In fact only if national sovereignty includes this capacity to enter into and accept binding obligations is any kind of international legal order possible.

b. According to an alternative view, national sovereignty is "an inherent characteristic of state existence as such, which is anterior to international law and membership in the family of nations, and which leaves its possessors always free in the last analysis to determine on the basis of interest alone the extent to which they shall observe the requirements of international law and of their engagements to other nations." On the basis of this conception an agreement to adhere to an international organization would not entail any real obligation, as it would leave the state free to determine its conduct on the basis of considerations of national interest. Such a conception of national sovereignty appears to be incompatible with the existence of an international legal order. It would lead necessarily to international anarchy.

c. A third view holds that the term "national sovereignty" has no application, "that the Family of Nations is the only real sovereign, and that the so-called sovereign nations are in the contemplation of international law merely its organs and appendages." Such a theory has little historical support, but nevertheless clearly interposes neither logical nor legal difficulties in the way of even a complete merging of existing nations into a world state.

THE THREAT TO NATIONAL SOVEREIGNTY [4]

In a world that is, de facto, a community of nations, the claim of each national state to sovereignty, or unbridled freedom, is as fantastic as the proposal of our political "anarchists" to dispense with civil law. Anarchy has never been seriously tried in any large community of men. Its most probable results are just too probable. Yet in the community of nations it is the prevailing system, and its actual results are exactly what one should expect. Where no law prevails, no higher authority than each member's own will determines rights and obligations, and the only duty of states is to advance their own interests, every neighbor is a potential enemy. Friendly neighbors are states that share some vital fear, and must needs make common cause against a foe whom neither could keep in check unaided. But when that fear is removed, there are no real bonds between nations; so the stanch allies of yesterday may be rivals and antagonists tomorrow.

The greatest obstacle to any help from this anarchy, i.e., to the creation of any worthwhile civil order, is the fact that national sentiment has made unlimited, ruthless egotism a moral ideal instead of a moral failing to be countered and controlled by institutions of justice. It is the "duty" of each state to advance its own interests even at the cost of untold suffering among other peoples; to take, by force if necessary, any strategic place that covers its borders; to withhold from others even the surplus of its wealth; and, above all, to brook no criticism,

[4] From "Make Your Own World," by Susanne K. Langer, author and philosopher. *Fortune*. 31:156-60+. March, 1945. Reprinted by permission.

respect no "natural rights" of others, and generally think of itself first, last, and always.

This complete rejection of all social responsibilities is the principle of sovereignty, which all patriots will defend with their lifeblood. Sovereignty is the "national honor"; not only dictation by another power, but even the thought of a universal authority, which would treat all states alike as legal persons, offends against that "honor." The highest expression of nationalism is the pride of sovereignty.

Now the sovereignty of a state is only as good as the power that defends it. It is not a "right" in any legal or moral sense because, as long as states do not recognize laws or moral obligations as binding upon them, there is no principle on which a right could rest, and no authority that could grant it. Sovereignty is simply a claim which is valid as long as no one is in a position to flout it. In the concert of nations, states are quite properly referred to as "powers," for that is all they are to each other—each one a sheer physical power, to be evaded, overcome, or pressed into use for one's own business.

The only way to avoid enslavement in a society without rights is to be beholden to nobody; and that means to be self-sufficient. This makes the scope of each country's needs practically unlimited. There are about sixty sovereign states, which have to share the world among themselves, each with the conviction that it "ought" to have the most desirable portions. Since each is afraid of becoming somebody else's vassal, each one must strive for self-sufficiency. It requires not only sources of food, oil, coal, and all other necessities, but exclusive control of these sources—in other words, possession.

As long as the states of Europe were the only "powers" they could go abroad for their resources. Europe is a tiny portion of earth; the outside world was so great that the mighty anarchists could allow each other's claims for a while. But now their expansion has reached its limit, and as their technology and their nationalist ideals spread over the globe, the non-European nations have themselves become powers, so the mushroom growths of European empire are shrinking again before those new claims of sovereignty.

That self-defeat of imperialism marks the end of the European era. For at this point the ideal of sovereignty, demanding as it does the self-sufficiency and mutual independence of all states, is operating in defiance of the world's actual, present setup. Economically the nations are more dependent on one another today than they have ever been in the world's history. Politically they are so involved with each other that the occupation of the remotest island by any power may cause a crisis or even a war among the nations.

NEW DELEGATION OF SOVEREIGNTY [5]

The oft-repeated objection to any system of collective security, that we must never sacrifice our sovereignty, is, in my opinion, a very red herring. In the minds of many the word "sovereignty" has some mystical connotation in some way associated with divinity.

In days gone by, when men were slaves, their masters imposed their will by an appeal to the divine right of kings. "Your sovereign by appointment from the All Highest" was the doctrine. By some peculiar quirk, today in this republic men talk as if the Federal Government is a sovereign body, above and apart from the people. Of course it is not. If sovereignty means anything, and resides anywhere, it means control over our own affairs and resides in the people. The people, according to our republican principles, are sovereign. They may delegate all, or any part, of the power to manage their affairs to any agency they please. So far they have delegated part to their city government, part to the county, part to the state and part to the Federal Government. We may recall that, under the Articles of Confederation, in 1781, our people delegated certain limited powers to the central government. When these powers proved inadequate, for the purpose of preserving order and tranquility, further powers were delegated under the Constitution of 1787. Does it make sense to say that in creating the Constitution and

[5] Excerpts from a radio broadcast by the Hon. J. W. Fulbright, U. S. Congressman from Arkansas, transcribed by the World Wide Broadcasting Foundation. New York. Program Number 19. Reprinted by permission.

establishing order our people sacrificed their sovereignty? On the contrary, they acquired through that delegation the means of preserving order and their individual freedom.

Certainly it cannot be denied that twice within twenty-five years we have been forced, against our will, into wars which have seriously threatened our free existence. To this extent, the supreme control over our affairs, over our destiny, is at present incomplete. Our sovereignty is imperfect. Therefore, if we can remedy this defect by a delegation of limited power to an agency designed to prevent war, to establish law and order, in which we participate fully and equally with others, how can this be called a sacrifice, a giving up of anything? Rather, I should say, it is the acquisition of something infinitely precious to civilized man. It is, of course, true that in saving our own freedom we may inevitably benefit other peoples of the world. But surely we will not refuse to save ourselves simply because in doing so we may help save others.

SOVEREIGNTY AND THE UNITED STATES [6]

The thirty-four cooperating groups which reported on this problem are almost completely agreed that there are no serious obstacles in the concept of "national sovereignty" or in the Constitution of the United States which need interfere with full participation by this country in a general international organization. They are inclined to believe that United States entry can be achieved by means of a treaty approved by two thirds of the Senate, and they tend to favor this method. However, the groups are almost unanimously agreed that an executive agreement, approved by a majority vote of both houses, would be entirely constitutional, and they hold that, should a recalcitrant group of Senators constituting a small minority block our entry by the treaty route, it would be desirable to overcome such a violation of the majority will by the joint resolution-executive

[6] From "American Membership in a General International Organization: Constitutional Difficulties," summary of the reports of 34 cooperating groups of the Universities Committee on Post-War International Problems. Released for publication, January 26, 1945. Reprinted by permission.

agreement procedure. Most of the groups believe that, eventually, but not in time for use on this occasion, a constitutional amendment can and should be adopted providing for the making of treaties by the President with the approval of a majority of both houses. . . .

Most of the groups regard the term "sovereignty" as variable in its meaning. For many people, its import is almost completely emotional. For nearly all, such cognitive meaning as it has is far from definite. Internally it signifies the supremacy of the state over rival claimants to power. Externally it denotes one thing for a small power, something else for a great power. As far as a state's relations to an international organization is concerned, the concept is in the developmental stage. Some six groups are inclined to believe that in practice many states regard sovereignty as a characteristic which leaves them "free in the last analysis to determine on the basis of interest alone the extent to which they shall observe the requirements of International Law and of their engagements to other nations." This view is generally deprecated as inconsistent with the reign of law among states and the moral obligation of states to observe their agreements.

The vast majority of the groups believe that states should regard sovereignty as limited by the obligations which international law imposes upon them including the obligation to observe their contractual engagements with one another. According to this view a state would be less than sovereign if it could not enter into binding agreements or join an international organization and assume obligations as a member of it. This is the view, most of the groups agree, which law-abiding states have professed and, in the main, have followed. . . .

The groups are almost unanimously agreed that there are no principles inherent in the Constitution which are inconsistent with our entrance into an international organization for the maintenance of peace. There is no opposition whatever to the view that the supreme power of the Federal Government in foreign affairs is well established both in practice and by judicial ruling. Nor is there any belief that our entrance into an international organization would conflict with any private rights guaranteed by our Constitution.

THE CONCEPT OF PEACE [7]

Much harm has been done to the cause of a constructive peace by the popular misunderstanding of the nature of peace and by the tendency to identify the term "peace" with the maintenance of the status quo. If peace is to be no more than a negative term, indicating the repression of violence without any reference to the conditions that make for violence, if it is to mean the absence of war on the battlefield when all the while economic and social forces are preparing the way for military conflict, then clearly what we have is merely an "armed peace," which is but the prelude to future war.

But even if "peace" is coneived in its broader and positive meaning, as the "tranquillity of order" based upon justice, it is clear that if any community, whether individual nation or family of nations, is to attain that happy conditions its primary task must be the repression of violence. Here the analogy with the domestic law of the state is not only suggestive but compelling. Long ago it was recognized that there can be no peace within the state if each citizen is to be allowed to take the law into his own hands and enforce his claims by his own armed might. It matters not how good he believes his claim to be, violence is forbidden him, and any resort to it is unlawful and punishable even though it should subsequently appear that the claim itself, by judgment of the courts, was a just one. To this extent the law of the state defends existing personal and property rights, it protects the status quo, to use the phrase of international law; and it does so even when, on occasion, there is reason to believe that abstract justice might call for a different decision. The state makes no compromise with violence, simply because it recognizes that if resort to violence is permitted to the individual citizen, nothing but anarchy would result, and whatever minor injustices might attend the status quo would be outweighed a hundred times by those attending a general condition of lawlessness.

[7] From "The Concept of Peace," by Charles G. Fenwick, Professor of Political Science, Bryn Mawr College, and writer on international law. *Preliminary Report and Monographs.* Commission to Study the Organization of Peace. New York. p. 182-4. Reprinted by permission.

As between citizens, so between nations the repression of violence must be the paramount obligation of the international community, to which all others are subordinate. The old right of each nation to be the judge in its own case must be definitely repudiated; the old right to declare war at will must be rejected without compromise. Under no circumstances must a nation be permitted to take the law into its own hands; and if it should do so; it must find ranged against it the organized community of nations which will see in its act of violence an attack upon the principle of law and order and, therefore, an attack upon each member of the community individually.

But if the international community is to be able to repress violence successfully it must first of all make provision for the ordinary administration of justice, that is, it must set up agencies of pacific settlement competent to adjust the claims of states upon the basis of principles accepted as the law of the community. Not all disputes between nations are of such a character; those arising out of political, as distinct from legal, issues require separate treatment. But the controversies arising out of differences of opinion as to legal rights, i.e., rights based upon the application of accepted general principles to concrete situations, can properly be required to be submitted to arbitration or to regularly established institutions, such as the Permanent Court of International Justice. The pacific settlement of controversies that have come to be known as "political disputes" may require adjustment by less formal methods, such as the procedure of conciliation as distinct from arbitration. The existence of these political disputes is due to the fact that international law has failed to develop rules covering many of the most important relations of states, so that it is impossible to refer them to "judicial settlement" for lack of a legal basis of decision. In turn, the failure of international law to develop these rules is due to the defective organization of the international community and the inadequate conceptions of law, order, peace, and justice which have hitherto prevailed. . . .

So must it be also between nations. Unless international law can be developed so as to become a means of remedying wrongs, an agency for the needs of each and every member of the international community, there can be little hope of preventing re-course to violence by those members of the community who believe themselves to be the victims of intolerable wrongs. "Peace" is thus conceived to be something dynamic, something which can only be obtained by the constant effort of the international community to make its rules of law correspond with the changing conditions in the relations of states and the growth of new needs for which the existing law has made no provision simply because they did not exist at the time its rules were formulated. Here we are confronted with the most important and the most difficult task of a constructive peace movement—the most important task because unless it is undertaken, there is no hope of repressing violence, and the most difficult task because of the many conflicts of national interest and the complicated character of the issues that must inevitably be presented to the organized community for solution. What shall constitute "tolerable conditions of living" for nations is more complicated than the corresponding problem between individual citizens. It may well be that there is no solution for a number of the present conflicts of national interest on the basis on which the particular nations take their stand; and it is possible that the solution may have to be sought by changing the underlying conditions that give rise to the dispute, by creating a new body of interests common to the whole community which will make the particular national interest seem less pressing.

Such must be the legislative task of the organized international community if it is to build a constructive peace capable of standing whatever strains may be put upon it. It is a task which calls not only for statesmanship of the highest order, but for a recognition on the part of the leading governments that many of the national interests which they have hitherto sought to advance by isolated national action may in the future have to be advanced by cooperation with other nations in the pursuit of the common good of the international community. If this means that a price must be paid for peace; it also means that if such a peace can be obtained, the price that has been paid for it will be many times repaid. A stable peace, a peace based upon justice, a peace in which the great majority of nations have such a stake that their overwhelming weight can be counted upon on the side of law and order—such a peace awaits the world when public opinion in the leading countries comes to realize what it would mean in terms of their own ideals and material interest.

THE SECURITY BASIS FOR PEACE [8]

International peace means not merely the absence of war, but justice and order in international relations. Justice is not to be achieved by yielding to each what he demands nor by preserving for each what he has but by submitting every controversy to a fair and adequate procedure for dealing with claims upon their merits. This means not merely the utilization of existing procedures to apply the law to the facts, nor even the continuous utilization of existing procedures to improve the law, but also improvement of procedures of international adjudication, conciliation, legislation, and administration whenever the justice of the existing procedures is challenged or has become obsolete. Order does not mean the perpetuation of a status quo (which would prevent progress), the elimination of controversy (which would prevent variety), nor even elimination of the use of force (which would prevent self-defense or law enforcement), but the adherence by individuals, nations, and international institutions to established procedures in settling disputes, in administering services, in making and enforcing law, and in changing such procedures themselves when justice requires and knowledge permits.

Peace will continually be endangered if certain states persistently attempt to augment their own power so as to dominate over others. Such attempts at domination are likely if the government or people accept the theory that the state exists for itself alone. The remedy for this condition lies in general acceptance of the theory that the state exists for the benefit of its people and of humanity. Such acceptance implies practical guar-

[8] From "Peace and Political International Organization," by Quincy Wright, Professor of International Law, University of Chicago. *Preliminary Report and Monographs*. Commission to Study the Organization of Peace. p. 240-47. New York. Reprinted by permission.

anties by the international order for assuring respect for fundamental human rights. The problem of peace may, therefore, be
approached from the political, the economic, the social, and the
legal points of view.

The desire of states to augment national power relative to
others is the immediate cause of many wars. This danger will
persist so long as it is not controlled by the superior power of
the family of nations, properly organized, giving greater security
to all. The lack of such organization encourages the hopes and,
therefore, the ambitions of aggressive-minded governments, and
sustains the popular opinion identifying the individual's welfare
with the power of his state.

Self-sufficient national wealth may provide the objective of
which power is the instrument, or the instrument of which power
is the objective. In either case demand for economic self-sufficiency often lies in the background of war, and must be met by
freer trade assuring more opportunity and more wealth for all
through division of labor.

Depression and unemployment lead to misery and discontent,
attitudes favorable to philosophies of revolution and violence.
Such attitudes may be directed toward a striving for national
power as an escape and a striving for national self-sufficiency as
a defense. Far from remedying conditions which gave rise to
them, such efforts often make the situation worse precipitating a
downward spiral toward war. . . .

A sense of injustice in domestic and international relations
adds fuel to fires kindled by political and economic rivalries and
social misery, and may engender popular support for tyranny and
conquest in the name of equality but subversive of liberty, or for
revolution and insurrection in the name of freedom but subversive of equity. Either may contribute to war and can only be
remedied by the development of law and procedure, better to
assure justice both to individuals and to nations. . . .

Security, whether economic or political, results from confidence in the stability and continuity of the whole by all or nearly
all of its parts. In the present interdependent world, security,
both for individuals and nations, depends on confidence in the
stability and continuity of the world order as a whole. The

powers of individuals, groups, and nations must be so limited that the function of each in the world society, and the procedures which will be used to effect changes are known in advance. Security implies the existence of a society and that implies the existence of a law. National security, therefore, depends upon a general respect for and confidence in international law, and the establishment of such respect and confidence requires a better organization of the world community.

The experience of human history shows that political institutions do not flourish if wholly lacking the support of custom. New institutions may establish themselves in time, if they serve essential interests, but those will do so most rapidly which avoid radical breach in continuity with the past—evolutionary changes are more likely to be lasting than revolutionary changes. Thus, institutions to improve the organization of the world community should, so far as possible, be natural developments from those that already exist.

One important exception exists in the case of material sanctions to enforce law. Such sanctions are either adequate to enforce the law in so large a number of cases that they create confidence among those subject to the law, or they are not. If they are not adequate, subjects of the law will not abandon the right of self-help, or if they do abandon it will become victims of their own confidence in an inadequate system as did Ethiopia and Czechoslovakia. If the force of a state is adequate to defend its own right, it will also be sufficient in some cases to defy the law. Consequently an unorganized balance of power system contains no guaranty against lawlessness. As a result of these circumstances, the establishment of a system of international sanctions assuring that the power behind law is greater than the power of any lawbreaker or any probable combination of lawbreakers, cannot take place gradually. Unless such sanctions are made sufficiently powerful all at once, they may be worse than useless.

Material sanctions whereby the community as a whole preserves the continuity of its law by preventing or remedying departures therefrom by the members have been classified in the international field as positive or negative in character. Positive

sanctions imply a military or police force, permanently constituted
or developed ad hoc through contribution of contingents by the
members, capable of subduing the law violator and thereby
inducing him by threats or by coercion to desist from wrong-
doing and to remedy injuries due to his acts. Negative sanctions
imply a withholding from the law violator of advantages which
he would otherwise have received, particularly of the economic
requirements essential for carrying on his aggressions. The two
may be combined, as in a naval blockade, which may contribute
on the one hand to disarming the enemy and occupying his
territory and on the other hand to withholding from the enemy
the materials of international trade which would contribute to
his aggressions and even to his life. Positive sanctions always
imply action against the law violator's territory or armed forces,
while negative sanctions may be carried out entirely by commercial or other regulations within the territory of sanctioning
governments.

Positive or military sanctions decrease in effectiveness as the
area within which they function increases. A military force
becomes less effective in proportion as its line of communication
from its base increases. Governments have, therefore, tended to
limit their policies dependent on military support to regions
near their homelands or capable of control through their navies.
Furthermore, governments are less interested in conditions in
remote regions and so are more reluctant to assume the burden
of military action in such regions. It appears, therefore, that
military sanctions in international organization are more likely
to be effective if regionally organized.

Negative or economic sanctions, on the other hand, increase
in effectiveness as the number of states applying them increases.
A lawbreaking government can draw supplies from all quarters
of the world. One large state may be able to supply the aggressor
with what it needs and discourage the application of economic
sanctions by the others. Consequently, if sanctions are to applied,
not by navies but by embargoes, they must be universal. . . .

Unless there is sufficient general unification to make resorts
to violence or breach of the common law rare, authoritative
central control of any particular function is likely to prove im-

practicable, because such control involves sacrifices of liberty or local autonomy which will not be willingly accepted by any, unless all can be sufficiently controlled to assure the general benefit which would arise from fulfilment of the objective. Without general confidence that the objective will be achieved, neither individuals nor nations will voluntarily give up their liberties to a superauthority. For this reason proposals for improved world organization involving sacrifices of national sovereignty must be sufficiently thoroughgoing to make success relatively certain if the proposal is once accepted. Sovereignty will not be given up with respect to even a few functions unless the authority vested with these functions operates in an organization assuring general observance of law and order.

For this reason international cooperation, developing as it has in a milieu of little general security, has seldom established world-wide authorities with power to act, but has relied on parallel action by national governments on the basis of general treaties or on coordinating systems designed to secure general agreement of all interested governments at every stage of action. Such systems have been effective in noncontroversial matters, such as postal service and narcotics control, but in matters affecting national power, such as armament and trade regulation, they have not been effective. Central authorities with powers of action might under suitable conditions be more efficient in all such cooperative activities, but they are not likely to be set up, nor would they be able to function in any field, until there is greater confidence that law and order has been secured in the world.

PROBLEMS OF ORGANIZING FOR PEACE [9]

In the community of nations today there is some organization. There is the body of international law, the network of treaties, the system of diplomacy, the numerous international

[9] From "Fundamental Problems of International Organization," by Quincy Wright, Professor of International Law, University of Chicago. *Preliminary Report and Monographs*. Commission to Study the Organization of Peace. p. 255-74. New York. Reprinted by permission.

unions, the International Labour Organization, the Permanent Court of International Justice, and the League of Nations, all of which recognize the status of some or all states and define many of their relationships. . . .

The phenomena of a shrinking world and of rapid change have increased the probability both of conflict and of violence developing from it, unless the effectiveness of community regulation increases comparably. Transition from the horse-and-buggy age to the automobile age would result in more frequent collisions and accidents, unless an adequate system of traffic regulation were adopted by the community. The serious conditions of conflict and disorder in the world today are due to the inadequacy of international organization. . . .

More organization seems particularly necessary in the fields of international adjudication, military preparation and action, and economic regulation. . . .

International controversies have become more frequent and more serious. While as a result of these changes many states have ratified arbitration and conciliation treaties, the optional clause of the Statute of the Permanent Court of International Justice and the General Act of Geneva agreeing to submit future disputes to some form of adjudication or conciliation, this system is not complete. Some states are bound by very few such obligations and few states are bound to submit all disputes to a peaceful procedure assuring a definitive settlement. . . .

War has become more destructive of life, property, and economic processes in proportion as it has become totalitarian. Military inventions have made it practicable to attack the national economy and morale directly while political and economic development has made it possible to coordinate the activities of the entire population and the national economy to a unified military effort. These changes have induced the acceptance of certain conventional obligations limiting armaments, qualifying the right to resort to armed force, or renouncing war altogether, but these conventions have been limited in scope, short in life, or lacking in observance. . . .

Among the important developments of the modern world have been the increase in population; the invention and use of rapid means of communication, travel, and transport; the increase in the proportion of people engaged in industry; the movement from subsistence to cash-crop agriculture; the increase in international trade; the growth of dependence of the industrialist, the laborer, the farmer, and the consumer for his income and the articles which he uses, or consumes, upon distant foreign markets and sources of raw material. This has created new insecurities, especially when interruption of the delicate mechanism of economic exchange is threatened by unexpected political actions in raising tariffs, modifying exchange rates, imposing embargoes, or resorting to war or violence. The latter often results in complete isolation of certain areas from international commerce.

Under general international law it is within the domestic jurisdiction of the sovereign state to regulate its external trade, its merchant marine, the navigation of its ports, its immigration as it sees fit. While most states are bound by many treaties providing for most-favored-nation treatment in matters of commerce and navigation or even limiting the height of tariffs or eliminating commercial barriers of certain types, they have usually reserved powers in many important questions, have limited the applicability of the treaties in time, or have excluded war, neutrality, or sanctions from their operation. The insecurities resulting from the vulnerability of international trade, through the arbitrary action of a single state, particularly since the experience with World War blockades and embargoes, has induced many states to attempt to make themselves economically self-sufficient, either for purposes of defense or in preparation for aggression. This effort has resulted in new barriers which, while economically injurious to the states imposing them, have often been even more injurious to the economy of other states. Thus, the downward spiral of economic insecurity, higher economic barriers, greater tensions, more political insecurity, further augmentation of economic insecurity has proceeded.

With the development of a more integrated economy, national governments have found it necessary increasingly to regulate economic life. Sometimes this regulation has been to secure freedom of economic enterprise under fair competition and sometimes to plan production and distribution directly. The first method has the longest experience back of it and requires less intensive control by centralized authority. The latter method seems to require the limitation of consumer demand and considerable control of opinion, both subversive of individual liberty. It thus appears that in the community of nations the first method of regulation would be more appropriate, and its essential feature is the restriction of monopoly, both private and public, and the assurance of fair methods of competition. It appears that the principle of limiting the power of states arbitrarily to interfere with international commerce needs a broader application in inter-tional affairs.

These three aspects of national sovereignty, the power of self-judgment in international controversies, the power to prepare and use armed force in international relations, and the power to impose arbitrary barriers to international trade, are in most need of limitation. Reciprocally, international organization should be developed to assure the definition, application, and enforcement of such limitations upon national sovereignty. . . .

Any international organization will have to start on the presumption of national sovereignties and the limitation of most governing authorities to the areas of those sovereignties. It is only where authorities so limited are clearly incapable of handling a problem which has become pressing, that international political organization should be considered.

Of those matters which come within the scope of international organization, there is no reason in principle why all should be handled by authorities with the same geographic competence. Some may require universal competence; others may require continental competence; others competence confined to the basin of a particular river or lake system, to an area subject to particular diseases or nutritional problems, to an area linked by a particular railroad network, to areas whose populations have similar standards of living, culture, or civil liberty, to areas peculiarly bound together by international trade and economic interdependence. Where an authority is needed with a competence transcending national boundaries, it is believed that the nature of the particular problem should determine the geographic limits of that competence. . . .

International legislation and international unions have usually been open to ratification by all states, but in most cases certain states have refused to ratify and by so doing have limited the area in which the organization can function, sometimes seriously affecting its efficiency. In recognition of this possibility general conventions have occasionally expressly asserted that they will not come into effect until ratified by a specified list of states. Thus, the Geneva Arms Trade Convention of 1925 was not to go into effect until ratified by the fourteen states mainly engaged in that trade. But, while the exclusion of a particular area may cause difficulties in efficient administration, the inclusion of an area inhabited by unwilling people may also cause difficulties. The question of whether the democratic principle of consent should be sacrificed to administrative efficiency, or whether the authoritarian principle of administrative efficiency should be sacrificed to consent of the governed, arises here as in all problems of government. . . .

In the present world each state may have controversies with any other, the effects of war, preparations for war and threats of war are world-wide, and no regional limits can be drawn to commercial interdependence. While subordinate regional authorities may be useful . . . particularly for organizing military sanctions, a world court, a world organization for limiting armaments and determining aggression, and a world economic authority are needed . . . .

Positive sanctions cannot be effective without a military or police force more powerful than any probable combination of law breakers. The efficacy of military force diminishes as the distance of its operations from its base increases. Such a force might be established, and be effective if national governments were in large measure disarmed, particularly if they were deprived of the most important instruments of aggression. . . .

While the initiation and definition of the competence of such an international police force should be a regional problem, the type of offenses which would render a government liable to the operation of military sanctions might best be determinable by world authority, thus assuring impartiality in judgment. That authority should be competent to decree interim or conservatory measures whenever aggression in violation of fundamental covenants is threatened and violation of such interim measures might be taken as the prime element in determining the aggressor. If the action of a regional police force were limited to occasions when such decisions had been made by world authority, the tendency for such a force to become an instrument for developing the hegemony of a particular power in the region could be reduced. . . .

The distinction between a league or confederation, in which central authority operates only upon states, and a union or federation, in which central authority operates on individuals with respect to certain functions is never a sharp one. Even in the community of nations some individuals, such as inhabitants of mandated territories and minorities, have a limited access to international procedures by petition, and the procedure of arbitrating international claims of individuals often approximates judicial action between a state and a foreign individual, though in theory the party is the claimant's state. Such institutions have reached such a development that some international lawyers consider that the individual is already a subject of international law. . . .

In regional international organizations a larger competence of the regional authority might be established directly over individuals in such matters as recruiting the regional police, certain forms of taxation, and the regulation of communication, transport, and commerce within the region. . . .

Another characteristic which may dangerously enhance the status of the members of a federation is the right of secession. Undoubtedly, the assumption, which arises from the existence of this right, that the organization is merely contractual and temporary, seriously militates against its capacity to preserve peace. This has been illustrated by the disposition of the members of the League of Nations to withdraw whenever serious opposition to their policies has been manifested within the League. On the other hand, the denial of the right of the states to secede from the American Union led to the Civil War. The British Commonwealth of Nations has moved toward recognition of the right of secession by the Dominions, and the Constitution of the

Soviet Union asserts that such a right belongs to the Soviet republics. . . . It appears that an organization designed to preserve peace should not recognize the right of secession. Peace can only develop if the members view the organization as permanent and organic and are prepared continually to adjust their policies of life within the union. The organization must be capable of yielding to demands for change soon enough, or of resisting them overpoweringly, so as either to satisfy or to eliminate the grievances which might lead to demands for secession, and to maintain the faith that problems can only be solved by the utilization of procedures which the organization permits. . . .

International organization has in the past been based on the hegemony of great states in a region, on an equilibrium between the Great Powers, or on a concert of the Great Powers, and the small states have existed only on sufferance slightly influenced by the precepts of international law or on mutual jealousies among the great. The League of Nations attempted a more democratic organization resting on the equality of states, though the more general influence of the Great Powers was recognized in the organization of the Council. Though the equality of states has been a dogma of international law, it may be doubted whether an organization based on the complete equality of states would be either practicable or in a broad sense democratic. It would greatly overweight the political influence of the citizens of small states. Thus, if Panama and the United States had equal influence in a world organization, each Panamanian could exercise a weight equal to more than two hundred citizens of the United States. Democracy would seem to require that the larger population should exercise more political influence. Federations have always compromised between the equality of states and the equality of individuals and an effective world organization would have to do the same. While in international organization, states as such should enjoy equality before the law, in the sense that each should have equal opportunity to enforce respect for its rights, it is doubtful whether they should have equality of political power. . . .

A political organization, however, to be effective must maintain a balance between procedures to enforce limitations of the power of the members, necessary to maximize the liberty of all, and procedures to exercise powers of the whole, necessary to equalize the opportunities of all. As societies become more integrated and more dynamic, the restrictive, police government, tends to give way to the constructive, service government. . . .

The advance of international cooperation beyond the stage of procedures for coordinating action in any given field must, therefore, await the organization of security against violence, of general respect for the common law, and of fundamental procedures for change.

The problem of international organization after the war should be to gain recognition, both internationally and constitutionally, of certain limitations of national sovereignty, and of the powers of international bodies, universal, regional, and functional, essential to a peaceful, stable, and progressive international order. Such international bodies may then gradually provide for exercising their powers in order to improve the lot of man and to develop a sense of loyalty to the world order.

THE BALANCE OF POWER CONCEPT [10]

The principle of the balance-of-power . . . means the balancing of potential enemies and potential allies among the nations of the world into two groups which are kept from springing at each other's throats by the equilibrium of their strength. Within such a scheme every great power strives to be in a position of holding the balance between the rival camps, so that by the threat of throwing its weight in one direction or another it can dominate world politics, and thus ride in the whirlwind and command the storm. There are many today who believe that we shall never transcend this principle: that on the one hand wars are inevitable because they are based on aggressive drives within the individual, and, on the other hand, that international cooperation on a world scale is a utopian pipe dream. They argue that the best plan for America is therefore to try to estab-

[10] From "International Organization After the War," analysis by Max Lerner, Professor of Political Science, Williams College; and Edna Lerner. Problems in American Life Series, Unit no. 15. p. 25-6. National Education Association. Washington. 1943. Reprinted by permission.

lish the sort of balance-of-power in the postwar world which it will be able to dominate. Thus a typical spokesman for this school of thought . . . urges that we plan to maintain in Europe a strong postwar Germany as a counterpoise to the strong Russia that will emerge from the war, and that we strive to maintain in the Far East a strong Japan as counterpoise to the strong China that will emerge from the war. This is exactly the tactic pursued in the past by one world power after another, more recently by Great Britain, and it is the tactic which has resulted in successive wars of annihilation.

A variant of this thesis is the proposition that world order can be established best by the might and prestige of one power. Some have urged that Britain and America together would constitute such a power and Anglo-Saxony could play the role for the modern world that the Pax Romana played in the ancient. Henry Luce, in a now famous editorial published in *Life* in February 1941 urged that the coming century be the "American Century": that we control the world sea-lanes and world trade, establish a world imperium, send out technicians to develop the world and educators to teach it, and food cargoes to feed it, and ideals to inspire it. Just why the Russians, the Chinese, and the anti-fascists all over the world should be fighting this war if this is to be its goal is not quite clear.

Others see American power as only one of the imperialistic forces in the world: they see a British, a Russian, and even perhaps a Chinese imperialism. They want America to assume the leadership of the American continent, including the Latin American countries and Canada, so that together we may outdo the other imperialisms. This concept has sometimes been called *Continentalism*. It is part of the balance-of-power scheme, except that it runs in terms of vast imperialisms in conflict, rather than in terms of alliances of nations.

In all these variants of the balance-of-power idea, the task of the postwar settlement would be that of a twentieth-century Congress of Vienna, with the great powers getting together to restore order and legitimacy and suppress the revolutionary forces which would threaten all the imperialisms. Such a program is blind to the fact that Europe has needed reorganization for centuries, and that her plight cannot be solved by a return to the Europe of 1938. Unfortunately, some of the commitments into which we have already entered—for example, the Atlantic Charter, which aims "to see sovereign rights and self-government restored to those who have been forcibly deprived of them"—plays into the hands of such a program. If this principle becomes the criterion of postwar organization, we run not only the danger but the virtual certainty of preparing the tinder for another world war.

REALISTIC APPROACH TO POWER POLITICS [11]

The Monroe Doctrine is the frankest and clearest declaration of an exclusive sphere of influence in the world. We say it is necessary to our security. We insist on it as a guarantee against aggression. At the close of the war we should, and probably will, insist on something similar in the Pacific. Can we blame other countries for doing the same thing? Can we say that in their case spheres of influence promote wars, while in our case the same principle is only a necessary safeguard of security? . . .

The problem of the sphere of influence always presents itself, and has always presented itself throughout human history, wherever there are small nations in proximity to relatively larger ones. . . .

Of course a sphere of influence may be abused. It may be employed to enable the larger power to dominate, exploit, and oppress the smaller one, meddle in its internal affairs, and in effect deprive it of self-government. We do not believe we have done that under the Monroe Doctrine, and impartial history will no doubt acquit us, but voices will not be wanting to challenge our innocence. As a matter of fact, whenever a sphere of influence is asserted, it will always be charged that the independence of the smaller power is impaired. It need not be, except in the one particular of preventing the smaller nation

[11] From an address entitled "Peace, Realism, and the Balance of Power," by Hon. John Dickinson, general counsel of the Pennsylvania Railroad and former Assistant Secretary of Commerce, before the midwinter meeting of the Maryland State Bar Association, January 20, 1945.

from making trouble, or letting itself be used to make trouble for the larger one. Such an impairment is essential in the interest of peace. If not imposed by a larger power itself, under the sphere-of-influence principle, some other and possibly more uncertain method of imposing it will have to be found.

The source of hostility to the sphere-of-influence principle is a sentimental insistence on the right of small nations to do as they choose and make as much trouble as they please, a right which is of course denied to larger countries. This sentimental claim of weak nations is one which throughout history, from the time of ancient Greece, has always been abused, and has in fact been one of the most prolific causes of war. . . .

What of the balance of power? The balance of power is simply the oldest and most elementary device to accomplish the object we are today pursuing in our war against Hitler—to keep one nation from ruling the earth. The principle of the balance of power is that no single power shall be allowed to dominate the international scene—that power should be so subdivided and balanced between nations that no nation shall be strong enough and dominant enough to threaten and overawe the freedom of the rest.

Thus the principle of the balance of power is the necessary corrective and counterpoise to spheres of influence and colonial empires. One of the strongest and most valid objections against these is that they encourage a tendency toward expansion, aggression, and excessive power. The principle of the balance of power sets itself in opposition to that tendency. It aims to insure that no sphere of influence shall be extended so far that no empire shall grow so great as to make a single nation the unrivaled arbiter of the destiny of the world or the dictator of civilization. It does this by strengthening new centers of power and promoting alliances between relatively weak states to counterbalance those nations which show signs of aggressive growth. . . .

Throughout history, the balance of power has been the most usual and effective form of insurance against aggression. For two centuries and a half it has been the agency through which western civilization has again and again saved itself from successive attempts on the part of ambitious rulers and nations to achieve world supremacy. It was the device by which Louis XIV of France . . . was kept from crushing Europe. It was the device whereby Napoleon was prevented from establishing universal empire. It was the device which, during the happy days of the nineteenth century, preserved the peace of Europe with only minor interruptions for a hundred years. It was the device which checked the ambitions of Germany in the First World War. . . .

Why, then, has the balance of power become anathema to international idealists and the chief bugbear of liberal thought. Simply, I believe, because of a basic misapprehension, a confusion of effect with cause. International idealists charge that the policy of striving for a balance of power is a cause of wars. It is not; rather it is the effect of the underlying rivalries and fears which may lead to wars, and it is their effect only in the sense that it is an attempt to counteract them in the interest of peace. . . .

However, the orthodox doctrine of international idealism today is that the principle of the balance of power must be given up; that it must be supplanted by some form of world association to keep the peace; that the only just and effective way to repress aggression is through a central agency supposedly representing the common interest and general good of all nations. . . . The point I wish to emphasize is that . . . its intended aim . . . must incorporate and make use of the balance-of-power principle and not seek to deny or ignore it. . . .

I submit that if one has even a slight knowledge of history or any acquaintance at all with the world about us today and with the way that men and groups behave it is clear that within any international organization or association that may be set up the principle of the balance of power will still continue to operate possibly in a different form and doubtless by somewhat different methods, but with the same inevitability as in the unorganized world of past and present day international politics. . . .

This does not mean . . . that it is therefore futile and useless to set up an international organization, or to seek to bring about a degree of closer international cooperation, and that attempts to do so should be abandoned. On the contrary the change in the environment which would be effected by the establishment of such an organization . . . may well produce highly beneficial consequences. . . . We can no more hope to build an international organization successfully without allowing for the continued balance of power, than we could undertake to improve the health of human beings without taking into account the circulation of the blood and the processes of metabolism.

A POSITIVE FOREIGN POLICY FOR THE UNITED STATES [12]

There was a time when the minting of Four Freedoms or the promulgation of an Atlantic Charter or the announcement of a set of general principles like those recently put together by Secretary of State Hull would have satisfied the American people that they and their leaders have a foreign policy. This is no longer the case. . . .

The only kind of policy Americans can use is one in which ideals and facts are fused into a working unity and freed from the excesses of these opposing trends. Taken alone, "America first" promises endless future friction, rivalry, and war. . . . But also, taken alone, "security first" means a policy which ties our hands, and still more, through alliance, our national conscience.

The policy of "security first" deserves a good look on its own merits, . . . just to see where it would take us. That we must have security is an axiom. So must an individual; but it is an empty and fear-ridden life whose primary object is to avoid getting killed. The security of living things is the incidental security of skill in managing the risks of action. The words "security," "defense," "alliance" are the great words for a moat-and-castle age, not for an age in which no moats can be dug and every all-round alliance so compromises policy as to cancel all that is distinctive of national character. . . .

[12] From "America's World Purpose," by William Ernest Hocking. *Life*. 16: 102-4+. April 17, 1944. Reprinted by permission.

The time requires a positive and outgoing policy built on radically different lines. In simplest terms, to have a positive policy is to make history instead of letting history happen to us or trying to fend it off. . . .

After we entered the last world war, we improvised a foreign policy that was positive and specific. We had fourteen points and several speeches. We tried to put the ideas contained in these documents into effect. We have been told that we failed. With strange meekness, we have accepted this dour and inaccurate verdict.

We did not wholly succeed, but who does? The point is, we did not wholly fail.

Our plan was indeed mutilated. Only five of Wilson's points were set into the Treaty. Our Armistice agreement was betrayed and our nation, unwisely but not without ground, declined to back the crippled program. We had lost our first battle, that of convincing the warmakers of Europe who were unfortunately also the peacemakers. The remnant of our plan was accepted with an undertow of cynical amusement; long after the Paris Conference our associates in Europe were still referring to "les idées wilsoniennes" with an indulgent shrug.

But the main thing to remember—aside from these vanities and struttings or even the massive disappointments of that time —is that a great experiment in international collaboration went forward, in part an American project. Every subsequent effort along this line will have the experience of the League of Nations to guide it. Because of the League, the whole problem of a future international structure is concrete, and not purely conjectural. The League's successes, and its failures as well, become the essential data for drawing specifications for a new attempt that must be made and will have American participation.

Let me make two passing remarks, one concerning hidden successes of the League, the other concerning hidden causes of its weakness.

The League influenced practice even where it did not officially act. For instance, in setting up mandates, it influenced the administration of colonies, which were wholly outside its field. When colonies and mandates existed side by side, as throughout Africa, two things were bound to happen; the mandate would slump toward the colony, the colony would rise toward the mandate. In spite of grave defects in the mandate system the average treatment of dependencies was improved and can never again revert to its pre-1914 level. That is something done.

The common criticism is that the League had no army to enforce its advice; its "military sanctions" were too far in the background to be effective. This is bad analysis. The makers of the League Covenant considered and definitely and wisely rejected the idea of a "League to Enforce Peace" which would have been a League with few members; its main reliance was to be public opinion. The hidden weakness of the League was not that it had no army, but that it had no public opinion. And the reason it had no public opinion was chiefly lack of time.

Further, the League itself, could not from the beginning exercise a moral authority which it required time to establish. In 1928 I made inquiries in Geneva about the causes of the League's backwardness in dealing with insistent boundary problems. One answer by a League official went far: "Give us ten years," he said. "Your Supreme Court had to build its prestige before it could decide issues between states; so must the League. In ten years the great powers will accept our judgment but not yet."

A weakness which time will cure is not a weakness inherent in the idea. It becomes a fatal weakness only if the needed time is denied. This is precisely what the blow of Japan in Manchuria in 1931 intentionally achieved. During that year the League was arranging a program of effective support to China, both in education and finance. This great new republic was perceptibly unifying its vast and shambling group of provinces. The war party of Japan saw in a strong China and a strong League in Asia an end to its hopes of domination. It timed its stroke to wreck both these prospects. Its action is strong evidence for my contention that, in spite of all other handicaps, time was bringing to the League political effectiveness.

In 1932 the balance between success or failure of the League's system of collective security in the Far East was very close, even to Japan. I was there during that year and witnessed the tension between parties, and the strength of League supporters even while the Lytton Commission was doing its work, and Japanese forces were carrying on their "incident" in Shanghai. After Japan announced its withdrawal from the League and Italy undertook its campaign in Abyssinia, the disintegration was rapid. But we cannot wisely forget the nearness of success, the accidents which turned the scale and the immense influence of the factor of time. . . .

We have no right to hang around our necks the disabling tokens of failure so far as our first essay in international co-operation is concerned. We may turn free of mind to the thought of a positive foreign policy for the present moment.

Foreign policy is necessary because the activities of states overflow their own borders. They have always done so, they do so now with increasing range and tempo.

This is obviously true of the private activities of citizens in trade and travel. Norway could once do very well with off-coast fishing. As sewing machines and motorcars became staples of life she began to deal with America. As coffee and tea, tobacco and citrus fruits entered her menu she took on half a dozen more distant relationshhips. As she developed an electro-chemical industry, she required technical and scientific contributions from many lands and has made her own contributions to them in return. Before the war, Norway had the fourth merchant fleet in the world; she was using what the world had to offer.

Now with this growing back-and-forth of goods, services and ideas, there has to go an increasing back-and-forth of political concern.

Whenever men and goods travel, there must go some understanding of rights and duties, some way of adjusting disputes, some basis of law accepted by both sides. Hence the picture of commercial and cultural interdependence is at the same time a picture of the advance of political activity. There is no standing frontier for American political concern, say at the Rhine or at the coast of China. The boundary moves outward in all directions until, having covered the earth, it annihilates itself. Each state, in terms of its political concern and influence, tends to be everywhere.

Today even the domestic legislation of any great power sends instant tremors through all the others. It is not surprising that this aggressive, outgoing action of state-wills arouses frequent resentment. But the rule of expansion of political life can hardly be curbed or reversed without reversing the trend of civilization.

The result of this expansion is friction of various sorts and degrees. Since humanity commonly learns things the hardest way, history is largely a record of the hostile clash of rival political expansions. In the age of America's colonial settlement, European states were overflowing into a relatively empty region, spilling their men and energy into the New World. These expansions clashed at the outer edges and we had a series of colonial wars.

In the last two centuries what we had was not so much the migration of men as the overflow of a system. The economic systems of Europe have been less and less capable of running to best effect without sweeping into their circuits outside regions and peoples as suppliers of materials and markets. Foreign policy took the form of empire building. World history was bearing out Machiavelli's view that a vigorous state can remain healthy only if it expands; and since expansion meant to him conquest, this empire-building policy bore little promise of peace. As the world filled up, rival expanders would have to collide. The era of empire building was bound to ripen into an era of wars among empires and empire-aspirants. That is where we are today.

And as we look ahead, the law of expanding state action seems to promise little better than struggles on a still more colossal scale, unless we can find an alternative to the head-on opposition of the outreaching purposes of states.

In the world of physics, there is such an alternative. Migrating billiard balls cannot pass through one another: encounter means displacement. But migrating waves from different centers (as on the surface of a pond) can pass through one another without conflict, adding themselves to one another as they pass.

And ordinarily, two gases, released into the same closed space, will expand through one another until each fills the entire space. In the physical world there are numerous examples of "interpenetration." Is it conceivable that political expansions might also interpenetrate like waves, rather than collide like billiard balls?

Let us answer this question by asking another. Is it true that the purposes of states are based solely on self-interest? And that the self-interests of states are at bottom contrary or competitive? If this is the case, then the result of their encounter can only be hostility, however honeyed over by diplomatic palaver. This is the great and traditional game of foreign policy whose essence is undercover warfare and whose stakes are the inchings up or down of the lives of nations. Current "realism" accepts this picture.

If, however, the purposes of states are based indeed on self-interest but not solely on self-interest; and if the self-interest element is not necessarily competitive, but can be so shaped that A's gain is also B's gain, the outlook is radically different. There can be an interpenetration of purposes on the analogy of the waves. A positive policy becomes possible, a policy in which a state, not abandoning its self-interest, would devise a way to create an identity of self-interests in precisely those spots where, apart from this inventiveness, conflict must have occurred. And the old game may acquire an aroma of honesty in place of its ancient smell of clever deceptiveness.

But is any such policy practicable? The best answer is that it has occurred, and that it has worked. And as a fact of interest to Americans, the best examples seem to be those in which an American mind has been a decisive factor. The Open Door Policy is a case in point.

Everybody connects with that policy the name of John Hay; but just what the policy meant is variously misunderstood. The popular understanding is that it was a claim on our part, put forward in 1899 when settlements among rival powers were going on in China, to share on equal terms with these other powers in Chinese trade. Owen Lattimore regards it as a rather self-righteous operation in which we claim a share of the fruits of

British, Dutch, French imperialism without assuming any imperial responsibilities. But there was another side to the policy. China was protected from imminent dismemberment. The essence of the Open Door Policy was a new idea, one in which the interests of the competing powers were met, our interests were promoted, the interests of China were satisfied and China herself protected. The stoke of genius was the invention whereby interests which had been competing were made noncompeting and, in fact, interpenetrating.

The time has now come when the mutual intrusions of political wills are so widespread that a policy of interpenetrating purposes has become essential to world peace. Cultural interests are in their own nature interpenetrating; to spread a scientific idea creates no friction. Economic interests have a competitive base, and they are among the chief roots of trouble. But they are also among the most plastic to invention of lines of mutual advantage. Oppositions of interest are still the rule and will remain so long as we allow it. But since this situation can be changed, it becomes the most insistent task of foreign policy to change it. It is a task for which we believe this country has a peculiar gift.

The foreign policy of this nation has never been inclined to busy itself systematically with the economic troubles of other peoples, and for good reasons. The economic picture of each region of earth is unique. Each has a unique and crooked bit of geography, in which unique human qualities are applied to unique soils, resources, climates—all with unique results. No economy on the planet is interchangeable with any other. The Eskimo does not campare his lot with that of the Dakota farmer, nor wish to go there. If he did he would then have to stop being an Eskimo.

Hence the protection of a high standard of living, joint product of a good soil, high human ability and hard work, is not unmitigated selfishness. The world would be poorer, not richer, if standards were leveled off. Philanthropy on a world scale is an impossible policy; also highly unwelcome. Minding one's business is not a bad way of serving the general good.

These traditional American reflections are sound in principle; but they have now become incomplete. For however much we are willing to mind our own business, a great economy will not and cannot mind its own business.

The international version of laissez faire would be "let every nation look out for itself," with perhaps a pious addendum to the effect that God means the strongest people to survive. But the hurt done to other peoples, if it is serious enough, gets around home and suggests a prudential modification: Avoid economic policies which materially damage your good customers and your debtors.

This puts a brake upon the complete carefreeness of tariff and currency legislation; but it still leaves us a long distance from any positive obligation to the outside world, such as:

Every nation has a duty to shape its economic policies so that their impact on other nations shall be useful to both. This strikes us at first as a counsel of perfection, too far away from the counsel of prudence. But between the two there is this:

No nation dare any longer be indifferent to the economic situation and destiny of other nations.

It was here that we, in common with England and France, failed in the between-wars period. We failed to see that in the story of growing interdependence the critical turn had been reached at which the prosperity of Europe, including Germany, had become a necessary part of our own prosperity. Indifference to the European living standard, though it looked like the realest brand of realism, was no longer even common sense. Had we seen and acted on this, the breach of world peace might never have occurred. This failure we share with our allies. It is visible in our unconscionable tariffs, in our ruining with a tweak of the presidential thumb the London Economic Conference of 1933, in the thwarting of reviving industrial life in Germany by the fears of France, halfheartedly seconded by an England which under false pretenses had materially aggrandized her empire at the cost to Germany of her African colonies.

Now the important thing at that time as always, was not to find the final answer to a complex economic problem, but to give attention to it. Nobody yet knows what "just distribution" is inside a nation, still less in a society of nations. It is less important for world peace that justice be found than that it be sought. The explosive factor in history is not suffering; it is indifference to suffering on the part of nonsuffering.

We may have learned by this failure of our pseudo realism. There are signs that at least in one or two spots we are ready to set up a positive policy in the economic field.

As to the redistribution of industry; we in America are about ready to some extent to promote industry, even industry which will compete with our own, in regions which require industrial developments for their own economic balance. Taking a long view, we see this not as altruism but as good business.

Another phase of economy which has an equally great and more immediate field of possibility is agriculture, especially as bearing on standards of living in eastern and southern Asia. These standards as measured by per-capita income are the lowest among civilized peoples; in prewar China, per-capita income ran in the neighborhood of 20c per day; in India about 5c per day. These two peoples account for over a third of the population of the planet, upward of 800,000,000 people. And of these, at least 80 per cent are on the land.

Rebellion against poverty has not been the rule in Asia. It is beginning to be the rule now. Aside from its plain human significance, the stability of the Far East is involved. At stake also is the drift of the thought of these masses toward one or other of the economic systems around them. An improvement in the standard of living of this large population would add materially to the market for all industry, their own and others'. There is no point in which so many postwar issues are knotted together.

We, as a nation, are in an extraordinarily favorable position to loosen this knot. Remember the transformation of Russian agriculture during twenty years. In 1917, 85 per cent of the population was on the land, only 15 per cent free for other occupations. The efficiency of agriculture was so low that it required 85 per cent of the population (as compared with about 30 per cent in the United States) to raise food-stuffs and raw materials for the whole. By 1939 this proportion had made an astonishing change: only 68 per cent were on the land; 32 per cent were free for other things, an increase of 25,000,000 people. Without this transformation Russia could not have been in the war today. American machines, methods and personnel materially helped in that transformation. We have here indications of functions which we can exercise in China and India and throughout the Far East not only privately, but as a part of national policy, if we have the foresight, imagination and inventive power.

These are but two of the many aspects of the economic picture. Here at least there are economic situations in which national purposes are ready to interpenetrate. And with a devised agreement on the level of material interest there will come also an increase in that indispensable substance called goodwill, which commercial realism recognizes as an intangible asset and which a sound political realism will not ignore.

Turning now to "international law," this term is likely to bring a shiver of discomfort to the well-trained legal mind. Law to the lawyer is an affair of the statute book or of actual court decisions behind which there are lawmaking bodies, authoritative courts and an apparatus of power to check or punish disobedience. There are no such institutions at the moment for the so-called law of nations. There are merely some common practices among nations, especially in the Law Merchant, which are accepted as useful reference points for settlements.

If international law is to mean something important for the order and peace of the world, it must achieve a far more authoritative position. It must be a source of command so august that sovereign states, great and small alike, will admit its authority over them. This involves a profound wrench to a popular conception of what a sovereign state is—a power which recognizes no law beyond its own will. International law has no chance unless we see that states are sovereign not because they are above all law but because, like mature men, they have sense enough to observe law, i.e., to act in a rational manner without compulsion.

Within any nation, law counts for far more than we commonly think, because most of its work is done without intrusion. Nine tenths of the time law is asking of men only what their own good sense is asking of them. To be rational in one's behavior, respecting the rights of others, is to be law-abiding without knowing it. Why may not the same be true of the behavior of states in a community of states?

For a certain distance, this analogy certainly holds good. There are for states as well as for individuals certain rules of prudence and ordinary justice which can be, and are, taken directly over from private morals or common law, such as paying debts and keeping agreements. And on the whole, the self-interested reasons which support such action are stronger for states than for individuals. An individual may retrieve a low credit rating; a state seldom can. For the most part, modern statesmen observe these reasonable rules unless there are "reasons of state" to the contrary. But perhaps, if the rights of nations were recognized as well as the rights of individuals, these disastrous exceptions might be overcome.

Such was the sanguine view which prevailed among liberals until after the First World War. As late as 1916 a "Declaration of the Rights of Nations" was put out by the American Institute of International Law, on the analogy of the French Declaration of the Rights of Man. But the vital points at which the analogy breaks down had already begun to appear. "Reasonable" conduct is conduct which assumes a certain equality among states which differ so extremely. Among persons, because of equality, comparison is an argument for rights: "If you have a right to a job or a vote, so have I." Among states, comparisons are not alone impertinent, but for the most part plain nonsense. Brazil's possession of a seacoast is no argument for Bolivia's right to a seacoast. In fact, while for domestic law there is something like a standard man, for the world community there is no such thing as a standard state.

Any law has to know what the units are to which it is ascribing "rights" and to whom it is doing "justice." But what are the units for international law? Is the British Empire one state or a dozen? Is the Soviet Union one or 16? Is the United States one or 48? The boundary of an animal or a man has an organic fixity. But the meltings and splittings of states are commonplaces of world history. The unit of law is elusive, variable, plastic.

From this it follows that the chief troubles of international society begin at a prelaw level, i.e., in setting up the units with which law has to work. India, for example, objects to continuing as a 400,000,000 abdomen for a 45,000,000 British head-and-chest. Where will you find legal precedents to deal with such an issue? Surely not within domestic law?

Hence, these issues, with all others involving the existence of states and their "vital interests," are set aside as "nonjusticiable" —out of the reach of the law. But since it is just these issues which are the war-breeders, international law, when these are omitted, sinks to the level of a mere lubricant.

It is necessary to recognize the deep difficulties in which international law is caught. It is also necessary to recognize what the alternative is, if there can be no authoritative law for nations. It is that the order among nations rests on the I-will of the strongest power. In this case, aggression could not be called unjust; it could only be called, in the present case, bad judgment. I press the alternative: you either exonerate the Nazi-Jajanese outburst on every ethical ground, or else you hold that even in these nonjusticiable problems of existence, status and boundry, there is a discoverable reason, a discoverable right-and-wrong, and therefore a basis for law. For law is the coinage of the ethical sense of mankind.

There can be no doubt of the decision. We cannot believe in the finality of any appeal to an arbitrary I-will. Those who profess to believe in it, when it comes to an appeal to their own people to fight, always trump up an ethical motive. There is a deeper reason: law is the way the human mind works. No human act can reject the question, "Why did you do it?" as impertinent. If states are to grow or decline, or to combine or divide, still more there must be assignable reasons. And if there are reasons, there is the raw material of law.

Hence the demand for a working international law arises with new vigor after every setback. Even in the absence of all institutions, the will-to-law operates on national behavior: it is seen in the concern for the "opinion of mankind," in the groping toward defensible practice, in the very hypocrisies of statesmen who dare not avow themselves naked of justification. It is obligatory upon us to revitalize its foundations. Just because its prestige is at low ebb, it becomes all the more an object of positive policy to promote the necessary new thinking and plan the appropriate institutions.

We cannot begin by setting up a world government with legislative and executive departments, armed with force. For even if there could be found men of sufficient caliber to run the world—which I doubt—and a firm public opinion to back them, it puts things in the wrong order to begin enforcing a justice not yet thought out in principle. The first institution should therefore be a world court, capable of applying such law as exists and a commission auxiliary to that court for working out a code, not of specific laws, but of fundamental principles of international law. We can reach principles here long before we can reach a finished code.

The important thing is to begin. For to have any institution devoted to this end is to make visible the resolve of nations to live under law and to set up the first law: "the law that there shall be law."

Law has to grow tough with time and application. It needs this far more than it needs force. As it becomes a working law, it bears directly on security. For as respect for law is effectively present in all men and nations, the habit of referring to law constitutes an unwritten alliance of every nation so committed with every other such nation. There would be a reasonable relaxing of military security just so far as the spirit of legality gained visible form, prestige and general effect. It is a matter of human pride to shake free from the mean presumption that a reasonableness native to mankind must always be handed out by an irresistible military coalition.

So long as men must stand on the defensive, free institutions can neither thrive at home nor spread abroad. For defense in terms of modern war implies a total organization of the resources of the state about a highly centralized executive. We must choose between complete safety and freedom. It lies near to the American genius to take the risk for freedom and to justify its faith by assuming leadership in setting up a working international law.

One difference between this war and the last is that this time there is a whole planet to be put into order. We are justly humbled by the immensity of the task. But there are two propitious circumstances at this moment of history. International law has today a factual and emotional support which it formerly lacked. The volume of common goods and ideas among all peoples, the common techniques of civilization, and the common enterprises of the family of nations have given substance to the frame within which all law operates. Clashes of interest continue to exist. But the question of aggressive self-assertion for any power has become altered. It is no longer What can I gain by asserting my separate will? but What is the net gain if, in doing so, I break down the existing frame?

The other propitious circumstance is an ingredient of the American spirit itself, a peculiar ability to take the other man's point of view. Wherever I have traveled I have found Americans at home in foreign parts. Merchants, consuls, teachers, engineers, dentists or scientists, they have friends among the people with whom they are living. I mean friends. The reason for this seems to me much the same in all cases. Two things go to make a good teacher: a knowledge of his subject and a knowledge of the difficulties his pupil is going to have with that subject. Everywhere abroad it is the American dentist who is in demand. Two things go to make a good dentist: a knowledge of his art and a knowledge of the susceptibilities of his patient. All of them, besides being good in their specialty, need to be practical psychologists to the extent of knowing where it is going to hurt! This means doing your job and at the same time taking the other man's point of view.

Possibly a little more of this exceedingly simple quality can make the chief turn required in our diplomacy today. It is well adapted to make the difference between seeing the point of "interpenetrating purposes," and cherishing under the laudatory name of realism the illusion that the normal and necessary relation between national wills is at bottom competitive. In my opinion the most successful ventures of American statecraft, from the Monroe Doctrine onward, have come from the exercise of this faculty, which is the essence of all faith in man, and also the point at which the spirit of religion touches the spirit of world politics. It is the necessary backing for any extension of human rights or liberties we may promote. And it has the advantage of calling out all the native shrewdness, factuality and inventiveness we can muster; for he who thinks for two has a bigger job than he who thinks for himself alone. And he is the only genuine realist; for he alone sees things as they are.

In politics all motives are mixed. Our record in the Philippines has been no pure poem of political altruism. But it has had enough of this saving human quality to make it outstanding in the treatment of dependencies. That experience gives us one base from which to meet the inescapable problem of transforming empire. That problem, thorny as it is, is a composite of elements we now have in hand—economy, law, human rights, world stability. These elements are interdependent. But the key which unlocks them is a direct corollary of the human quality we are speaking of and a condition of all interpenetration of purpose: As no man can be the property of any other man, so no nation can be the property of any other nation. The "our owns" are out.

THE PUBLIC TREND TOWARD WORLD ORDER [13]

In October, 1937, when the Gallop Poll was less than two years old, this question was asked: "Do you think the United States should have joined the League of Nations after the last war?" The same question was repeated in August, 1941—four months before Pearl Harbor—and a similar question was asked eleven months later in July, 1942.

During this five-year period Americans with definite attitudes on the subject completely reversed their opinions:

	1937	1941	1942
All Voters Favoring U. S. Membership in League	33%	50%	73%

Gallup reports (December, 1942): "Should the government take steps now, before the end of the war, to set up with our Allies a world organization to maintain the future peace of the world? Yes......73%

Since Pearl Harbor, whenever a public opinion poll has asked a question regarding some type of postwar world organization, a majority of the American public have expressed approval of the idea in principle.

[13] From "The Public Looks at World Organization," report No. 19, National Opinion Research Center, University of Denver. April, 1944. p. 5-6. Reprinted by permission.

NORC reports the following trend question has been used several times over a period of more than a year with results so similar that opinion on the issue is quite definitely crystallized:

"If a union of nations is formed after the war, do you think it would be a good idea or a bad idea for the United States to join it?"

	Sept. 1942	Jan. 1943	June 1943	Sept. 1943
Good idea	68%	70%	70%	81%
Qualified answer	3	5	4	—
Bad idea	15	16	13	11
Undecided	14	9	13	8

NORC asked:

"In general, what chance do you think a union of nations will have to prevent wars—good, fair, or no chance at all?"

Good chance..... 52%	Fair chance...... 38%
No chance....... 10%	Undecided 6%

Fortune reports (June, 1943):

"Which of these statements comes closer to what you would like to see us do when the war is over?"

"Stay on our side of the oceans, and have as little as possible to do with Europe and Asia	13.0%
"Try to keep the world at peace, but make no definite agreements with other countries.....	25.2
"Take an active part in some sort of international organization with a court and police force strong enough to enforce its decisions"	56.6
Don't know	5.2

FORTUNE SURVEY [14]

Which one of these comes closest to expressing what you would like to have the United States do after the war?

a. Enter into no alliance and have as little as possible to do with other countries	12.7%
b. Depend only on separate alliances with certain countries	7.7
c. Take an active part in an international organization	68.1
d. Don't know	11.5

[14] From "The Fortune Survey." *Fortune.* 29:94+. March, 1944. Reprinted by permission.

To find out whether the U.S. people want an international organization to be a sort of town-meeting-of-the-world or a club-within-a-club, all of those interviewed—whether they wanted an international organization or not—were asked this question:

If we should take part in an international organization, which do you think would be better?

To let certain countries have more say at the start than
    other countries 39.8%
To let all member countries have the same say 50.3
Don't know 9.9

The large majority wanting some countries to have more to say at the start quite clearly had certain countries in mind—the Big Four, and no others. Presented with the list of fourteen countries previously used—with the United States added to it—those who wanted a dominant group of countries within an international organization were asked:

Which of these countries would you want to have the most say?

United States 85.4%
Great Britain 85.4
Russia 71.7
China 63.4
Australia 18.9
Remaining 10 countries ..... Less than 10% each
Don't know 1.6

Wishing for an international organization may be an easy sort of wishing. The test of seriousness comes with ground rules that people are willing to accept for such an organization. Accordingly *Fortune* presented to all of those interviewed a sheaf of possible ground rules—and received answers that are nothing short of amazing. Not until the people are confronted with an actual international organization will it be possible to say for certain whether these confident opinions are only misty daydreams or are bold realism.

If a general international organization should be set up, which of these things do you think it should and should not be organized to do—?

	Should	Should not	Don't know
Prevent any member country from starting a war of its own against an outside country	79.0%	7.0%	14.0%
Decide which country is right if two members get into a dispute	75.9	8.2	15.9
Decide what taxes individual member nations must pay to support the organization.......	69.7	8.9	21.4
Decide what military strength each member nation can have..	69.0	13.6	17.4
Regulate the rights of airplanes from one member nation to land on airfields in other member nations	61.1	14.0	24.9
Have a permanent military force of its own, stronger than any single nation	54.0	23.3	22.7
Decide what tariff rates should be charged by member nations..	44.8	23.3	31.9
Decide which side is right if a civil war breaks out in a member nation, and support that side	43.0	31.7	25.3
Decide minimum standards for working conditions in member countries	32.0	44.7	23.3

THE OUTLOOK FOR PEACE TOMORROW [15]

Two facts render the world outlook quite different today from what it was in the nineteenth century. First, war is infinitely more destructive. Secondly, once it starts no country can count on escaping it. Both changes are due to the unparalleled multiplication of man's power by science and machinery—a multiplication which is abolishing distances.

Peace becomes, under such conditions, an absolute necessity. If the Great Powers cannot combine to secure it, they will be ground to powder under a series of wars; and what is left of humanity in a blasted world will eventually accept peace, as in Rome's day, from some single hand.

[15] From "World Peace Hope Seen in 'Big Three,' " by "Scrutator," pen name of commentator of the Sunday Times of London. *New York World-Telegram.* 77:10. March 24, 1945. Reprinted by permission.

Is there any stopping place short of this terrible consummation? I have never been able to see but one. It is that, instead of peace being enforced by a single conqueror, it should be secured by a concert of contented great powers. That is, of powers "contented" enough never to want to provoke war themselves, and "great" enough to insure their being able, in concert, to prevent any other power from doing so.

It is within this framework that Anglo-American relations fall. The older ways of regarding them must give way to it. In the nineteenth century the United States and Great Britain saw each other with very different eyes.

Not only was any idea of another war with America excluded as fratricidal—a view strikingly exemplified nearly eighty years ago when Great Britain accepted and abode by the Alabama arbitration—but the power of the British Navy, then unrivaled, was consistently ranged in support of the Monroe Doctrine, of which it was, in reality, the most effective guardian. In the United States there was no equivalent feeling for Great Britain. But in the twentieth century much has occurred to modify this condition.

Who are the possible "contented great powers," on whose cooperation with herself the United States must rely to save her from suffering another war? They are four—Great Britain, Russia, France and China. There may be sufficient reasons for associating China with this group from the outset, and there are, I think, overwhelming ones for associating France.

But when we get to the bedrock task of vetoing war and guaranteeing peace, neither of those countries can, for a long time to come, contribute much. They simply will not be strong enough. The task will fall upon three—the United States, Great Britain (with her Commonwealth and Empire) and the Soviet Union. The world's supreme need, therefore, is for close understanding and permanent mutual support between these three.

What are the prospects of it? Many grounds exist for hope. The British world-unit is "contented"; it desires no annexations anywhere, and its concerns with "spheres of interests" are only what have been well known and recognized for long past.

Russia, it is true, having suffered so terribly from invasion, will naturally insist on a measure of special control over the lands adjacent to it—a demand which it will be neither reasonable nor practicable to oppose. Uninvaded and unbombed America has no similar need; the Monroe Doctrine and the leased bases already cover her case.

What then will be the difficulties? Frankly, I think the greatest will come from the United States. First there is the constitutional one—that treaties and agreements made by the executive branch of the government are not valid until ratified by a two-thirds majority of the Senate. No such inhibition clogs the cooperation of any great power. Even if the Senate's record had been quite different from what it has, this would still not be a practical way for a great power to do its international business.

It has only lasted on, because, before distance was abolished, it did not much matter to the United States how badly her international business was done.

This last point explains what I think is a still greater danger —the exceptional irresponsibility of American opinion upon foreign affairs, alike in Congress and in the press. European public men much less often wag their tongues idly on this subject, because for centuries they have known that words may bring war. American tongues underwent no similar discipline, because in a sense they did not need it. They do need it now.

As between Great Britain and the Soviet Union there are, of course, initial difficulties. But both nations have been through the fire in this war, and sincerely desire peace. I am sure the British government will be disposed to take generous views toward Russia, and the signs are that Stalin will reciprocate. Harmony will not be automatic, yet it should be attained.

America is very popular in Great Britain today, and deservedly so. The British are grateful for what has been done and admiring towards those who have done it. The fine young manhood of the United States, who sojourn here in their hundreds of thousands before crossing to the continent for battle, have left a vast volume of friendly feeling behind them. Here are the raw materials for precious new ties between the nations. I would say to my friends in America: "Take note of them, treasure them, join hands over them. But above all do not let them be destroyed by your politicians."

EXCERPTS

National security is a twofold political problem, that of defense against war after it has begun and of prevention against its outbreak. Of these two measures it is only the second which offers any guaranty of safety, because science, by inventing the airplane, has made defense against actual attack extremely uncertain and perilous. But prevention calls for more than measures of police or disarmament, because it must offer substitutes for war by procedures for the pacific settlement of disputes, for otherwise the peace will ultimately be broken by nations to whom its conditions would have become intolerable.

Disputes that can be settled by diplomacy must therefore be submitted to political settlement which means by mediation, inquiry, conciliation and other conference methods for multilateral agreement, or by judicial settlement through court or arbitration. These institutions must be developed until nations can resort to them with confidence; and the way to insure genuine cooperation in their development is to make resort to these devices obligatory and then to designate the resort to war by any nation against another except for the maintenance of peace as aggression, and then to designate such aggression as a crime against humanity to be put down by cooperative action.—*James T. Shotwell, special adviser to the State Department and Chairman of the Commission to Study the Organization of Peace. Radio broadcast transcribed by the World Wide Broadcasting Foundation. New York. Program Number* 19.

"Buffer states" used to be dear to the secret diplomacy of a century ago: they were countries set up to keep apart great powers which could not get along together. Today, the idea of a buffer state is as dead as a dodo. You cannot have "buffer states" in air warfare. Any buffer state, or any belt of buffer states, which could be built around Russia could be flown over by a modern air force in a few minutes, and probably demolished in a few hours.—*Sumner Welles, Former Under Secretary of State. Letter to Professor Ralph Barton Berry, April 2, 1943, Quoted in "War and Peace Aims," special supplement II of the United Nations Review. p.* 74.

CHAPTER II

THE ROAD TO DUMBARTON OAKS

After more than two thousand years of striving for the establishment of a peaceful world, the road ahead for the first time seems clear of any major obstructions. When the representatives of the United States, Great Britain, Russia and China met at Dumbarton Oaks to set down on paper a practical program of world organization for peace, they were in effect charting a known course. They had before them the sum of man's experience in the field of international relations and attempts at international organization. They knew to what extent nations would cooperate with other nations. They knew the obstacles, and in the main the areas of agreement. But, the major accomplishment of the Dumbarton Oaks discussions was their ability to combine realism and idealism in a practical formula. It has taken two thousand years, and even now the Oaks planners make it clear that their "plan" is most certainly subject to revision, to amendment—in fact, no nation is forced to accept any of it, unless it so desires.

It would be a major task to set down the past efforts at world organization. Most were impractical and unrealistic. The practical programs which were effected were usually unjust and therefore unworkable. All were dependent upon world conditions which were not ripe for international cooperation of any sort. To build a world organization requires some common meeting ground of all nations. We have learned, unfortunately perhaps, that the most effective meeting ground, common to all nations, is that of common defense in wartime.

For awhile it seemed that the common defense in World War I would be sufficient. But even before the Armistice the Allied political unity was dissolving. And by 1919 the major powers were almost irrevocably divided. The realism expressed at the Peace Table, unfortunately, was not a true realism based upon future considerations. The peace planners who built the League were "realistic" only in dealing out retribution and in dividing the spoils of war. Yet, their very actions conclusively proved to the world, or that part of it which did not participate in the spoils, that the old order was dead. A new order was in the offing. Even the most optimistic statesmen of those first postwar years did not see the League of Nations as the instrument which would create the new order. And within a few years, the breakdown of disarmament conferences, the rise of power politics again as a potent factor, brought disillusionment in its wake, but a disillusionment that was largely anticipated. The planners of the League realized that it might fail . . . but its failure would prove only that the world was not quite ready for unity in thought and action. Few of those leaders closely associated with the League, even in its darkest days—the Ethiopian war, the Manchukuo episode, the Spanish revolt—few of them gave up hope. Eventually, they hoped that nations would recognize the pressing need of cooperation . . . and in the interim they worked and planned to make what they could out of what they had. The machinery was weak in spots, but it could be strengthened. One thing, however, was essential, and that was the need for cooperation by *all* nations. The League, to be effective, required universal representation. Without it, the battle was lost. And among those not willing to accept the responsibility of cooperative internationalism was the United States. Some agency was needed to weld the nations together. The universal catalyst—war—effectively solved the problem.

Now, for the first time in two thousand years of civilized history, the time is ripe. The nations are not only united as never before—but we have a practical blueprint before us. We have the pattern of the old League—plus the lessons of its problems and its successes. In addition, and most important, we have the *will,* based upon a realization of the need for all nations to work together. The Dumbarton Oaks Proposals lay the foundation of a new organization. The plan still cannot be perfect at its inception. But it can be the first step toward world organization. From now on the job should be merely to work out the details and begin operation.

HISTORICAL BASIS OF WORLD ORGANIZATION [1]

In the Old Testament Isaiah and Micah tell us of their dream and aspirations of a world at peace, bound together under the fear of God.

Again, the city states of ancient Greece were formed into a league, and there was a similar organization of Latin city states under the general leadership of the city of Rome. We saw emerge the entity of the Roman Empire, and finally, upon its collapse, the next power of universal strength, the Catholic Church, which exercised temporal as well as spiritual authority.

Then the Dark Ages. In the 1300's we find a Frenchman writing of an association of nations governed by a common council.

In the 1600's Henry IV of France, with his Foreign Minister, promulgated to the Western world a rather remarkable proposal of a similar character—that there should be a federal association of states of Europe governed by a common council. Of course, he envisioned only the Christian states in that concept; but there was another crusader about the same time, far advanced in his own age, who conceived that the non-Christian states also should be admitted into the association of nations.

After the Napoleonic Wars came the concept of an ordered Europe out of the Congress of Vienna and succeeding congresses.

So from time to time in almost every nation there has been some farseeing writer envisioning a unity of nations and people which would make possible a peaceable and prosperous world.

It may be interesting to recall at this time, when Germany has been so anti-social in her actions and concepts, that it was the philosopher Kant of Germany that was the first to suggest that the foundation of the federation of states must not be the sovereigns, but the people themselves, who must associate themselves into an effective new order.

Here in this hemisphere, late in the nineteenth century, a very significant step forward occurred. That was the calling, by James

[1] From "A More Perfect United Nations—How and When?" by Claude Pepper, United States Senator from Florida. *The Annals of the American Academy.* 228:40-6. July, 1943. Reprinted by permission.

G. Blaine, a distinguished American Secretary of State, of the first Pan American Congress. As early as 1815 a great American, too little noticed and honored, Simon Bolivar, in writing a letter to a British gentleman who had given him asylum in Jamaica, envisioned a time when the nations of this hemisphere should come together on the Isthmus of Panama, and representatives of the British Empire should be included in the conference.

Then in 1899 began the Hague Conventions. There were two of them, the second of which occurred about the beginning of World War I. There was almost a universal attendance at this meeting devoted to the settlement of disputes by arbitration and dedicated to the principles of national disarmament. These conventions also failed, but they were in the direction of great events of the inevitable future, not so far ahead.

We often forget that when the First World War broke upon the earth, we had achieved an international stability which lured many wise men into the belief that never again could war smite the race of man and the fair earth. I believe there were only two countries in Europe that required passports, and that artificial barriers of trade were hardly an obstruction to the natural commerce of the Continent. Still, war occurred, and with its pitiful and painful devastation shocked the whole race of man into a consciousness of the necessity for at last doing something about this social institution of war. . . .

The climax of all this long struggle for a better world was the League of Nations. I am willing to take the considered judgment of Dr. Shotwell, a participant at Versailles, that in the six months within which the Covenant of the League was produced there was done one of the most creative jobs in all the history of the world.

WILSON'S FOURTEEN POINTS [2]

1. Open covenants of peace openly arrived at, after which there shall be no private international understandings of any kind, but diplomacy shall proceed always frankly and in the public view.

[2] As set forth in an address before a joint session of Congress, January 8, 1918.

2. Absolute freedom of navigation upon the seas outside territorial waters alike in peace and in war, except as the seas may be closed in whole or in part by international action or the enforcement of international covenants.

3. The removal, so far as possible, of all economic barriers and the establishment of an equality of trade conditions among all the nations consenting to the peace and associating themselves for its maintenance.

4. Adequate guarantees given and taken that national armaments will be reduced to the lowest point consistent with domestic safety.

5. A free, open-minded and absolutely impartial adjustment of all colonial claims based upon a strict observance of the principle that in determining all such questions of sovereignty the interests of the populations concerned must have equal weight with the equitable claims of the government whose title is to be determined.

6. The evacuation of all Russian territory, and such a settlement of all questions affecting Russia as will secure the best and freest cooperation of the other nations of the world in obtaining for her an unhampered and unembarrassed opportunity for the independent determination of her own political development and national policy, and assure her of a sincere welcome into the society of free nations under institutions of her own choosing; and, more than a welcome, assistance also of every kind that she may need and may herself desire. The treatment accorded Russia by her sister nations in the months to come will be the acid test of their goodwill, of their comprehension of her needs as distinguished from their own interests, and of their intelligent and unselfish sympathy.

7. Belgium, the whole world will agree, must be evacuated and restored, without any attempt to limit the sovereignty which she enjoys in common with all other free nations. No other single act will serve as this will serve to restore confidence among the nations in the laws which they have themselves set and determined for the government of their relations with one another. Without this healing act the whole structure and validity of international law is forever impaired.

8. All French territory should be freed and the invaded portions restored, and the wrong done to France by Prussia in 1871 in the matter of Alsace-Lorraine, which has unsettled the peace of the world for nearly fifty years, should be righted, in order that peace may once more be made secure in the interest of all.

9. A readjustment of the frontiers of Italy should be effected along clearly recognizable lines of nationality.

10. The peoples of Austria-Hungary, whose place among the nations we wish to see safeguarded and assured, should be accorded the freest opportunity of autonomous development.

11. Rumania, Serbia and Montenegro should be evacuated; occupied territories restored; Serbia accorded free and secure access to the sea; and the relations of the several Balkan States to one another determined by friendly counsel along historically established lines of allegiance and nationality; and international guarantees of the political and economic independence and territorial integrity of the several Balkan States should be entered upon.

12. The Turkish portions of the present Ottoman Empire should be assured a secure sovereignty, but the other nationalities which are now under Turkish rule should be assured an undoubted security of life and an absolutely unmolested opportunity of autonomous development, and the Dardanelles should be permanently opened as a free passage to the ships and commerce of all nations under international guarantees.

13. An independent Polish state should be erected which should include the territories inhabited by indisputably Polish populations, which should be assured a free and secure access to the sea, and whose political and economic independence and territorial integrity should be guaranteed by international covenant.

14. A general association of nations must be formed under specific covenants for the purpose of affording mutual guarantees of political independence and territorial integrity to great and small states alike.

THE LEAGUE EXPERIMENT [3]

The League of Nations may be regarded as an episode in a continuing evolution toward international, and eventual world, government. This movement, whose roots lie deep in the past, has not yet reached its culmination. The growth in the nineteenth century of international law and legislation, of international administrative agencies, and the scores of private international organizations, were all portents of a closer world integration which was bound to become more organized in the twentieth century.

Through World War I this movement was precipitated into the first League of Nations. In its technical aspects, the League was already long overdue; politically, however, it was born prematurely, or more accurately it was projected into a world psychologically and politically unready to receive it.

Political evolution in recent decades had been hard pressed to keep pace with technical advances. This uneven development created a tension in international life which proved to be incapable of peaceful adjustment. In the present conflict this tension has again reached the breaking point. But seen in perspective it can hardly be doubted that it will have the effect of hastening the tempo of political evolution toward further integration. The great uncertainty, however, is whether this impulse will be directed toward free federation or toward rigid domination in regional or world-wide areas.

The experience of the League in its first phase will doubtless be of value to those who may be engaged in projecting new blueprints of world organization following the conflicts now in progress in Europe and the Far East. But whether the unit in the new organization will be the fully sovereign or modified nation-state, and, if the latter, what the number and nature of those nation-states will be, will have a very great bearing as to the amount of material from the existing League which can be built into the

[3] From "An Appraisal of the League of Nations," by Benjamin Gerig, member of League of Nations secretariat. *Preliminary Report and Monographs.* Commission to Study the Organization of Peace. New York. p. 102-14. Reprinted by permission.

new and—unless the course of evolution is set in reverse—the
more highly integrated structures which must be created.

For, it cannot be too often repeated, there was very little integration in the League of 1920-40. It was a loose association
of states whose seat or meeting place was at Geneva, but whose
sovereign powers were retained largely intact in their respective
capitals. These states, whose numbers varied from year to year,
acted together according to a set of principles which were outlined in the Covenant in a manner generally more ambiguous
than precise. And if the lawyers attempted to make the obligations precise the governments still retained the power to render
them inoperative by the unanimity rule.

Thus the League in practice became an expression of the
maximum international cooperation that was possible at any given
time. This varied both with the subject matter under discussion,
and with the governments of the day which states happened to
have in office.

Nearly every appraisal of the League of Nations made in the
past twenty years points out that the first and principal handicap
was the failure to achieve a universal or near-universal membership. It was, therefore, only a truncated League lacking the basic
elements necessary to give effect to the two principles of stability
and change which alone could avert recurrent war. It required,
it was held, a great power like the United States, disinterested
and detached from Europe's internal differences, to press certain
states to make concessions, and others to modify their demands, if
the new situation which her participation in the war helped to
create, was not to revert to the condition of an armed truce and
eventually to renewed hostilities. Her absence, it will hardly be
denied, seriously weakened the guaranty function of the League,
for the other leading sea power, Great Britain, was unwilling to
assume this added responsibility and perhaps run afoul of the
now equally great United States navy in doing so.

This fateful decision of the United States, which deprived the
League from the beginning of a very great moral and material
influence, was accompanied by an equally fatal decision in Paris
in 1919 which kept Germany and the Soviet Union out of League
membership and on probation till 1926 and 1934 respectively.

This deliberate separation of the "sheep from the goats" was further reflected in the wording of the Covenant—designed to be the permanent charter or constitution of the new international order—which contained repeated references to "the Allied and Associated Powers." The psychological effects of these decisions doubtless went very far in poisoning the atmosphere in which the infant League was intended to grow and prosper. The constitutional effects were equally great since it prevented the systematic coordination of various international bureaus and world services in the League framework as was intended under Article 24.

Membership alone, of course, was not enough. To be effective it had to be coupled with wholehearted cooperation. And the history of the League shows that in some cases nonmembers, like the United States for example, cooperated more helpfully and effectively than did certain of the formal members. This was particularly true as regards the League's technical (as distinct from its political) activities where near-universality was achieved during the period 1926 to 1934 in the fields of health, social welfare, economic questions, and disarmament, with varying degrees of resulting success and failure. Cooperation, however, did not prove to be an adequate substitute for the assumption of corporate responsibility. And failure to agree on major political questions, like disarmament and security together with the League's condemnation of specific acts of aggression, led to the successive withdrawal of Germany, Japan, and Italy from the League, including, finally, withdrawal from its technical activities as well. Later still, the Soviet Union was expelled for her aggression on Finland.

This development led to an apprehension on the part of many remaining members of the League, notably Chile, Switzerland, and the Scandinavian countries, lest the League become a bloc or an alliance directed against a too-powerful group of nonmember states. They argued that the sanctions obligations of the Covenant had become too onerous in a League which no longer bound the majority of the Great Powers. Prolonged discussions consequently took place in the period 1936 to 1939 as to reforms which should be made in the Covenant (as if that instrument were to blame for the difficulties). These discussions, which mainly turned on the question of universality, resulted in a deadlock as to whether it was better to have a League without universality or universality without League principles.

Doubtless one reason why a larger degree of universal unity was not realized by the League was the general reluctance of all states to abridge their sovereignty. This was, and continues to be, the principal obstacle to effective world organization. The framers of the Covenant . . . introduced into the League's constitution as many elements of a corporate character as was possible without setting up a super-state on the ruins of its sovereign members. For example, in admitting and expelling members without unanimous consent, establishing a permanent secretariat, appointing certain committees by majority vote, limiting freedom of members to make war, providing for collective action in restraint of aggression, and in amending the Covenant against the will of a minority, the League founders went a long way in subordinating national independence to the collective will. At the same time, by admitting the right of secession, expressly refraining from domestic interference, by recommending instead of imposing most of its decisions, and by maintaining the general practice of the unanimous vote, the national sovereignties of member states were substantially safeguarded.

The League of Nations thus is clearly a corporate entity which is something more than the mere sum of its members in a permanent conference, but something less than an international government or even a confederation of states. . . .

One of the most difficult problems which harassed the peace-keeping and war-restraining efforts of the League was the retention of neutrality both by nonmembers and member states. It seems obvious, though it is not everywhere admitted, that the principles of neutrality and collective responsibility are incompatible. If the Covenant had been universally supported no neutrality would have been permissible before the maximum nine-month period had elapsed for attempting peaceful settlement under Article 12. After that members might have been neutral though not necessarily impartial. But if war was resorted to in spite of this delay, no neutrality was permissible; instead, the immediate severance of trade and other relations was required.

In practice, however, this neat arrangement never worked out. A special exception was first made when Switzerland was permitted largely to retain her traditional neutrality though agreeing to cooperate in economic measures against a covenant-breaking state. Later, it was seen that certain Latin-American states, members of the League and parties to the Pact of Paris, freely entered into neutrality treaties despite their obligations under the Covenant. Later still, after the failure of sanctions against Italy and the withdrawal of more Great Powers from the League, certain of the Scandinavian powers announced that the new situation required them to return to their previous position of neutrality.

THE FAILURE OF THE LEAGUE [4]

There were effective reasons for the failure of the League. There was a faulty conception of the problems involved in organizing the world for peace; there were deficiencies in the League machinery which were to make impossible the enforcement of League decisions. The constituent nations' refusal to limit their jealously guarded national sovereignty made League failure in crisis inevitable. But America was not concerned with such criticisms. We found even the pastel commitments involved in joining the League too compromising. American hostility to the Covenant of the League (which constituted the first twenty-six articles of the Versailles Treaty) blocked the ratification of the Versailles Treaty. And Wilson, who had played the leading role in drawing up the Treaty, who had conceived the idea of the League, and whose prestige had sold it to the rest of the world, saw the pledge of full American cooperation repudiated, and returned to America a defeated man.

In the next twenty years the United States staged a number of international peace shows and cooperated in others—the Washington Disarmament Conference in 1921, the Coolidge Conference in 1927, the Nine-Power Treaty, the Briand-Kellogg Pact in 1928, the London Five-Power Naval Conference in 1930,

[4] From "International Organization After the War," analysis by Max Lerner, Professor of Political Science, Williams College, and Edna Lerner. Problems in American Life Series, Unit no. 15. p. 10-13. National Education Association. Washington. 1943. Reprinted by permission.

the League of Nations Council in 1931 on the Manchuria crisis, and others. But these gestures toward international peace remained gestures. The United States consistently showed itself lacking in the imagination or will to involve herself in the economic and political commitments which would make the stated aims of the conferences more than pious hopes.

The world failure to achieve some kind of solution to its economic and political problems after World War I must thus be attributed largely to our fatal inability to see ourselves as an integral part of the world, and to our rejection of responsibility for world order which went with our position as a major world power. The planners of the League had in mind the United States as a major member. Our refusal to join was a blow from which the League could not hope fully to recover.

But the League was not wholly a failure. In the early years it settled a number of disputes involving Sweden and England, Greece and Bulgaria, Danzig and Poland. It organized and directed valuable reconstruction work in Austria and Hungary, protected racial minorities in Central and Eastern Europe, successfully fought disease in Africa, South America, and Asia, and cut down drug and white-slave traffic throughout the world. The International Labor Organization, part of the League machinery, did effective work in reducing working hours, abolishing child labor, and introducing protective health measures for the industrial worker. The Permanent Court at the Hague settled over thirty disputes between nations from 1922 to 1940, and gave advisory opinions in many other disputes which arose during this period.

But while the successes of the League were worthy, her failures were spectacular. They began with her failure to act decisively in such comparatively minor disputes as those between Poland and Lithuania over Vilna, and between Greece and Italy over indemnity to be paid Italy for the murder of an Italian commission on Greek territory. But such failures, trivial in themselves, set the classic pattern of appeasement that was followed in Manchuria, Ethiopia, the German occupation of the Rhineland, and Spain. Each time the boldness of the aggressor was met by protests from the League. And each time the protests were made meaningless by the refusal of the League powers to apply sanctions—the economic and military measures which alone could stop aggression. The Western democracies were attacked by a paralysis of will which left them just strength enough to rationalize their inaction. The pattern established in Manchuria, Ethiopia, and Spain was followed with pitiless consistency as Hitler took over Austria, swallowed Czechoslovakia in two gulps, and occupied Memel and Danzig. Not until he had invaded Poland did the remaining democracies feel called upon to act.

There have been numerous explanations of the League's failures, most of them emphasizing the fact that the member states retained full sovereignty. A world government must be able to enforce its decisions—even in the face of the objections of powerful individual member states. Otherwise . . . it becomes the machinery for random instances of cooperation which would take place just as well without it. E. H. Carr points out that one of the limitations of sovereignty was never seriously considered—largely because the unspoken premises of the League were those of enlightened self-interest. They carried over into international politics the attitude that characterized eighteenth- and nineteenth-century economic thinking. They assumed that each nation in following what seemed its own best interests was in the long run promoting the world's best interests. And they framed a government in which rational thought was to decide where the world's best interests lay and the enlightened nations were to cooperate. Unfortunately this sweet and reasonable principle broke down in the face of national interests, irreconcilable and untractable. The planners had not been tough-minded enough to prepare for such an eventuality. It is true that France made sporadic attempts to strengthen the Covenant provisions in order to insure decisive punishment of aggressors. Both the Draft Treaty of Mutual Assistance in 1923 and the Geneva Protocol a year later were framed with this in mind. But the opposition of Britain and the British Dominions doomed both attempts. . . .

Later, of course, it was the opposition of the fascist nations —Italy, Germany, and Japan—which gave the League its final blow.

An even more serious criticism of the League was that its whole conception of international relationships was a narrowly political one, and ignored the psychological and economic realities on which it should have been based. The "right of self-determination," which had been one of the most successful slogans of the war, led in practice to boundaries being determined largely on political and "moral" grounds, even in the face of economic logic; crushing financial reparations were demanded of countries economically unable to meet them; and no arrangements were made to insure each nation access to vital food and raw material supplies. The sterility of the 1919 peace plans was due to the fact that the planners failed to understand the forces at work in their world. They superimposed a static political building on a shifting economic quicksand. Our victory—when and if it comes —must find us aware of the revolutionary demands of our age, ready with revolutionary answers.

THE LEAGUE OF NATIONS TODAY [5]

The League of Nations came into existence (Jan. 10, 1920) through the coming into force on that date of the Treaty of Versailles. Its purpose, as stated in the Covenant, is "to promote international cooperation and to achieve international peace and security." From 42 members the League grew to include 60 nations (1935). Sixty-three nations have at one time or another been members. The United States and Saudi Arabia are the only nations which have never been members. The roll of states which are still officially members of the League follows:

Afghanistan	China
Albania	Colombia
Argentina	Cuba
Australia	Czechoslovakia
Belgium	Denmark
Bolivia	Dominican Republic
Bulgaria	Ecuador
Canada	Egypt

[5] From "The League of Nations," explanation in the *World Almanac*. p. 754. 1944. *New York World-Telegram*. New York. Reprinted by permission.

Estonia
Ethiopia
Finland
France
Greece
Haiti
India
Iraq
Ireland
Latvia
Liberia
Lithuania
Luxemburg
Mexico
Netherlands

New Zealand
Norway
Panama
Persia (Iran)
Poland
Portugal
Siam (Thailand)
South Africa
Sweden
Switzerland
Turkey
United Kingdom
  (Great Britain)
Uruguay
Yugoslavia

Reasons for withdrawal from the League have been varied. Japan, the first of the great states to give notice of withdrawal, left the League because it adopted the report of the Lytton Commission which reaffirmed Chinese sovereignty over Manchuria and condemned Japan's aggressive action. Germany, which had entered the League (1926) at the time of the Locarno Treaties, gave notice of withdrawal (1933) when the powers represented at the Disarmament Conference refused to grant her equality in arms. Italy gave her notice of withdrawal (1937) because during her war with Ethiopia the League applied economic and financial sanctions against her and refused later to recognize her sovereignty over Ethiopia. The Soviet Union was expelled from the League at a special session of the Assembly (Dec. 1939) because of her aggression against Finland. There have been no meetings of the Assembly since 1939.

Other nations not members of the League, either through failure to join or withdrawal, are:

Brazil
Chile
Costa Rica
Guatemala
Honduras
Hungary

Nicaragua
Paraguay
Peru
Spain
Venezuela

A part of the League Economic and Financial Organization is now established in Princeton, N.J., where it is pursuing research and publishing important documents. The Central Opium Board is operating from a branch office in Washington, D.C. Thus, from the United States and from Geneva, some of the non-political work of the League still continues even under wartime conditions.

The League Assembly (1938) gave emergency powers to a Supervisory Commission enabling it to vote a budget and to carry on reduced activities in absence of regular Assembly and Council meetings. Dr. Carl J. Hambro, former President of the Norwegian Storting, is Chairman of this Supervisory Commission. The Acting Secretary-General is Sean Lester of Ireland.

There are established within the framework of the League the *International Labor Organization* and the *Permanent Court of International Justice* with headquarters at The Hague, the Netherlands.

The object of the International Labor Organization is the establishment of social justice throughout the world. Membership in the League carries with it membership in the Labor Organization. Membership also includes certain countries which do not belong to or have ceased to remain in the League. The present membership is 54 countries. The Labor Organization consists of the International Labor Conference which meets annually in Geneva, and the *International Labor Office,* which is controlled by a Governing Body. The Conference and the Governing Body consist of representatives of Governments, employers and workers. The decisions of the Conference are in the form of draft conventions which each country is obliged to submit to the proper authority for the enactment of legislation or other action. The membership report at each annual meeting on the enactment of legislation.

The Permanent Court of International Justice (usually referred to in the United States as the *World Court*) was created under article 14 of the Covenant of the League, which provided that:

"The Council shall formulate and submit to the members of the League for adoption plans for the establishment of a Permanent Court of International Justice. The Court shall be competent to hear and determine any dispute of international character which parties thereto submit to it. The Court may also give an advisory opinion upon any dispute or question referred to it by the Council of the Assembly."

The court consists of 15 judges, elected by the Assembly and Council of the League in independent sessions. The judges are elected for periods of nine years and are eligible for re-election. Before assuming his duties each judge must take an oath in open court that he will exercise his powers impartially and conscientiously. It is the common practice for the full court of 15 judges to sit but a quorum of nine is sufficient to constitute the Court. The judges when engaged on the business of the Court enjoy diplomatic privileges and immunities. They may not engage in any other occupation of a professional nature or exercise any administrative or political function.

The Court held its first session (1922) and since then sixty cases have come before it. The opinions are in many respects similar to judgments but they are made to the Council or Assembly of the League on points of law on which one of these bodies consults the Court.

The expenses of the Court are paid by the League of Nations and public sessions are held in which cases are heard and judgments delivered.

The organization of the League comprises three principal bodies: the Assembly, the Council and the Secretariat. When the League was still functioning fully, the Assembly met annually in September and was in session for some three weeks. Every member state was entitled to one vote at Assembly deliberations and to send three delegates, either men or women. The Council, or cabinet of the League, met at least three times a year. The Secretariat, which comprises the civil service of the League, up to 1939 had some 700 persons on its staff. It was organized in sections according to special phases of League work, such as political, economic, mandate, minorities, opium traffic, etc. Since now it operates under a greatly reduced budget and since much of its normal work is not at present possible, the Secretariat has been reduced until it comprises slightly less than 100 persons. Of these about 30 are working in the United States.

THE SEARCH FOR SECURITY OUTSIDE
THE LEAGUE [6]

The League of Nations, as proposed by President Wilson, was to be an agency which would insure its members against invasion by other powers. France, from the beginning, desired that the League should be made a powerful body, with an international army under League direction strong enough to oppose any efforts at aggression. But this concept of the League did not have the support of its other members. So France, fearful of another German attack, made every effort to secure guarantees of security outside of the League organization, as such. In 1919, she induced the United States and Great Britain to sign a treaty guaranteeing the Franco-German frontier and agreeing to come to the aid of France in the event of German attack. The treaty was not ratified by the United States, and as a consequence, Great Britain withdrew its adherence. So France turned to other nations of Europe, and attempted, through alliances, to build a "ring of steel" around Germany. Mutual assistance alliances were concluded with Belgium in 1920, with Poland in 1921, and with Czechoslovakia in 1924. Poland, in turn, made similar treaties of alliance with the Little Entente allies, Czechoslovakia, Jugoslavia, and Rumania.

In 1925 Germany, perhaps herself alarmed by the rapidly increasing power of France, proposed that the powers, by joint treaty, guarantee the Franco-German border. The result was the series of treaties known as the Locarno Pacts. Germany, France and Belgium undertook to keep peace with each other and to settle their differences by arbitration. Germany concluded similar treaties of arbitration with Poland and Czechoslovakia. In addition, France, Belgium, Italy, Germany and Great Britain signed a treaty guaranteeing the inviolability of the existing frontiers between Germany and Belgium and between Germany and France, and providing for the demilitarization of German territory west of a line fifty kilometers east of the Rhine. Each of

[6] From "Anglo-American Agreement," compiled by H. B. Summers. p. 31-3. (The Reference Shelf. Vol. 12). H. W. Wilson Co. New York. 1938. Reprinted by permission.

the signatories agreed to support the agreement with armed force, if need be.

During the next few years, the number of treaties of alliance, treaties of arbitration, and treaties binding their signatories to non-aggression increased greatly. France signed non-aggression pacts with Rumania and Jugoslavia; Russia concluded treaties binding each signatory to remain neutral in the event of a war involving the other with Turkey, Germany, Lithuania, Finland, Estonia and Poland; Italy negotiated treaties of friendship and neutrality with the Little Entente nations and with Albania, Hungary, Austria, Turkey and Greece.

With practically every nation in Europe a signatory to one or more non-aggression pacts, the situation was ripe, in 1928, for the Kellogg Peace Pact. In 1924, the Assembly of the League of Nations adopted a Protocol or amendment to the League Covenant, providing that private war be outlawed between nations, that disputes be submitted to arbitration, and that the members of the League enforce the arbitration awards by armed force if necessary. But the Protocol arrangement came to nothing, through refusal of the British government to agree to it—on the ground that, under the pact, Great Britain might be forced to take part in a European war for a cause which did not affect her own interests.

The Kellogg Pact did not go so far as the Protocol of 1924. It provided simply that the signatory nations should "renounce war as an instrument of national policy." The pact came into being as a result of a proposal from Briand that France and the United States conclude a treaty renouncing war between the two nations. Secretary Kellogg agreed to the idea, but proposed that the treaty be entered into jointly by all of the powers, rather than by France and the United States alone. As a result, the Pact was signed at Paris by representatives of fifteen major nations; it was later ratified by 62 governments, including practically every independent nation in the world.

While no provision was made in the Kellogg Treaty for concerted action against aggressor nations, many of the nations adhering to the pact apparently believed that some sort of joint action was implied. The London Agreements of 1933, signed by Soviet Russia and the Balkan states, expressed the conviction that the Kellogg Pact forbade all aggression, and bound the signers to proceed jointly against any Balkan state which joined an outside power that had committed an act of aggression against one of the signatories. Likewise, in the dispute between Russia and China in Manchuria, and later on the occasion of the Japanese invasion of Manchuria, the American government protested the action of the aggressors as violation of the Kellogg Pact, and in the latter case, refused to recognize Japanese title to territory gained by conquest. In each case, the United States called for the support, in the measures taken, of other signatories to the Kellogg Treaty.

THE ATLANTIC CHARTER [7]

The President of the United States of America and the Prime Minister, Mr. Churchill, representing his Majesty's Government in the United Kingdom, being met together, deem it right to make known certain common principles in the national policies of their respective countries on which they base their hopes for a better future for the world.

1. Their countries seek no aggrandizement, territorial or other.

2. They desire to see no territorial changes that do not accord with the freely expressed wishes of the peoples concerned.

3. They respect the right of all peoples to choose the form of government under which they will live; and they wish to see sovereign rights and self-government restored to those who have been forcibly deprived of them.

4. They will endeavor, with due respect for their existing obligations, to further the enjoyment by all states, great or small, victor or vanquished, of access, on equal terms, to the trade and to the raw materials of the world which are needed for their economic prosperity.

5. They desire to bring about the fullest collaboration between all nations in the economic field with the object of securing, for all, improved labor standards, economic advancement and social security.

[7] As promulgated by President Roosevelt and Prime Minister Churchill on August 14, 1941.

6. After the final destruction of the Nazi tyranny, they hope to see established a peace which will afford to all nations the means of dwelling in safety within their own boundaries, and which will afford assurance that all the men in all the lands may live out their lives in freedom from fear and want.

7. Such a peace should enable all men to traverse the high seas and oceans without hindrance.

8. They believe that all of the nations of the world, for realistic as well as spiritual reasons must come to the abandonment of the use of force. Since no future peace can be maintained if land, sea or air armaments continue to be employed by nations which threaten, or may threaten, aggression outside of their frontiers, they believe, pending the establishment of a wider and permanent system of general security, that the disarmament of such nations is essential. They will likewise aid and encourage all other practicable measures which will lighten for peace-loving peoples the crushing burden of armaments.

DECLARATION BY UNITED NATIONS

The governments signatory hereto,

Having subscribed to a common program of purposes and principles embodied in the joint declaration of the President of the United States of America and the Prime Minister of the United Kingdom of Great Britain and Northern Ireland dated August 14, 1941, known as the Atlantic Charter, being convinced that complete victory over their enemies is essential to defend life, liberty, independence and religious freedom, and to preserve human rights and justice in their own lands as well as in other lands, and that they are now engaged in a common struggle against savage and brutal forces seeking to subjugate the world, declare:

(1) Each government pledges itself to employ its full resources, military or economic, against those members of the tripartite pact and its adherents with which such government is at war.

(2) Each government pledges itself to cooperate with the governments signatory hereto and not to make a separate armistice or peace with the enemies.

The foregoing declaration may be adhered to by other nations which are, or which may be, rendering material assistance and contributions in the struggles for victory over Hitlerism.

Done at Washington, January First, 1942.

Original Signatories:

Australia
Belgium
Canada
China
 Costa Rica
Cuba
Czecho-Slovakia
Dominican Republic
El Salvador
Greece
Guatemala
Haiti
Honduras
India
Luxembourg

Netherlands
New Zealand
Nicaragua
Norway
Panama
Poland
Union of South Africa
Union of Soviet Socialist Republics
United Kingdom of Great Britain and Northern Ireland
United States of America
Yugoslavia

Later Signatories:

Bolivia
Brazil
Colombia
Ethiopia
France

Iran
Iraq
Liberia
Mexico
The Philippines

WARTIME ORGANIZATION OF THE UNITED NATIONS [8]

The urgent needs of war have led to bilateral and regional commitments, not between the United Nations as a coherent group, but between most of them and the United States separate-

[8] From "Problems of Economic Reorganization," by J. B. Condliffe, Professor of Economics, University of California; Chairman of Geneva Research Committee. p. 15-20. Commission to Study the Organization of Peace. New York, January, 1943.

ly, or between them and Britain which in turn negotiates with the United States. It is almost impossible to tabulate these commitments systematically. They are in part a continuation of prewar policies and in part war improvisations. Some are regional and others bilateral. Some have at least rudimentary executive organs to implement them, others are simply treaty instruments or executive commitments without any joint secretariat. . . .

Elements of the system of war trade and investment consist of the loans extended by the Treasury, the Import-Export Bank and the Reconstruction Finance Corporation to different members of the United Nations, . . . the purchasing agreements made by the subsidiaries of the R. F. C. . . . , by the Board of Economic Warfare and the allocation of export markets by the War Trade Committee.

It is apparent that all of these operations of economic warfare, involving many United Nations countries and many departments in the United States are, or ought to be, subordinate to decisions of policy and strategy. It is at this point, however, that much of the confusion of the war effort arises. There is no Supreme War Council of the United Nations. There is a Pacific War Council of some of them, a United States-Canadian Permanent Joint Board, a Joint Mexican-United States Defense Committee and an agreement with Cuba, . . . an Inter-American Defense Board, the Anglo-United States Combined Chiefs of Staffs, as well as mutual aid (lend-lease) agreements between the United States and ten of its allies. This does not by any means exhaust the list of the bilateral, regional and multilateral arrangements and agreements to which the United States has recently become a party. . . .

The most important of these joint organizations seem in practice to be the Anglo-American arrangements—the Combined Chiefs of Staff and the Combined Boards dealing with Munitions, Raw Materials, Shipping, Production and Resources, and Food. The Pacific War Council is consultative and does not possess executive power. The Combined Chiefs of Staff, indeed, do not seem to have the ultimate power of decision and the British members are not the ranking commanders. . . .

The situation may, however, be summarized somewhat as follows. The prewar trading system, confused and disordered

by the breakdown of its directive organs, survives both on the
side of business and of government. On top of it, for war
needs there has been imposed a temporary structure of war trade
(and investment) between the United Nations. This temporary
trade already accounts for much more than half the exports of
the United States and grows steadily as private trade shrinks. . . .
There has not, as yet, emerged any clear-cut pattern of organization designed to implement the strategy of United Nations policy.
There must come a time, if it has not already arrived, when
there will be need to develop such organization as will give
broader scope for consultation among all the United Nations
and will depend less upon personal concentration of power.
This organization, if and when it comes, will be the organization available not only for the conduct of the war, but also for
the transition from war to peace.

EXTENT OF INTERNATIONAL COOPERATION
IN WORLD WAR II [9]

A summary of these arrangements follows. It is arranged
geographically by areas; but needs to be interpreted with caution
since the practical development and organization of the various
agreements differs greatly.

1. INTER-AMERICAN:

1939, October	:	Inter-American Financial and Advisory Committee supplemented by Inter-American Development Commission (June 1940) and Inter-American Maritime Technical Commission (November 1941)
1942, January	:	Inter-American Defense Board
		Inter-American Commission for Territorial Administration
		Inter-American Juridical Committee
		Emergency Advisory Committee
February	:	Joint Mexican-United States Defense Committee
April	:	Agreement for Reciprocal Use of Air Bases
August	:	United States-Mexican Agreement on Seasonal Labor Migration
September	:	Cuba-United States Agreement for Defense Coordination

[9] From "Problems of Economic Reorganization," by J. B. Condliffe, Professor
of Economics, University of California; Chairman of Geneva Research Committee.
p. 15-20. Commission to Study the Organization of Peace. New York, January,
1943.

2. UNITED STATES-CANADIAN:

   1940, August   : Permanent Joint Defense Board
   1941, May   : Materials Coordinating Committee
         June   : Permanent Joint Economic Committee
         November: Joint War Production Committee

3. UNITED STATES-UNITED KINGDOM:

   1942, January : Combined Munitions Assignment Board
                    Combined Raw Materials Board
                    Combined Shipping Adjustment Board
         February : Combined Chiefs of Staff
         March   : Anglo-American Caribbean Commission
         June   : Combined Production and Resources Board
                    Combined Food Board

4. UNITED STATES-CHINA:

   1942, March   : Financial Agreement

5. UNITED NATIONS:

   1941, August   : Atlantic Charter
   1942, January : Declaration of the United Nations; Rio de Janeiro Conference Resolution **XXXV** in support of the Atlantic Charter
         March   : Pacific War Council
         April   : Middle East Supply Center
                    Allied Supply Council in Australia
                    Southwest Pacific Command
                    South Pacific Command

6. LEND-LEASE AGREEMENTS:

   1942, February : United Kingdom
         June   : China
                    USSR
                    Belgium
         July   : Poland
                    Netherlands
                    Greece
                    Czechoslovakia
                    Norway
                    Yugoslavia
         September: Reciprocal Lend-Lease Agreements with Australia, Fighting France, New Zealand and the United Kingdom

U.S. HOUSE OF REPRESENTATIVES
RESOLUTION, NO. 114 [10]

That the Congress hereby expresses itself as favoring the creation of appropriate international machinery with power

[10] Introduced by Representative J. W. Fulbright (Arkansas) Passed, September 21, 1943, by a vote of 360 to 29.

adequate to establish and to maintain a just and lasting peace, among the nations of the world, and as favoring participation by the United States therein.

THE MOSCOW DECLARATION [11]

The governments of the United States of America, the United Kingdom, the Soviet Union and China:

United in their determination, in accordance with the declaration by the United Nations of January 1, 1942, and subsequent declarations, to continue hostilities against those Axis powers with which they respectively are at war until such powers have laid down their arms on the basis of unconditional surrender;

Conscious of their responsibility to secure the liberation of themselves and the peoples allied with them from the menace of aggression;

Recognizing the necessity of ensuring a rapid and orderly transition from war to peace and of establishing and maintaining international peace and security with the least diversion of the world's human and economic resources for armaments;

Jointly declare:

1. That their united action, pledged for the prosecution of the war against their respective enemies, will be continued for the organization and maintenance of peace and security.

2. That those of them at war with a common enemy will act together in all matters relating to the surrender and disarmament of that enemy.

3. That they will take all measures deemed by them to be necessary to provide against any violation of the terms imposed upon the enemy.

4. That they recognize the necessity of establishing at the earliest practicable date a general international organization, based on the principle of the sovereign equality of all peace-loving states, and open to membership by all such states, large and small, for the maintenance of international peace and security.

[11] Joint Four-Nation Agreement of Foreign Ministers. Molotov, Eden, Hull, Foo Ping-sheung. Moscow, October 30, 1943.

5. That for the purpose of maintaining international peace and security pending the re-establishment of law and order and the inauguration of a system of general security, they will consult with one another and as occasion requires with other members of the United Nations with a view to joint action on behalf of the community of nations.

6. That after the termination of hostilities they will not employ their military forces within the territories of other states except for the purposes envisaged in this declaration and after joint consultation.

7. That they will confer and cooperate with one another and with other members of the United Nations to bring about a practicable general agreement with respect to the regulation of armaments in the postwar period.

U.S. SENATE RESOLUTION, NO. 192 [12]

RESOLVED, That the war against all our enemies be waged until complete victory is achieved.

That the United States cooperate with its comrades-in-arms in securing a just and honorable peace.

That the United States, acting through its constitutional processes, join with free and sovereign nations in establishment and maintenance of international authority with power to prevent aggression and to preserve the peace of the world.

That the Senate recognizes the necessity of there being established at the earliest practicable date a general international organization, based on the principle of the sovereign equality of all peace-loving states, and open to membership by all such states, large and small, for the maintenance of international peace and security.

That, pursuant to the Constitution of the United States, any treaty made to effect the purposes of this resoluion, on behalf of the Government of the United States with any other nation or any association of nations, shall be made only by and with the advice and consent of the Senate of the United States, provided two thirds of the Senators present concur.

[12] Introduced by Senator Tom Connally (Texas). Passed November 5, 1943, by a vote of 85 to 5.

THE CAIRO DECLARATION [13]

The several military missions have agreed upon future military operations against Japan. The Three Great Allies expressed their resolve to bring unrelenting pressure against their brutal enemies by sea, land, and air. This pressure is already rising.

The Three Great Allies are fighting this war to restrain and punish the aggression of Japan. They covet no gain for themselves and have no thought of territorial expansion. It is their purpose that Japan shall be stripped of all the islands in the Pacific which she has seized or occupied since the beginning of the First World War in 1914, and that all the territories Japan has stolen from the Chinese such as Manchuria, Formosa and the Pescadores, shall be restored to the Republic of China. Japan will also be expelled from all other territories, which she has taken by violence and greed. The aforesaid three great powers, mindful of the enslavement of the people of Korea, are determined that in due course Korea shall become free and independent.

With these objects in view the three Allies, in harmony with those of the United Nations at war with Japan, will continue to persevere in the serious and prolonged operations necessary to procure the unconditional surrender of Japan.

THE TEHERAN DECLARATION [14]

We, the President of the United States of America, the Prime Minister of Great Britain, and the Premier of the Soviet Union, have met in these four days past in this the capital of our ally, Teheran, and have shaped and confirmed our common policy.

We express our determination that our nations shall work together in the war and in the peace that will follow.

As to the war, our military staffs have joined in our round-table discussions and we have concerted our plans for the destruction of the German forces. We have reached complete

[13] Statement on Conference of Roosevelt, Chiang Kai-shek and Churchill held in North Africa, November 22-26, 1943. Released, December 1, 1943.

[14] Three-Power Agreement. Signed at Teheran, December 1, 1943, by Roosevelt, Stalin, Churchill.

agreement as to the scope and timing of operations which will be undertaken from the east, west and south. The common understanding which we have here reached guarantees that victory will be ours.

And as to the peace, we are sure that our concord will make it an enduring peace. We recognize fully the supreme responsibility resting upon us and all the nations to make a peace which will command good will from the overwhelming masses of the peoples of the world and banish the scourge and terror of war for many generations.

With our diplomatic advisers we have surveyed the problems of the future. We shall seek the cooperation and active participation of all nations, large and small, whose peoples in heart and in mind are dedicated, as are our own peoples, to the elimination of tyranny and slavery, oppression and intolerance. We will welcome them as they may choose to come into the world family of democratic nations.

No power on earth can prevent our destroying the German armies by land, their U-boats by sea, and their war plants from the air. Our attacks will be relentless and increasing.

Emerging from these friendly conferences we look with confidence to the day when all the peoples of the world may live free lives untouched by tyranny and according to their varying desires and their own consciences.

We came here with hope and determination. We leave here friends in fact, in spirit, and in purpose.

REPUBLICAN PLATFORM OF 1944 [15]

We favor responsible participation by the United States in postwar cooperative organization among sovereign nations to prevent military aggression and to attain permanent peace with organized justice in a free world.

Such an organization should develop effective cooperative means to direct peace forces to prevent or repel military aggression. Pending this, we pledge continuing collaboration with the United Nations to assure the ultimate objective.

[15] Excerpts on Foreign Policy from Platform Adopted by the Republican Party in Chicago on June 27.

We believe, however, that peace and security do not depend upon the sanction of force alone, but should prevail by virtue of reciprocal interests and spiritual values recognized in the security agreements. The treaty of peace should be just; the nations which are the victims of aggression should be restored to sovereignty and self-government; and the organized cooperation of the nation should concern itself with basic causes of world disorder. It should promote a world opinion to influence the nations to right conduct, develop international law and maintain an international tribunal to deal with justiciable disputes.

We shall seek, in our relations with other nations, conditions calculated to promote world-wide economic stability not only for the sake of the world, but also to the end that our own people may enjoy a high level of employment in an increasingly prosperous world.

DEMOCRATIC PLATFORM OF 1944 [16]

We pledge:

To join with the other United Nations in the establishment of an international organization based on the principle of the sovereign equality of all peace-loving states, open to membership by all such states, large and small, for the prevention of aggression and the maintenance of international peace and security;

To make all necessary and effective agreements and arrangements through which the nations would maintain adequate forces to meet the needs of preventing war and of making impossible the preparation for war and which would have such forces available for joint action when necessary.

Such organization must be endowed with power to employ armed forces when necessary to prevent aggression and preserve peace.

We favor the maintenance of an international court of justice of which the United States shall be a member and the employment of diplomacy, conciliation, arbitration and other like methods where appropriate in the settlement of international disputes.

[16] Excerpts on Foreign Policy from Platform Adopted by the Democratic Party in Chicago on July 20.

THE END OF THE PREPARATORY STAGE [17]

If the Moscow Agreement was the act of governments the votes of the Senate and House on the Connally and Fulbright Resolutions showed that the principles set forth in it had the support of a united people. Over ninety per cent of the total membership of Congress voted their adherence to the principle of collective security and this support came from all parts of the nation. In the representation of thirty-four states not a single vote in either house was cast against these Resolutions, and in eleven other states there were only one or two opposed. Therefore, we have before us the all-important fact that the action of the government this time will not be subject to the hazard of partisan debate. It is a free expression of the people themselves and has been taken out of the arena of domestic politics by the joint action of leaders conscious of their responsibility to the country as a whole.

"The Joint Four-Nation Declaration" issued in the names of the governments of the United States of America, the United Kingdom, the Soviet Union and China covers only part of a wide field of international relations. It is limited to the problems of security and does not deal with those of economic and social welfare and international justice. These are left for future consideration, and properly so, because the establishment and maintenance of peace is the indispensable condition for progress in all other matters.

THE DUMBARTON OAKS PROPOSALS [18]

PROPOSALS FOR THE ESTABLISHMENT OF A GENERAL INTERNATIONAL ORGANIZATION

There should be established an international organization under the title of the United Nations, the charter of which

[17] From "Fundamentals of the International Organization: General Statement," Fourth Report of Commission to Study the Organization of Peace. November, 1943. p. 22-3. Reprinted by permission.

[18] From "Texts of Statements on Dumbarton Oaks and Documents Giving Tentative Security Plans," *The New York Times*. 93:12. October 10, 1944. Reprinted by permission.

should contain provisions necessary to give effect to the proposals which follow.

CHAPTER I. PURPOSES: The purposes of the organization should be:

1. To maintain international peace and security, and to that end to take effective collective measures for the prevention and removal of threats to the peace and the suppression of acts of aggression or other breaches of the peace and to bring about by peaceful means adjustment or settlement of international disputes which may lead to a breach of the peace;

2. To develop friendly relations among nations and to take other appropriate measures to strengthen universal peace;

3. To achieve international cooperation in the solution of international economic, social and other humanitarian problems; and

4. To afford a center for harmonizing the actions of nations in the achievement of these common ends.

CHAPTER II. PRINCIPLES: In pursuit of the purposes mentioned in Chapter I the organization and its members should act in accordance with the following principles:

1. The organization is based on the principle of the sovereign equality of all peace-loving states.

2. All members of the organization undertake, in order to insure to all of them the rights and benefits resulting from membership in the organization, to fulfill the obligations assumed by them in accordance with the Charter.

3. All members of the organization shall settle their disputes by peaceful means in such a manner that international peace and security are not endangered.

4. All members of the organization shall refrain in their international relations from the threat or use of force in any manner inconsistent with the purposes of the organization.

5. All members of the organization shall give every assistance to the organization in any action undertaken by it in accordance with the provisions of the Charter.

6. All members of the organization shall refrain from giving assistance to any state against which preventive or enforcement action is being undertaken by the organization.

The organization should insure that states not members of the organization act in accordance with these principles so far as may be necessary for the maintenance of international peace and security.

CHAPTER III. MEMBERSHIP: 1. Membership of the organization should be open to all peace-loving states.

CHAPTER IV. PRINCIPAL ORGANS: 1. The organization should have as its principal organs:

    A. A General Assembly;
    B. A Security Council;
    C. An International Court of Justice; and
    D. A Secretariat.

2. The organization should have such subsidiary agencies as may be found necessary.

CHAPTER V. THE GENERAL ASSEMBLY: *Section A—Composition*: All members of the organization should be members of the General Assembly and should have a number of representatives to be specified in the charter.

Section B—Functions and Powers: 1. The General Assembly should have the right to consider the general principles of cooperation in the maintenance of international peace and security, including the principles governing disarmament and the regulation of armaments; to discuss any questions relating to the maintenance of international peace and security brought before it by any member or members of the organization or by the Security Council; and to make recommendations with regard to any such principles or questions. Any such questions on which action is necessary should be referred to the Security Council by the General Assembly either before or after discussion. The General Assembly should not on its own initiative make recommendations on any matter relating to the maintenance of international peace and security which is being dealt with by the Security Council.

2. The General Assembly should be empowered to admit new members to the organization upon recommendation of the Security Council.

3. The General Assembly should, upon recommendation of the Security Council, be empowered to suspend from the exercise of any rights or privileges of membership any member of the organization against which preventive or enforcement action shall have been taken by the Security Council. The exercise of the rights and privileges thus suspended may be restored by decision of the Security Council. The General Assembly should be empowered, upon recommendation of the Security Council, to expel from the organization any member of the organization which persistently violates the principles contained in the Charter.

4. The General Assembly should elect the non-permanent members of the Security Council and the members of the Economic and Social Council provided for in Chapter IX. It should be empowered to elect, upon recommendation of the Security Council, the secretary-general of the organization. It should perform such functions in relation to the election of the judges of the International Court of Justice as may be conferred upon it by the statute of the court.

5. The General Assembly should apportion the expenses among the members of the organization and should be empowered to approve the budgets of the organization.

6. The General Assembly should initiate studies and make recommendations for the purpose of promoting international co-operation in political, economic and social fields and of adjusting situations likely to impair the general welfare.

7. The General Assembly should make recommendations for the coordination of the policies of international economic, social and other specialized agencies brought into relation with the organization in accordance with agreements between such agencies and the organization.

8. The General Assembly should receive and consider annual and special reports from the Security Council and reports from other bodies of the organization.

Section C—Voting: 1. Each member of the organization should have one vote in the General Assembly.

2. Important decisions of the General Assembly, including recommendations with respect to the maintenance of international peace and security; election of members of the Security Council; election of members of the Economic and Social Council; admis-

sion of members, suspension of the exercise of the rights and privileges of members, and expulsion of members; and budgetary questions should be made by a two-thirds majority of those present and voting. On other questions, including the determination of additional categories of questions to be decided by a two-thirds majority, the decisions of the General Assembly should be made by a simple majority vote.

Section D—Procedure: 1. The General Assembly should meet in regular annual sessions and in such special sessions as occasion may require.

2. The General Assembly should adopt its own rules of procedure and elect its president for each session.

3. The General Assembly should be empowered to set up such bodies and agencies as it may deem necessary for the performance of its functions.

Chapter VI. The Security Council: *Section A—Composition*: The Security Council should consist of one representative of each of eleven members of the organization. Representatives of the United States of America, the United Kingdom of Great Britain and Northern Ireland, the Union of Soviet Socialist Republics, the Republic of China and, in due course, France, should have permanent seats. The General Assembly should elect six states to fill the non-permanent seats. These six states should be elected for a term of two years, three retiring each year. They should not be immediately eligible for re-election. In the first election of the non-permanent members three should be chosen by the General Assembly for one-year terms and three for two-year terms.

Section B—Principal Functions and Powers: 1. In order to ensure prompt and effective action by the organization, members of the organization should by the Charter confer on the Security Council primary responsibility for the maintenance of international peace and security and should agree that in carrying out these duties under this responsibility it should act on their behalf.

2. In discharging these duties the Security Council should act in accordance with the purposes and principles of the organization.

3. The specific powers conferred on the Security Council in order to carry out these duties are laid down in Chapter VIII.

4. All members of the organization should obligate themselves to accept the decisions of the Security Council and to carry them out in accordance with the provisions of the Charter.

5. In order to promote the establishment and maintenance of international peace and security with the least diversion of the world's human and economic resources for armaments, the Security Council, with the assistance of the military staff committee referred to in Chapter VIII, Section B, Paragraph 9, should have the responsibility for formulating plans for the establishment of a system of regulation of armaments for submission to the members of the organization.

Section C—Voting: NOTE: The question of voting procedure in the Security Council is still under consideration.

Section D—Procedure: 1. The Security Council should be so organized as to be able to function continuously and each state member of the Security Council should be permanently represented at the headquarters of the organization. It may hold meetings at such other places as in its judgment may best facilitate its work. There should be periodic meetings at which each state member of the Security Council could if it so desired be represented by a member of the government or some other special representative.

2. The Security Council should be empowered to set up such bodies or agencies as it may deem necessary for the performance of its functions including regional subcommittees of the military staff committee.

3. The Security Council should adopt its own rules of procedure, including the method of selecting its president.

4. Any member of the organization should participate in the discussion of any question brought before the Security Council whenever the Security Council considers that the interests of that member of the organization are specially affected.

5. Any member of the organization not having a seat on the Security Council and any state not a member of the organization, if it is a party to a dispute under consideration by the Se-

curity Council, should be invited to participate in the discussion relating to the dispute.

CHAPTER VII. AN INTERNATIONAL COURT OF JUSTICE: 1. There should be an International Court of Justice which should constitute the principal judicial organ of the organization.

2. The Court should be constituted and should function in accordance with a statute which should be annexed to and be a part of the Charter of the organization.

3. The statute of the Court of International Justice should be either (a) the statute of the Permanent Court of International Justice, continued in force with such modifications as may be desirable, or (b) a new statute in the preparation of which the statute of the Permanent Court of International Justice should be used as a basis.

4. All members of the organization should ipso facto be parties to the statute of the International Court of Justice.

5. Conditions under which states not members of the organization may become parties to the statute of the International Court of Justice should be determined in each case by the General Assembly upon recommendation of the Security Council.

CHAPTER VIII. ARRANGEMENTS FOR THE MAINTENANCE OF INTERNATIONAL PEACE AND SECURITY, INCLUDING PREVENTION AND SUPPRESSION OF AGGRESSION: *Section A—Pacific Settlement of Disputes*: 1. The Security Council should be empowered to investigate any dispute or any situation which may lead to international friction or give rise to a dispute in order to determine whether its continuance is likely to endanger the maintenance of international peace and security.

2. Any state, whether member of the organization or not, may bring any such dispute or situation to the attention of the General Assembly or of the Security Council.

3. The parties to any dispute the continuance of which is likely to endanger the maintenance of international peace and security should obligate themselves, first of all, to seek a solution by negotiation, mediation, conciliation, arbitration or judicial settlement or other peaceful means of their own choice. The

Security Council should call upon the parties to settle their dispute by such means.

4. If, nevertheless, parties to a dispute of the nature referred to in Paragraph 3 above fail to settle it by the means indicated in that paragraph they should obligate themselves to refer it to the Security Council. The Security Council should, in each case, decide whether or not the continuance of the particular dispute is in fact likely to endanger the maintenance of international peace and security and, accordingly, whether it should take action under Paragraph 5.

5. The Security Council should be empowered, at any stage of a dispute of the nature referred to in Paragraph 3 above, to recommend appropriate procedures or methods of adjustment.

6. Justiciable disputes should normally be referred to the International Court of Justice. The Security Council should be empowered to refer to the Court, for advice, legal questions connected with other disputes.

7. The provisions of Paragraph 1 to 6 of Section A should not apply to situations or disputes arising out of matters which by international law are solely within the domestic jurisdiction of the state concerned.

Section B—Determination of Threats to the Peace or Acts of Aggression and Action With Respect Thereto: 1. Should the Security Council deem that a failure to settle a dispute in accordance with procedures indicated in Paragraph 3 of Section A, or in accordance with its recommendations made under Paragraph 5 of Section A, constitutes a threat to the maintenance of international peace and security, it should take any measures necessary for the maintenance of international peace and security in accordance with the purposes and principles of the organization.

2. In general the Security Council should determine the existence of any threat to the peace, breach of the peace or act of aggression and should make recommendations or decide upon the measures to be taken to maintain or restore peace and security.

3. The Security Council should be empowered to determine what diplomatic, economic, or other measures not involving the use of armed force should be employed to give effect to its decisions, and to call upon members of the organization to apply such measures. Such measures may include complete or partial interruption of rail, sea, air, postal, telegraphic, radio and other means of communication and the severance of diplomatic and economic relations.

4. Should the Security Council consider such measures to be inadequate, it should be empowered to take such action by air, naval or land forces as may be necessary to maintain or restore international peace and security. Such action may include demonstrations, blockade and other operations by air, sea or land forces of members of the organization.

5. In order that all members of the organization should contribute to the maintenance of international peace and security, they should undertake to make available to the Security Council, on its call and in accordance with a special agreement or agreements concluded among themselves, armed forces, facilities and assistance necessary for the purpose of maintaining international peace and security. Such agreement or agreements should govern the numbers and types of forces and the nature of the facilities and assistance to be provided. The special agreement or agreements should be negotiated as soon as possible and should in each case be subject to approval by the Security Council and to ratification by the signatory states in accordance with their constitutional processes.

6. In order to enable urgent military measures to be taken by the organization there should be held immediately available by the members of the organization national air force contingents for combined international enforcement action. The strength and degree of readiness of these contingents and plans for their combined action should be determined by the Security Council with the assistance of the Military Staff Committee within the limits laid down in the special agreement or agreements referred to in Paragraph 5 above.

7. The action required to carry out the decisions of the Security Council for the maintenance of international peace and security should be taken by all the members of the organization in cooperation or by some of them as the Security Council may determine. This undertaking should be carried out by the members of the organization by their own action and through action of the appropriate specialized organizations and agencies of which they are members.

Plans for the application of armed force should be made by the Security Council with the assistance of the Military Staff Committee referred to in Paragraph 9 below.

9. There should be established a Military Staff Committee the functions of which should be to advise and assist the Security Council on all questions relating to the Security Council's military requirements for the maintenance of international peace and security, to the employment and command of forces placed at its disposal, to the regulation of armaments, and to possible disarmament. It should be responsible under the Security Council for the strategic direction of any armed forces placed at the disposal of the Security Council. The committee should be composed of the Chiefs of Staff of the permanent members of the Security Council or their representatives. Any member of the organization not permanently represented on the committee should be invited by the committee to be associated with it when the efficient discharge of the committee's responsibilities requires that such a state should participate in its work. Questions of command of forces should be worked out subsequently.

10. The members of the organization should join in affording mutual assistance in carrying out the measures decided upon by the Security Council.

11. Any state, whether a member of the organization or not, which finds itself confronted with special economic problems arising from the carrying out of measures which have been decided upon by the Security Council should have the right to consult the Security Council in regard to a solution of those problems.

Section C—Regional Arrangements: 1. Nothing in the Charter should preclude the existence of regional arrangements or agencies for dealing with such matters relating to the maintenance of international peace and security as are appropriate for regional action, provided such arrangements or agencies and their activities are consistent with the purposes and principles of the organization. The Security Council should encourage settlement of local disputes through such regional arrangements or by such regional agencies, either on the initiative of the states concerned or by reference from the Security Council.

2. The Security Council should, where appropriate, utilize such arrangements or agencies for enforcement action under its authority, but no enforcement action should be taken under regional arrangements or by regional agencies without the authorization of the Security Council.

3. The Security Council should at all times be kept fully informed of activities undertaken or in contemplation under regional arrangements or by regional agencies for the maintenance of international peace and security.

CHAPTER IX. ARRANGEMENT FOR INTERNATIONAL ECONOMIC AND SOCIAL COOPERATION: *Section A—Purpose and Relationships*: 1. With a view to the creation of conditions of stability and well-being which are necessary for peaceful and friendly relations among nations, the organization should facilitate solutions of international economic, social and other humanitarian problems and promote respect for human rights and fundamental freedoms. Responsibility for the discharge of this function should be vested in the General Assembly and, under the authority of the General Assembly, in an Economic and Social Council.

2. The various specialized economic, social and other organizations and agencies would have responsibilities in their respective fields as defined in their statutes. Each such organization or agency should be brought into relationship with the organization on terms to be determined by agreement between the

Economic and Social Council and the appropriate authorities of the specialized organization or agency, subject to approval by the General Assembly.

Section B—Composition and Voting: The Economic and Social Council should consist of representatives of eighteen members of the organization. The states to be represented for this purpose should be elected by the General Assembly for terms of three years. Each such state should have one representative, who should have one vote. Decisions of the Economic and Social Council should be taken by simple majority vote of those present and voting.

Section C—Functions and Powers of the Economic and Social Council: 1. The Economic and Social Council should be empowered:

a. To carry out, within the scope of its functions, recommendations of the General Assembly;

b. To make recommendations, on its own initiative, with respect to international economic, social and other humanitarian matters;

c. To receive and consider reports from the economic, social and other organizations or agencies brought into relationship with the organization, and to coordinate their activities through consultations with, and recommendations to, such organizations or agencies;

d. To examine the administrative budgets of such specialized organizations or agencies with a view to making recommendations to the organizations or agencies concerned;

e. To enable the secretary-general to provide information to the Security Council;

f. To assist the Security Council upon its request; and

g. To perform such other functions within the general scope of its competence as may be assigned to it by the General Assembly.

Section D—Organization and Procedure: 1. The Economic and Social Council should set up an economic commission, a social commission, and such other commissions as may be required. These commissions should consist of experts. There should be a permanent staff which should constitute a part of the secretariat of the organization.

2. The Economic and Social Council should make suitable arrangements for representatives of the specialized organizations or agencies to participate without vote in its deliberations and in those of the commissions established by it.

3. The Economic and Social Council should adopt its own rules of procedure and the method of selecting its president.

CHAPTER X. THE SECRETARIAT: 1. There should be a secretariat comprising a secretary-general and such staff as may be required. The secretary-general should be the chief administrative officer of the organization. He should be elected by the General Assembly, on recommendation of the Security Council, for such term and under such conditions as are specified in the Charter.

2. The secretary-general should act in that capacity in all meetings of the General Assembly, of the Security Council, and of the Economic and Social Council and should make an annual report to the General Assembly on the work of the organization.

3. The secretary-general should have the right to bring to the attention of the Security Council any matter which in his opinion may threaten international peace and security.

CHAPTER XI. AMENDMENTS: Amendments should come into force for all members of the organization when they have been adopted by a vote of two-thirds of the members of the General Assembly and ratified in accordance with their respective constitutional process by the members of the organization having permanent membership on the Security Council and by a majority of the other members of the organization.

CHAPTER XII. TRANSITIONAL ARRANGEMENTS: 1. Pending the coming into force of the special agreement or agreements referred to in Chapter VIII, Section B, Paragraph 5, and in accordance with the provisions of Paragraph 5 of the four-nation declaration signed at Moscow Oct. 30, 1943, the states parties to that declaration should consult with one another, and as occasion arises with other members of the organization, with a view to such joint action on behalf of the organization as may be necessary for the purpose of maintaining international peace and security.

2. No provision of the Charter should preclude action taken or authorized in relation to enemy states as a result of the present war by the governments having responsibility for such action.

Note: In addition to the question of voting procedure in the Security Council referred to in Chapter VI, several other questions are still under consideration.

THE PRESIDENT'S ENDORSEMENT [19]

The projected international organization has for its primary purpose the maintenance of international peace and security and the creation of the conditions that make for peace.

We now know the need for such an organization of the peace-loving peoples and the spirit of unity which will be required to maintain. . . . From the very beginning of the war, and paralleling our military plans, we have begun to lay the foundations for the general organization for the maintenance of peace and security.

It represents, therefore, a major objective for which this war is being fought. . . . The projected general organization may be regarded as the keystone of the arch and will include within its framework a number of specialized economic and social agencies now existing or to be established.

The task of planning the great design of security and peace has been well begun. It now remains for the nations to complete the structure in a spirit of constructive purpose and mutual confidence.

[19] From "Washington Conversations on International Organization," statement by President Franklin D. Roosevelt, released to the press by the White House, October 9, 1944. Reprinted in the *Department of State Bulletin*. 11:265. October 8, 1944.

COMPARISON: THE "PROPOSALS" VERSUS THE LEAGUE COVENANT [20]

League of Nations Covenant

1. The League of Nations Covenant was a part of the Treaty of Versailles, and was not drawn up until after the end of the war, with no opportunity for previous public discussion.

2. The Covenant became an issue of party politics in this country.

Dumbarton Oaks Proposals

1 The Charter of the United Nations outlined at Dumbarton Oaks will be a separate document, not tied to the peace treaties.

The United Nations Organization may come into being before the war ends, transforming the present wartime cooperation of the United Nations into a permanent Organization for peace and security.

The peoples and governments of the United Nations have been given the opportunity to discuss the plans for the Charter of the United Nations Organization before the final text is drafted.

2. The State Department consulted with congressional leaders of both parties before the Dumbarton Oaks Conference was held; also, political leaders of both parties have endorsed the Proposals and expressed the strong determination which exists throughout the country to prevent the

[20] From "The Dumbarton Oaks Proposals, A comparison with the League of Nations Covenant," issued by the United Nations Educational Campaign, New York. Reprinted by permission.

League of Nations Covenant   *Dumbarton Oaks Proposals*

United Nations Charter from becoming a party issue.

Already Congress through both the Fulbright and Connally resolutions is on record favoring American participation in world organization.

3. The obligations of the Covenant were not universal; however, the Covenant provided that non-member states were to accept the obligations of League membership for the purpose of settlement of disputes in which they were involved.

3. The United Nations Organization would be empowered to ensure that non-members act in accordance with the basic principles of the Charter, so far as may be necessary for the maintenance of peace and security.

4. The Assembly was composed of representatives of the members of the League, each member having one vote.

4. The General Assembly is to be composed of the members of the Organization, each member having one vote.

5. The Covenant provided that the Council should consist of the Principal Allied and Associated Powers (U.S., British Empire, France, Italy, Japan) together with representatives of four other member states selected by the Assembly from time to time in its discretion. The number of non-permanent members was later increased to eleven.

5. The Proposals recommend that the permanent members be the United States, Great Britain, China, Russia, and in "due course" France, and that the Assembly select the six non-permanent members for a term of two years each.

6. The League of Nations Assembly and Council had the same general powers.

6. Primary responsibility for the promotion of international cooperation in political,

League of Nations Covenant

Dumbarton Oaks Proposals

economic and social fields will rest with the General Assembly.

Primary responsibility for maintenance of peace and security will be centered in the Security Council, which will have no other functions. The Council would be in continuous session, unlike the League's Council which was required by the Covenant to meet at least annually, and did in fact meet three times a year, with special sessions when occasion required.

7. There was no specialized body to deal with social and other non-political activities of the League.

7. An Economic and Social Council, under the authority of the General Assembly, will be set up, as well as such subsidiary agencies as may be found necessary. In addition, autonomous agencies dealing with economic and social questions will be brought within the framework of the world organization, such as the Food and Agriculture Organization, the Monetary Fund and International Bank for Reconstruction, etc.

8. Both the Assembly and Council required a unanimous vote in all important matters.

8. The question of voting procedure on the Security Council has been postponed for future decision, but in all probability a unanimous vote will not be required.

League of Nations Covenant

Dumbarton Oaks Proposals

The General Assembly will vote by a 2/3 majority on important questions, such as membership on the Councils, recommendations with respect to peace and security, etc.; by a simple majority vote on other questions.

The Economic and Social Council will vote by simple majority on all matters.

9. The Covenant provided for pacific settlement of disputes through arbitration, judicial settlement, or action by the Council.

9. The Proposals recommend pacific settlement of disputes through mediation, conciliation, arbitration, judicial settlement or action by the Security Council.

10. The League of Nations and World Court were separate institutions. A nation could belong to either, neither, or both.

10. Every member of the world organization will automatically become a member of the international court of justice. The Court's constitution will be part of the Charter of the United Nations Organization.

11. The League Covenant provided for action only in case of war or in the event of a dispute likely to lead to war.

11. The Security Council will be empowered to investigate any dispute or any *situation* which may threaten peace and security.

12. The League had no force actually at its command. In each separate case, the Council could only *recommend* to the governments what military, naval or air force each should contribute for joint action.

12. The Security Council will have at its command armed forces, facilities, and assistance contributed by the members; and national air force contingents immediately available for emergency measures. These contributions will

League of Nations Covenant   *Dumbarton Oaks Proposals*

not be specified in the Charter but worked out by special agreement among the nations, ratified by each according to its own constitutional procedure.

A Military Staff Committee will be set up to advise and assist the Security Council.

13. War was not completely outlawed by the League Covenant. Under certain circumstances League members could resort to war as a policy of their own, separate from collective action.

13. Under the United Nations Charter, any threat or use of force by any nation on its own will be illegal. The only use of force recognized as legal is *force used by collective action.*

14. The League guaranteed as against aggression the territorial integrity and political independence of its members.

14. The Proposals do not specifically make this statement, yet practically they go further. They provide against change by force, and the Organization will have power at its command to enforce that pledge. However, change by peaceful means is provided for.

15. The Covenant provided for review of treaties and consideration of international conditions whose continuance might endanger the peace of the world.

15. The Proposals recommend consideration of questions for the purpose of adjusting situations likely to impair the general welfare, and of facilitating solutions of economic, social and other humanitarian problems; also, the investigation of any situation which may lead to international friction or give rise to a dispute.

League of Nations Covenant

16. The Covenant provided that acceptance of membership constituted the abrogation of all obligations and understandings among the members which were inconsistent with the terms of the Covenant.

17. The League recognized the validity of regional understandings like the Monroe Doctrine for securing the maintenance of peace.

18. The League of Nations Covenant stressed reduction of armaments for the maintenance of peace.

19. A mandate system was set up for non-self-governing peoples.

Dumbarton Oaks Proposals

16. No specific statement is made on this point, although this is implied in the provision that all members agree to fulfill the obligations assumed by them in accordance with the Charter.

17. The Proposals devote more attention to regional arrangements, but recommend that no enforcement action should be taken under regional arrangements or by regional agencies without authorization of the Security Council.

18. The Proposals place less emphasis on reduction of armaments, yet provide for the regulation of armaments and "possible disarmament."

19. This question was postponed for future decision. The Commission to Study the Organization of Peace suggests: (1) A United Nations declaration of principles guaranteeing the advancement of non-self-governing peoples; (2) regional commissions, with consultative and advisory functions, designed to promote the economic and social wellbeing of the peoples of the region; (3) A Permanent Trusteeship Council, within the

League of Nations Covenant   *Dumbarton Oaks Proposals*

Organization, to direct the administration of existing mandated territories and other dependent territories taken from enemy states.

20. No specific provision was made concerning human rights.

20. The obligation to "promote respect for human rights and fundamental freedoms" is recognized.

21. Amendments to the Covenant required a unanimous vote of the Assembly, and came into effect when ratified by all members of the Council and a majority of the Assembly.

21. Amendments to the Charter will require a 2/3 vote of the General Assembly, and ratification by the permanent members of the Security Council and a majority of the other members of the Organization.

Chapter III

THE DUMBARTON OAKS PROPOSALS MEET THE PUBLIC

From their first publication in October, 1944, the Dumbarton Oaks Proposals have been the subject of the greatest discussion in history. In this country, the Department of State set forth on a long and well-planned crusade to develop public understanding. But, their "propaganda campaign" made it clear from the start that while the Proposals were the best and most well-intentioned efforts of planners, they did not constitute a final draft. The public was invited to discuss the Proposals, criticize, amend, and generally dissect them. By so doing, the Department of State obviated the necessity of "selling the American people" on the Proposals themselves. In all of the debate throughout the nation, rarely has a voice been raised against the principles involved. Quite naturally, the questions raised have dealt with specific features of the Proposals—but the main purpose of the Dumbarton Oaks Proposals, that of creating a world organization, has met with no opposition. For a time, in the very beginning, Congress debated the general subject, but the opposition gradually weakened and died altogether. The public was committed to an organization of some kind—the problem now was to work out details—opposition as such was out of the question. And so the matter stands to date. The Dumbarton Oaks Proposals laid the foundation, outlined the general framework of the organization. Roosevelt, Churchill and Stalin worked out a few details at Yalta. But the specific organization is to come from San Francisco—for that will be the first opportunity for the small nations to speak.

Criticisms of the specific amendments have poured in a steady stream from all quarters, but the majority of those criticisms are based upon a sincere desire to strengthen rather than weaken the organization itself. And that is the key to whatever success the Proposals will have in the final outcome. The problem is not "should we or should we not approve the Dumbarton Oaks Proposals?" But "how can we make them more effective?"

THE PROPOSALS EXPLAINED [1]

We know . . . as individuals that the mere desire for peace and security is not enough. We must possess the will to seek the ways of peace and security and the collective intelligence to define clearly the machinery, the techniques, the methods and requirements of peace and security. Peoples and governments must be willing to make the measure of sacrifice necessary to their attainment.

The Dumbarton Oaks Proposals represent a partial crystallization of these basic beliefs and hopes of humanity.

They are, at this stage, the joint product of the thought and discussion of the spokesmen of the nations participating in the recent conference. Several years of serious study by responsible officials of each of the governments preceded the conference. Eminent world authorities in the fields of security and world organization were frequently consulted, and the articulate will of the masses of our people provided a constant guide.

Since the conference, every effort has been made to explain the Proposals to the public. As a result of these efforts, we have received splendid advice and ripe judgments, which will undoubtedly reflect themselves in the finished instrument.

This reciprocal relationship between the government and the people is a major aspect of democracy. . . . The Proposals in their present tentative form were described by former Secretary of State Hull as representing the "highest common denominator rather than . . . the plan of any one nation." And President Roosevelt expressed his pleasure that so much had "been accomplished on so difficult a subject in so short a time." From these substantial beginnings, it becomes our common task to subject the document to the closest scrutiny with the aim of making it a still more effective instrument for the attainment of its objectives.

[1] From "A General Peace and Security Organization: Analysis of its Major Functions," by Andrew W. Cordier, Division of International Security Affairs, Office of Special Political Affairs, Department of State. From a radio speech delivered on the Southwest Radio Forum, Tulsa, Okla., February 17, 1945, and reprinted in the *Department of State Bulletin.* 12:253-5. February 18, 1945.

The proposals outline two major tasks for a general international organization—to maintain or restore peace and security and to promote the solution of international economic, social, and humanitarian problems. The first task is essentially preventive; the second curative and creative. . . .

The responsibility for maintaining or restoring peace and security under the Proposals would be jointly assumed by the Security Council and the member states.

The members of the Organization in discharging their obligations for the keeping of the peace would submit to a series of principles determining their course of action. They would pledge that they would settle their disputes by pacific means in such a way that international peace and security would not be endangered.

They would be obliged to refrain in their international relations from the threat or use of force in any manner inconsistent with the purposes of the Organization. They would likewise refrain from giving assistance to any state against which preventive or enforcement action was being undertaken by the Organization.

Positively they would undertake to give every assistance to the Organization in any action undertaken by it. They would oblige themselves particularly to accept and carry out the decisions of the Security Council.

The member states would be pledged to carry out all of these obligations in accordance with the purposes and provisions of the Charter.

To make their contributions to enforcement measures effective to a maximum degree, they would be pledged to act not only directly and in their individual capacity as member states but also through the various international arrangements and technical agencies of which they are members.

These obligations and responsibilities of member states would be coordinated at many points with responsibilities assigned to the Security Council. Within the Organization the Security Council is clothed with the special task of maintaining peace and security. It would be empowered to keep a constant vigil over disputes or situations whose continuance might endanger the peace. It would call upon states to use peaceful processes of their own choice to settle their disputes. At any stage in such efforts at a solution the Security Council itself is empowered to recommend methods of adjustment.

It would be empowered to determine at what stage a dispute, if not settled by peaceful means, might be designated a threat to the peace, a breach of the peace, or an act of aggression. If once it determined that a threat to the peace existed, it could decide upon the measures to be taken to maintain or restore peace and security. It would be enabled to call upon members to apply the diplomatic, economic, or other non-military measures to give effect to its decisions, or it might, if necessary, take action by such air, land, and naval forces as might be required to restore peace and security. The contribution of armed forces by the member states is to be regulated by special agreement among the states themselves.

In this important realm of the pacific settlement of disputes, and of enforcement action in cases where disputes are not settled amicably, the procedures and facilities of regional arrangements and agencies might be utilized in accord with the purposes and principles of the Organization. Thus universal and regional machinery for maintaining the peace would be correlated to mutual advantage. Through these new relationship, the inter-American system could strengthen its own machinery, processes, and procedures and contribute strength to the general Organization.

You will observe the balance between the flexible and inflexible in the pacific settlement of disputes and in the character of enforcement action. Many avenues of pacific settlement would be open to the use of member states, but once a threat to the peace is determined, enforcement action would follow speedily and within well-defined lines of procedure.

To facilitate action, the Security Council would be assisted by a military staff committee which would advise it on military requirements, the employment and command of forces, and the regulation of armament. It would be responsible for the strategic command of any armed forces placed at the disposal of the Security Council.

Disputes of a justiciable character would be referred to an international court of justice which would be established as an integral part of the Organization.

The General Assembly would be empowered to assist the Security Council by making recommendations concerning the maintenance of peace and security.

The second major function of the Organization—the promotion of the solution of international economic, social, and humanitarian problems—would be the responsibility of the General Assembly and of its subordinate body, the Economic and Social Council.

The Security Council is limited to 11 members, 5 of which would be the great powers. Power in the Organization is rightly harnessed to the responsibility for keeping the peace. In the General Assembly all members of the Organization would be represented on an equal footing. The small states, whose competence in the handling of economic, social, and humanitarian problems is so frequently in evidence, would enjoy equality with the great powers. Each member would have one vote.

The fundamental positions of the General Assembly in the Organization is further strengthened by its responsibility for certain electoral functions such as the admission of new members upon the recommendation of the Security Council, the election of the non-permanent members of the Security Council and the members of the Economic and Social Council.

The creative functions of the Organization are most clearly seen in the authority vested in the General Assembly and in the Economic and Social Council in their assigned task of seeking solutions to problems in the vitally important economic and social fields where the balance between peace and war so often finds its roots. Incipient wars require military action, but a world depression requires vigorous international economic cooperation. Acute economic crises marked by such expressions as bitter trade competition, clogged markets, currency collapses, industrial stagnation, mass unemployment, produce serious political disturbances, which, in turn, often lead to war. To raise levels of nutrition and standards of living, to improve labor standards, to contribute toward an expanding world economy, to promote exchange stability, to facilitate the expansion and balanced growth of international trade, are vital objectives for world organization. In the fields of health, education, and culture, intelligently pursued cooperative policies are not only the rightful pursuits of peoples who claim to be civilized, but they produce understandings which help to eliminate the psychological basis of conflict. These broad areas would be problems of concern for the General Assembly, the Economic and Social Council, and subsidiary organizations. . . . Such organizations might include, for example, the International Labor Organization, the proposed United Nations Food and Agriculture Organization, the International Monetary Fund, the International Bank for Reconstruction and Development, and the International Civil Aviation Organization. . . .

SUMMARY OF PROS AND CONS [2]

The United States is about to make one of the most important decisions in its whole history. Shortly after the San Francisco conference of the United Nations, a treaty will undoubtedly be offered the Senate proposing to bring this country into the new league. . . .

The chief arguments of those who say the United States should stay out may be summarized as follows:

The world is still ruled by selfish powers which have not actually renounced the sort of political and economic imperialism and power politics that have in the past tended to produce war and will continue to do so in the future. The organization of the new Security Council and, in particular, the voting procedure if a country is charged with aggression, both show that this is not a genuine world league but an organization dominated by the three chief Allies—who are presumably about to win this war—plus a window dressing of lesser Allies and neutrals. The neutrals, however, will not be permitted to attend the San Francisco meeting or the subsequent peace conference—which accounts for the haste with which some of them are now declaring war on

[2] From "America and Dumbarton Oaks," editorial, *The New Republic*. 112: 350-1. March 12, 1945. Reprinted by permission.

the Axis. Americans, especially, do not want the new organization to be empowered to make decisions including the use of American armed forces, without ratification by Congress. Some alarm is also expressed lest the new plan be used to freeze the status quo so firmly that even revolution against a dictatorship, or freedom for a conquered territory, like India, might be impossible.

Certain of the smaller states, while supporting the new league, have offered criticism of details. Thus the Poles in London have asked the inclusion of the Atlantic Charter and the Four Freedoms, a council of fifteen members instead of eleven, no regional subdivisions and no action regarding disarmament or boundaries. Latin America wants more power for the Assembly, a world-wide bill of rights, registration of all treaties, and formal adoption by every state of the principles of international law. It is reported that Latin America also wants at least one of its republics to be sitting at all times on the Security Council.

Those who argue that the United States should join the new organization make, in general, these points:

It is true that the new organization is imperfect, but this is an exceedingly imperfect world, in which progress is almost invariably by evolution, not revolution. If the new organization can get under way, we have at least a chance of doing something about imperialism, whereas if there is no organization, such efforts must depend upon the dubious and tedious matter of increased social enlightenment within each of the imperialist powers. Moreover, if there is another war every couple of decades, progress in the emancipation of colonial peoples will at least be suspended temporarily, if not completely halted.

One of the pronounced evils of the world today is competitive private capitalism operating internationally. The new league, it is argued, provides the best and indeed the only present hope of curbing the excesses of international competition—and of international monopolization—and thereby increasing the likelihood of prosperity and peace. While it is true that none of the great powers has surrendered or appears willing to surrender any part of its national sovereignty, all of them have made some concessions—probably about as many as are to be expected in this stage of world development. . . .

Moreover, the new plan contains important provisions that were left out of the old one. The Economic and Social Council of eighteen members, elected by the Assembly, to handle social, economic, labor and humanitarian agencies, should go far toward remedying the worst mistake of the former League, which was to center its attention of political matters and almost ignore economic ones.

SOMETHING BETTER THAN DUMBARTON OAKS [3]

What will be the effect of the Dumbarton Oaks agreement upon the maintenance of peace? The answer is that it will be almost negligible. Indeed it will be hurtful if it gives to the peoples of the world delusions about the price of peace, or if it makes them accept the doctrine that any sort of international alliances labelled "cooperation," no matter how precarious their basis or how much resented by the exploited peoples, will somehow bring us peace. The cure for a dangerous isolation is not a more dangerous membership in an international gang of exploiters.

To be sure, there are features of the Dumbarton Oaks agreement, disappointing as it is, which *in the proper setting* might be a beginning of better things. It is good that they should begin to think in terms of collective well-being and security. It is not good that the final power should be in the hands of three great empires already engaged in the sharpest sort of competition for advantage. And this reflects on the underlying philosophy of the agreement and cannot be cured by any changes in voting procedure for dealing with an aggressor.

It is, however, conceivable that some improvements may be made in the agreement. Thus aggression may be defined and some judicial process established for determining it. The present arrangements for international police power may be made at once more meaningful and less dangerous. The agreement should be made easier of amendment.

[3] From "Something Better Than Dumbarton Oaks," excerpts from a speech broadcast over CBS, March 10, 1945, by Norman Thomas, presidential candidate of Socialist party.

But none of these things nor any other improvement in the Charter of Dumbarton Oaks will make that agreement adequate to peace *in its present setting.* Indeed a worse agreement than Dumbarton Oaks might be useful in the setting of proper peace terms, while a better agreement would fail in the present setting of power politics as played by Messrs. Churchill, Stalin and Roosevelt.

Our hope for something better than Dumbarton Oaks lies in four proposals which, as the Post War World Council has insisted, are basic to peace and effective international cooperation.

1. Self-government for liberated European states must be genuine. Their economic and political independence cannot be maintained as against London and Moscow except by regional federations, preferably a United States of Europe. This should be encouraged and not discouraged. The relief work by UNRRA must be hastened and improved to bring to liberated peoples strength for freedom.

2. Independence within a framework of regional and world-wide federation must be promised to all peoples of every race and color.

3. To enemy peoples, disarmed, stripped of conquest and purged of marauding leadership, must be offered inclusion at the earliest possible moment in the benefits, economic and political, of organized cooperation. There must be an end to the bankrupt slogan, "unconditional surrender," which only strengthens resistance. There must be no divisions of the homelands of enemy peoples or enslavement of their workers.

4. An essential condition of collective security or any quota system of police must be progressive national disarmament following the establishment of peace, and the universal abolition of military conscription. This Stalin himself recognized in 1927.

FIVE POWER COOPERATION [4]

In reply to a question put to him yesterday in the House of Commons, Mr. Churchill agreed that under the Yalta agreement on world security "there is nothing at all" to deal with aggression

[4] From "The Great Powers," editorial. *The New York Times.* 94:14. March 16, 1945. Reprinted by permission.

by the Great Powers. Asked then by his questioner whether the British delegates to the forthcoming conference at San Francisco would propose some plan to fill this gap, Mr. Churchill replied: "No, sir. As far as we are concerned, we made a perfectly voluntary agreement with other Great Powers that were gathered at Yalta and that does prescribe for a differentiation between the treatment of the greatest powers in these matters and of the smallest powers. We may deplore, if we choose, that there is a difference between the great and small, between the strong and weak in the world. There is undoubtedly such a difference and it would be foolish to upset the good arrangements proceeding on a broad front for the sake of trying to attain immediately to what is a hopeless ideal."

Before this blunt and typically Churchillian piece of plain-speaking is too widely deplored as another instance of British faith in "power politics" or as further evidence of a callous intention on the part of the Great Powers to "dominate" the smaller ones, there are several considerations which should be kept in mind:

First, while it is true that there is nothing in the Yalta plan to prevent aggression by any of the five Great Powers—Britain, Russia, France, China and the United States—this omission is more important in theory than in practice. Surely the reality of the situation is that if a point is ever reached when one of the five Great Powers must be coerced by force, then peace will have been lost anyway, beyond the possibility of salvage by any voting procedure that can possibly be devised, and a new world war will be in the making. The Yalta plan provides a method of preventing smaller wars which could easily grow into larger ones. That is the way many large wars have started. Beyond this the Yalta plan bases its hope of peace on the good faith of the Great Powers and their ability to get along together. If they cannot get along together, then no machinery of voting in the proposed new Security Council, however elaborate or however ingenious on paper, will suffice to keep the peace.

Second, while the Yalta plan does thus give the Great Powers what Mr. Churchill describes as "differential treatment," it does not give these powers a high hand. For the Yalta plan provides that any nation, however small, may at any time call any nation, however great, on the carpet for any policy or action which it believes threatens the world's peace, and get a hearing on its case. The Yalta plan further provides that before the Great Powers themselves can initiate any action which requires the use of force they must enlist the support of at least two of the six Small Powers which are represented on the Security Council. By maintaining a united front, the Small Powers can therefore command a veto power over the larger nations in any proposed enforcement action.

Finally, while the Yalta plan provides a formula for voting, it also provides something more important than this. It provides a method by which all five of the Great Powers, upon which must inevitably rest the chief burden of providing men and arms to prevent aggression, if force is needed for that purpose, may keep in close and confident cooperation, from the very start, in a new effort to keep the peace. And here surely, rather than in any voting formula, is the real difference between the proposed new league and the old League.

For it was the chief defect of the old League of Nations that three of these five Great Powers did not participate as full partners, or did not participate at all, in the initial efforts to preserve the peace that followed the last war. Russia was excluded. The United States voted itself out, preferring to believe that what happened in Europe or in Asia was none of its own business. China was in the League, but not as a full partner; rather, as a poor relation whose territory was divided into "spheres of influence" by foreign powers, some of which did not wish to see China become too strong lest they lose their "extraterritorial rights," their special "concessions" and their opportunities for economic exploitation.

In this respect the present situation, as reflected in the plans made at Yalta, differs radically from the situation prevailing after 1918. This time, at San Francisco, Russia will be one of the principal sponsors and founders of the new league. So will the United States. And so will China; for the nations of the West have come at last to see clearly what should have been evident for a generation—that without a strong, prosperous and united China there can be no real hope of peace in Asia.

It is in these fundamental facts, rather than in the degree of perfection of any voting procedure, that Yalta and San Francisco offer the greatest hope of a new era of peace and international order.

EDITORIAL OPINION: *THE NEW REPUBLIC* [5]

The draft of the international security organization of the United Nations agreed upon at Dumbarton Oaks deserves careful scrutiny. It ought to be improved if it can be. Some constitutions last a long time, and it is impossible to devote too much care to the attempt to foresee eventualities to which they may have to be applied. Even at best, however, it is impossible to draft a constitution without defects, or one that will please everybody concerned. The basic question is whether on the whole it is better to have a constitution of the general sort proposed, or none at all.

On the whole, the plan seems to us a distinct improvement over the covenant of the League of Nations. It is so, first because the Soviet Union and the United States will be members from the beginning if it goes into effect, second because it embodies the declared intention of those who are capable of using adequate force to do so promptly when the need arises and to act in unison, and third because it strips away as many as possible of the hampering inhibitions and formalities which might impede this action. It is a practical device, suited to the realities of the situation, rather than an idealistic dream put on paper. As long as these characteristics are maintained, we need not worry too much about details.

EDITORIAL OPINION: *THE NATION* [6]

The results of the Dumbarton Oaks conference have been laid before the public for judgment. The submission is accompanied by a warning that "the proposals in their present

[5] From "The Dumbarton Oaks Plan," editorial. *The New Republic*. 111: 510-11. October 23, 1944. Reprinted by permission.

[6] From "Great Power Hegemony," editorial. *The Nation*. 159:451. October 21, 1944. Reprinted by permission.

form are neither complete nor final." But this apparent frankness is far from disclosing either the extent of their incompleteness or the degree of their finality.

Many questions long under discussion have been definitively answered. The general organization will embrace economic and social welfare as well as security. Regional associations will be coordinated with the general organization. There will be no world federation. There will be no world legislature. There will be no world force at the direct and immediate disposal of a central command. The Security Council calls upon the member states to take the measures and supply the forces necessary to stop aggression but how it reaches decisions has not yet been determined; and this leaves a gaping hole in the structure.

Agreement was reached that the Council's decisions would generally require the unanimous vote of the United States, Britain, the Soviet Union, China—and eventually France—its permanent members. Any one of these countries could thus impose an absolute veto on action. On the other hand, if all five agreed, only one vote among the six non-permanent members would be necessary to make their decision operative. So privileged a position corresponds of course to the inevitable responsibilities of the great powers, but it reduces to a farce the "sovereign equality" announced as the first principle of the organization. One far-reaching exception was supported by the United States, Britain, and China. Even a permanent member would lose its vote if it were accused of aggression. This proposal the Soviet Union steadfastly rejected, and the voting system was left in suspense.

Moscow will probably maintain its opposition to a rule that would prevent its veto on action touching the Baltic States, Poland, or any other area bordering on Russia. But before we condemn Mr. Stalin, we must ask ourselves whether Congress would have surrendered the American vote in a dispute with a Latin American State, or whether Parliament would have accepted a provision silencing the British representative in a conflict over the Suez Canal. By accepting the proposal, and counting on Congress or Parliament to throw it out, Moscow might have shifted the odium of defeating the most equalizing and democratic clause in the draft. If, as now seems probable, each of the permanent members of the Council is to have a veto even when party to a dispute, then we shall have, not a democratic international organization, but a great-power alliance keeping order, as it understands order, in the world. The great powers and they alone will remain judges in their own cause. There are already in the text marks enough of hegemony. Under Chapter XI, for example, a single great power can prevent amendment of the charter, whereas it will take more than a third of the ordinary members at the voting stage, and more than half at the ratifying stage, to veto any amendment pushed by the four or five leaders. Once again, the only sovereign equality is that of the greatest powers.

The organization will be hard on the pride of the small nations and harder still on the prestige of those in the middle range. They will urge changes. Should they stay out? Should those of us who detest domination crusade for equality or nothing?

In the world as it is, they, and we, would get nothing. The proposed organization, on the other hand, offers order, backed by power as the League was never backed. It offers economic and social organization with a closer approach to equality. It imposes no inequality which the lesser states do not already suffer in fact.

Structurally, the proposed system is weak. Structure can never replace good-will; but if it is strong it can tide over temporary deficiencies in that commodity. The "United Nations" will depend utterly on agreement among the great powers and will be exposed to all the hazards that affect their relationships. But the way to strengthen the organization and to make it just is to work from within. There, using the rights allotted them, the lesser states can establish an influence in fact which will far exceed their prerogatives in law. Many times in the national domain we have seen the consultative function hardening into a strong share in decision. Moreover, the small nations will find natural support in liberal groups within all countries, whose growing political strength must be exerted without let-up to effect a more just and democratic organization of the peace.

SUMMARY OF THE HOOVER
AMENDMENTS [7]

The Dumbarton Oaks proposals are in most ways patterned upon the world's last great experiment—the League of Nations. The league was a partial success and its failures present vivid experience which it would be folly to ignore. In the light of these experiences, there are some important additions which should be infused into the Dumbarton Oaks proposals and thereby greatly strengthen this chart of peace.

I state them at once and I shall in later articles amplify the reasons for them.

First: Positive standards of the political rights of men and nations and the establishment of a world committee to promote these political rights, this committee to rank with the economic and social committees already proposed in the Dumbarton Oaks plan.

Second: Provision for revision of onerous treaties between nations at, say, ten-year intervals, in order to assure that the peace settlements are dynamic and not static.

Third: Regional organization of the organization to preserve peace in three areas, Asia, Europe and the Western Hemisphere, the regional organizations to be subject of course to the Security Council.

Fourth: Absolute disarmament of the enemy powers.

Fifth: Immediate relative disarmament of the United Nations and the establishment of maximum limit of armies, navies and air power among them.

Sixth: While it is probably not a part of the charter itself, when it is adopted by the Congress the authority to use force should not be given the American delegate on the Security Council, but that power should be delegated to the President of the United States with the provision that he be bound by the majority of the joint Foreign Relations Committees of the Senate and the House as to whether a vote to employ American force shall be submitted to the Congress as a whole.

[7] From "Wider Oaks Plan Urged by Hoover," first of a series of four articles by Herbert Hoover, former President of the United States, prepared specially for the North American Newspaper Alliance, published March 25, 1945. Reprinted by permission.

Seventh: Take enough time in formulating the charter of peace to do it right.

These proposals are not counsels of perfection. They are lessons of grim experience.

There are three general methods by which peace can be preserved:

First, through measures of force to stop aggression.

Second, through pacific methods, the immediate effect of which is to settle controversies between nations by negotiation, arbitration and judicial decisions.

Third, beyond all this, are the moral, spiritual, political and social forces, which either foment conflicts or allay them. If we are to have lasting peace we cannot rely wholly upon stopping quarrels. We must set in motion these forces which would build for peace.

The weakening of the power to stop military aggression in the Dumbarton proposals by the voting formula now agreed renders it even more imperative that the great underlying forces building for peace should be more greatly developed at San Francisco than they appeared at Dumbarton Oaks. The League of Nations proclaimed its base as the maintenance of honor and justice between nations. Even that wholly nebular enunciation of a standard of conflict between nations does not appear in Dumbarton Oaks.

The great principles of political rights of nations and men, the standards of conduct among nations and the curative functions which eliminate the cause of war are wholly absent from Dumbarton Oaks. These forces must underlie not only the whole basis of international law but of moral and spiritual progress of nations toward peace. We are in danger of setting up a purely mechanistic body without spiritual inspiration or soul.

THE FRENCH PROPOSALS [8]

The main purpose of the amendments is to insure that the French-Russian pact shall operate independently of the world security system.

[8] From "Oaks Amendments Offered by Paris," by Harold Callender. *The New York Times.* 94:10. March 16, 1945. Reprinted by permission.

A principal French proposal in its final form is for adding after the second division of Chapter VIII, Section C, in the Oaks text, which provides that enforcement actions taken under the regional arrangements must have the authorization of the Security Council, the following words:

"But application of urgent measures provided by treaties of assistance concluded between members of the organization and notified by them to the council of security will be exempt from this rule. However, the states signatory to such treaties shall render to the council as soon as possible an accounting of the measures they will have taken in the execution of said treaties."

This would mean that France and Russia could take military action against Germany under their pact without the authorization of the Security Council. Thus their pact would remain "automatic" in the sense that it would require no prior consultation with anyone except the two Powers concerned. The French regard this as vital in an age when rocket-bombs, if used in sufficient quantities, might wipe out Paris before the Security Council could even get together.

French concern for his treaty is revealed in several of the amendments they propose. In the first section of Chapter I, where the purposes of the organization are defined, the French would insert a clause to the effect that peaceful settlement of international disputes should be sought "without losing sight of treaties binding those who have signed them, or of the fact that respect of these treaties constitutes one of the essential conditions of international order."

Again, in the first sentence of Chapter VIII, after the words "security council," the French would insert "without losing sight of respect for treaties."

In Section B of Chapter VIII, which deals with the determination of the threats to peace and the action to be taken, under Division 5, which describes the facilities to be placed at the disposal of the peace organization, the French would stipulate "notably the right of passage."

Russian troops, therefore, would have the right to pass through Poland to move against Germany under the French-Russian pact.

In the same division the French would provide that agreements regarding the forces to be lent to the world organization should specify "how soon they will be placed at the council's disposition and, where appropriate, the zone in which they normally will be stationed, and should define the facilities, the aid and the means of communication to be furnished."

In the next division—Six—in the first sentence, the French would provide that "national contingents of forces of all branches stationed in appropriate zones of security, or for which stations would be permanently prepared, should be permanently at the disposition of the council."

The French would also make an amendment to this effect:

"Every treaty of international engagement of a political character concluded in the future by a member of the organization shall be immediately registered with the secretariat and published by it as soon as possible. No treaty or engagement is to be binding before being registered."

The French recommend that in a case where the council does not succeed in adopting a resolution, the members of the organization retain the right to act as they deem necessary in the interest of "peace, law and justice." This means that if the great powers are not agreed on the action to be taken, all states are free to act on their own. A similar clause in the League of Nations covenant left the way open for a warlike action that would not violate the covenant.

In Chapter VI, Section A, dealing with the composition of the security council, where six non-permanent members are provided, the French propose to insert: "At least three to be chosen from among the states that will have undertaken, and will have the means, to participate in an appreciable degree—to be determined by the council—in the active defense of the international order."

Regarding the membership of the organization—Chapter III —the French would write the existing clause to read:

"Membership of the organization should be open to all states that prove they are peace-loving by their institutions, their international behavior and the effective guarantees they give to respect international engagements. Participation in the organization involves engagements incompatible with the status of neutrality."

In Chapter I, Division 3, which says the purpose of the organization is to achieve international cooperation in the solution of international, economic, social and other humanitarian problems, the French would add "and to watch over the respect of essential liberties for all, without distinction of race, language or religion."

Again, in Chapter VIII, Section A, Division 7, which exempts domestic questions from the jurisdiction of the organization, the French would add "unless manifest violation of essential liberties and rights of men constitutes in itself a menace calculated to compromise the peace"—as the Nazi and Fascist systems did.

In Chapter V, Section B, the French would replace the final sentence of Division 1 with this sentence:

"The General Assembly may always draw the attention of the security council to situations that may endanger the peace. But it may not take up questions touching the maintenance of peace and security that the security council has itself taken up."

In Chapter VIII, Section B, Division 9, dealing with the military staff committee to advise the council on regulation of armaments, the French would include also "all measures of control that are deemed appropriate."

To the composition of the committee, the French would add "one delegate from each member of the organization that has agreed to put substantial forces at the disposal of the security council."

In that part of the Oaks plan dealing with economic cooperation—Chapter I—the French propose several alterations. They suggest—Section A, Division 1—that the organization should press for the solution of social problems, and that the Assembly and Economic and Social Council under it should collaborate with the security council in doing this. They propose that at least half of the eighteen states represented in the Economic Council should be "the countries whose economic importance is greatest." Regarding the voting in this council—Chapter IX, Section B—the French suggest that, while decisions may be taken with a majority vote, at least two thirds of the members of the council must participate in any vote.

In Section C, dealing with the powers of the Economic Council, the French would authorize it "to envisage the creation and control of similar organizations concerning, especially, the distribution of raw materials." In the same section the French would provide that the Economic Council should present to the security council in emergencies "any humanitarian, economic or social or like question that it deems susceptible of endangering the peace, the security council to report to the assembly."

CANADA'S AMENDMENTS [9]

Ottawa, March 21—In all debates by the Canadian Parliament on the Dumbarton Oaks proposals, there has so far been general agreement with the four principal suggestions made by Prime Minister W. L. Mackenzie King for the direction of the delegation at San Francisco. These are:

1. If responsibility is to be fairly matched with power, as has been done in the case of the Great Powers, the position accorded to each state should correspond with the functions that it is able and ready to discharge. The method of selection to membership in the security council should therefore be planned with regard for the powers and responsibilities of secondary states.

2. States not represented in the security council should not be called on to undertake serious enforcement action without the opportunity of participating in the council's proceedings or without separate agreement to join in executing its decisions.

3. The relations between the security council and any interallied authority that may be set up to supervise any long-term measures of control of enemy countries should be clearly defined.

4. The charter should include a provision for its general review after a term of years.

While various parties in the House of Representatives have criticized the general policy of the government, these four pro-

[9] From "Canadians Agree on Parley Plans," by R. J. Philip. *The New York Times.* 94:17. March 22, 1945. Reprinted by permission.

visions, which have not yet been framed as definite amendments to be presented in San Francisco, are accepted as fairly representing the special view of Canada. Other suggestions have been made during the debate. Concern has been expressed regarding the method of taking over the institutions and work of the League of Nations in different domains.

Mr. Paul Martin, who headed the Canadian delegation to the recent International Labor Office meeting in London, told the House that, in his experience, the workers of the world would look very carefully, even suspiciously, at any attempt to delimit the scope and the status of the ILO. Ultimately, he said, the ILO must be subservient to the world security organization, but it must be subservient to a body that represents the ultimate power of government and not a body that has merely delegated power and one on which the workers and employers have no representative.

LATIN-AMERICAN COUNTER-PROPOSALS [10]

Mexico City, March 5—The Inter-American Conference approved in general today the objectives of the Dumbarton Oaks world security proposals, but suggested to the other United Nations that the American republics be permitted to solve their own disputes in this hemisphere in accordance with their own methods and procedures.

In a resolution adopted by the world organization committee of the conference a few minutes after Secretary of State Edward R. Stettinius, Jr. had read to them the compromise voting procedure reached at the Big Three meeting at Yalta, the representatives of twenty American nations agreed that "the Dumbarton Oaks proposals constitute a basis for and a valuable contribution to the setting up of a general organization which permit the achievement of a just peaceful order. . . .

The resolution added, however, that in the view of the conference, the Dumbarton Oaks proposals were "capable of certain improvement" and passed on to the rest of the United

[10] From "Meeting in Mexico Asks Oaks Changes," newsstory. *The New York Times*. 94:8. March 6, 1945. Reprinted by permission.

Nations and to the San Francisco conference a detailed list of the observations of delegates to the meeting here, including the following seven general suggestions, which were emphasized:

1. The world organization should strive more toward the ideals of universality.

2. The section in the Dumbarton Oaks proposal dealing with the principles and purposes of the world organization should be amplified and be made more specific.

3. The powers of the general assembly of the proposed world organization should be amplified and made more specific so that it could play a more effective part.

4. The jurisdiction and competence of the international tribunal or court of justice should be extended.

5. An international agency specially charged with promoting intellectual and moral cooperation between nations should be created.

6. An "adequate representation" in the world security council should be given to Latin America.

7. It would be "preferable" to solve "controversies and questions of an inter-American character in accordance with inter-American method and procedures."

The delegates here stressed the last point more than any other. They have maintained that "under the Act of Chapultepec," the American states would be obligated to take action against any American or non-American state that committed an act of aggression against another American state but that under the Dumbarton Oaks regulations this action could not be taken unless it were approved by the world security council.

Consequently certain resolutions have been introduced here to prevent the world security council from interfering in inter-American disputes unless they threatened the peace of other regions of the world, but in the last analysis the conference decided that it should merely pass on a vague suggestion on this point to the San Francisco conference and allow the connection between the regional and world security systems to be thrashed out there.

Mr. Stettinius strove to minimize reports of a conflict between the terms of the Act of Chapultepec and the Dumbarton

Oaks proposal by issuing a public statement today to the effect that there was no conflict between the documents.

"The act says specifically that the arrangements, activities and procedures referred to therein should be consistent with the purposes of the general international organization, when established," he said.

He did not refer to the fact that the Dumbarton Oaks proposals also state that no enforcement action should be taken against an aggressor by any regional organization such as the inter-American security system without the authority of the proposed security council.

Mr. Stettinius was warmly applauded when he disclosed the proposed voting procedure for the world security organization. Responding for the world organization committee of the conference, the Mexican Foreign Minister, Ezequiel Padilla, said, "An extraordinary advance has been made."

The small nations, he added, do not aspire to equal participation in a world of unequal responsibility, but at the same time they do not want to have their voices drowned through the solidarity of the great powers. The new voting procedure, he implied, removed that fear.

Elsewhere the delegates praised the fact that the Yalta Conference had taken away the veto power of the great states on questions of procedure and they also expressed themselves in favor of requiring an affirmative vote of seven on all decisions.

THE PROBLEM OF RATIFICATION [11]

To eleminate . . . political disputes involving boundaries, peace terms and treatment of national aspirations, it has been proclaimed that the San Francisco conference will not be concerned in any way with such discussions. The conference will be limited strictly to consideration of the mechanism of the postwar international organization, using the agreement at Dumbarton Oaks, as supplemented at Yalta by the Big Three leaders, as the sole basis for discussion. . . .

[11] From "Hurdles for the San Francisco Conference," by Lansing Warren. The New York Times. 94:3E. March 18, 1945. Reprinted by permission.

Issues that are pertinent to the San Francisco debates will thus be confined to questions relating to the machinery for maintaining and enforcing peace and issues involving the program for world cooperation. Even at that, it is admitted by those who have studied previous meetings that it will not be possible to exclude all thought of political considerations which are found to crop up in the corridors of the deliberations. Moreover, the mechanics of the new organization, presented to so many nations, are sure to offer ample field for disagreement and discussion.

Already many nations have prepared suggestions and amendments to the charter framed by the Big Three. France, Brazil, Canada, Norway, the Netherlands, Venezuela and Belgium, to name only a few, have announced their intention of proposing alterations. The Polish Government in Exile, prior to the decision of Yalta that made necessary its exclusion, had made public a general criticism, containing as many as twenty-two proposed reservations and amendments. The delegates in San Francisco will have the opportunity of hearing these and plenty more from the various nations.

A great many of these proposals, as they have been thus far aired, relate to minor details of the organization and the principal opportunities for major conflict now appear to be centered on a half dozen subjects that had already given rise to much debate and negotiation between the four leading powers that attended the conference at Dumbarton Oaks.

Thus, the main storm centers that may trouble the delegates may be considered to be gathering around the following debatable issues:

1. Voting power in the security council, the vote and representation of the middle and small powers.

2. The operation of regional arrangements, for which the charter provides in Chapter VIII.

3. Trusteeship for certain territories, understood to have been approved during the discussions at Yalta.

4. An expected move by the small powers to obtain sovereignty and territorial guarantees, which have been omitted from the purposes of the organization.

In addition to these chief centers for disagreement, there are a great number of subsidiary questions, mostly falling into a category that may be classed as ideological. They will be raised by critics of the charter, who regret its incisive "realism" and who would like to have the charter directed fundamentally toward an ideal solution of world problems.

These elements will suggest introduction of the principles of the Atlantic Charter and the Rights of Man, the theory of universal justice and the rights of peoples to select their forms of government. There will be proposals for the extension of the powers of the World Court to arbitrate all international disputes and there will be other suggestions for revision of the agreement, tending either to make it a super-state or to base the organization on the principle of federal union.

Then there will come the question of what is to be done with the organization of the old League of Nations. Most of the countries that will attend the San Francisco conference, with the exception of the United States and the Soviet Union, are still members of the League, and are still paying its dues. It still has numerous services functioning that could be merged with the new organization, and some effort will be made to see that it is done.

And finally, in the background of the whole discussion will arise the question of implementation of the organization—how will the military forces be apportioned, directed and brought into action?

This question is to form the basis for separate understandings, but in these negotiations all eyes will be fixed on the United States, for it is ever remembered that the League of Nations, which was fathered here, was abandoned by us on Europe's doorstep.

It will be up to the big powers to quiet concern among the smaller and middle powers with respect to the voting procedure, as established under the Yalta accord. The provision it contains for airing disputes in the council in a stage preliminary to any move for the use of force has done much to reduce the objections to the veto power over sanctions, which has been reserved for the five holders of permanent council seats. But there will remain objections to this unrestricted authority by the nations that will have to bear the brunt of any resort to armed force.

Several of the middle-sized powers will come to San Francisco prepared to press claims for permanent seats for themselves, and if this were to be accorded to Brazil or Canada or Australia or the Netherlands, it would require enlargement of the number of non-permanent seats and increase the cumbersomeness of the council. Another proposal will be that a permanent seat should be created that would be reserved for South American states in rotation, and another to be reserved for occupancy in turn by the leading empire powers among the smaller nations.

Next in order of conflicts will be those involving regional understandings, such as the Franco-Russian alliance in Europe, or the pact for mutual resistance to any aggression in the Western Hemisphere, which was signed by the inter-American meeting in Mexico City.

France is understood to maintain that her accord with Russia should be held to be automatic and independent of the world agreement, while Russia is thought to be ready to subordinate it to the approval of the council. Chapter VIII, Section C of the Charter provides that "no enforcement should be taken under regional arrangements or by regional agencies without authorization of the security council." The framers of the Mexico City agreement contend it conforms to this specification, but the provisions for regional action admittedly have only been broadly defined.

The provisions for trusteeship, approved at Yalta, have not been published in detail, but are likely to give opportunity for dispute. It is understood that under this plan a Pacific island might be placed under international trusteeship to allow several nations to use it as a base. Trusteeships might also be extended to apply to former mandates and even to colonies of enemy or liberated countries. If this is done, it cannot but occasion some heated discussion.

All the small countries, it is understood, regret the fact that the organization has deliberately abstained from offering guarantees of sovereignty and territorial integrity. At the Mexico

City conference this claim was admitted, but the larger powers, under the Dumbarton accord, have decided to limit action of the organization to preventing aggression and removing threats to peace.

With all these grounds for opposition to the proposals as they stand, it appears unlikely that the organization can obtain universal adoption without changes in some respects. But changes that are decided must be those that secure a widespread support before they will be considered.

The inviting powers, which have endorsed the proposals, hold in their hand the powers that will make or break the effectiveness of the plan. They will be reluctant to make alterations that will profit a single country or to accept changes that will increase the liabilities they will incur. They will, therefore, be expected to make the most strenuous efforts to obtain endorsement of the program as it stands. Their strength alone insures that without their approval and cooperation no organization can work or even hope to survive.

It was said at the outset that political considerations, no matter how great the effort to exclude them, would be bound to intrude, and they may be expected to play the deciding role in the final success of the United Nations treaty. Not all the nations can be offered assurances that will gain their wholehearted support, and there may in the end be some countries that will sign the agreement with reservations or may even refuse to sign.

Close observers of international negotiations, however, are convinced that though the meeting in San Francisco may be much prolonged beyond the month's duration scheduled, the bulk of the nations in the end will agree to a program for international organization that will not deviate much in its essentials from the basic proposals in the hands of the delegates now.

COMMENTS [12]

It meets the world demand for permanent peace machinery. It expresses the hope of peace-loving nations that civilization shall provide a method whereby future wars may be prevented

[12] From "The Dumbarton Oaks Proposals," reprinted from *World Affairs*. 107:237-51. December, 1944. Reprinted by permission.

and the treasure and the blood of peace-loving states may be conserved. . . .

As a whole, the plan adopted meets with my full approval. It's insistence upon the employment of peaceful measures of settlement is of the highest importance.—*Senator Tom Connally, Chairman of the Senate Foreign Relations Committee, October 9, 1944*

The Dumbarton Oaks agreement marks a long step forward in our government's policy, both international and domestic, for the establishment and protection of peace and for the assurance of our country's domestic prosperity and security.—*Nicholas Murray Butler, President of Columbia University*

The Dumbarton Oaks conferences mark a great progress because they give promise of an agreement among four powerful states to support a general international organization for the maintenance of peace and security. That achievement will supply a foundation without which effective organization could not proceed. If the "tentative proposals" advanced be judged in this light, there should be little hesitance in the accumulation of an enthusiastic popular support for them.—*Judge Manley O. Hudson, Member of the Permanent Court of International Justice*

The Dumbarton Oaks Proposals for the International Organization of Peace and Security are surely a substantial step towards the establishment of an international order. They justify the hope that from this beginning there will arise by mutual agreement a new basis of written international law for the prevention of world wars in the future and the greater security for all nations—this would be a substantial realization of the purposes for which the American Peace Society was founded 116 years ago.—*Major General Ulysses S. Grant, III*

For those of us who through long years have defended the Covenant of the League of Nations against active hostility and indifference the present prospects of its revival as outlined in the Dumbarton Oaks agreement and the popular demand for an organization of peace stronger, not weaker, than the League, all this seems almost too good to be true.—*James T. Shotwell, Director of the Division of Economics and History of the Carnegie Endowment for International Peace, and Chairman of the Commission to Study the Organization of Peace*

No friend of peace, and I assume that is the great majority if not the unanimity of American citizens, can fail to be gratified at the result of the Dumbarton Oaks Proposals. The fact that the Great Powers, who in population, productive capacity and material resources, possess, when united, overwhelming strength is a step forward in the substitution of law for force.—*Frederic R. Coudert, President of the American Society of International Law*

In the Dumbarton Oaks proposals we have the first and most important step toward effective world organization for the maintenance of peace and the establishment of international security. —*Leo S. Rowe, Director General of the Pan American Union*

The Dumbarton Oaks Conference has laid a basis for the formation of an international organization to secure an enduring peace. We have a grave responsibility to the young men and women of the United Nations who are giving their lives in order to make possible the achievement of an enduring peace. The opportunity which has now been presented must be firmly grasped now.—*Philip Murray, President, Congress of Industrial Organizations*

CHAPTER IV

MACHINERY OF DUMBARTON OAKS

The machinery of world organization as proposed at Dumbarton Oaks has been the focal point of all criticism of the Oaks plans, primarily in connection with the Security Council and the effectiveness of its powers to prevent war. The arguments have multiplied as time passed. First, the criticism resolved itself into a simple issue of whether we should delegate final authority to our representative on the security council. This has been for the time relegated to the rear shelves while the voting procedure has come into its share of criticism.

At this time, the recently released details of the voting procedure as established at the Yalta conference have almost effectively ended consideration of this issue. The next logical step had been mentioned briefly in the halls of Congress last October, but was almost completely forgotten in the latter discussions. Now, it would seem that the enforcement powers and the size and nature of the police force will soon come under discussion. The Proposals were necessarily vague on this point, but no doubt will be clarified in time. Criticism is gradually developing, largely around the commitments of a nation with regard to such a force, and what powers the council would have to enforce its decision, particularly against a major power.

Another major issue is that of the powers of the General Assembly. As outlined in the Proposals, the General Assembly lacks the wide jurisdiction of the League, and to a large extent is subordinate to the proposed Security Council, which was not included in the organization of the League. This basic difference has been a primary cause for alarm on the part of small nations who tend to look upon the Security Council as the exclusive property of the Big Powers. It is freely admitted that without unity of action among the Big Powers no security organization could operate. Yet the small countries would like a little more opportunity to voice their opinions. Even though they realize they can't hope to cope with antagonistic major powers, they hope to prevent the major powers from running the affairs of the little nations. Accordingly they ask for more power for the General Assembly, particularly more power with regard to discussion of security problems, at present limited except upon request of the Security Council itself to advice from the General Assembly. Also, the small nations want more power with regard to application of sanctions, instead of leaving that matter almost exclusively in the hands of the Security Council. There are many amendments. Most of them are protectionist measures, designed to guarantee small nations a stronger voice in international affairs.

The third, and probably the most important, issue, though the least mentioned in this country, is that relating to the economic controls established by the world organization. The Proposals outline a vague unit to be called the Economic and Social Council, which is to coordinate a number of quasi-independent bodies in a number of technical fields, such as the International Labor Organization operating under the old League. It seems evident that a new body dealing specifically with foreign trade problems will be set up. A number of commissions and authorities have been proposed, the most important of which in recent discussion has been the civil air authority which is intended to set the rules for international air transport.

The field of economic controls is of utmost importance to the small nations, who realize their extreme vulnerability to economic aggression by a major power. They wish protection against unwise tariff legislation, against dumping of surpluses, against inflation and cartels. Foreign trade is the life-blood of many small nations, such as Czechoslovakia, Norway, and the Netherlands. And they further feel that the primary causes of war are economic, so desire a strong Economic and Social Council. The apparent belief is that with a powerful council with all-inclusive powers, the causes of war could be eradicated, and the dependency of the small nations on the Security Council to a certain extent obviated.

One other feature of the machinery remains to be discussed—the International Court of Justice. There will undoubtedly be amendments and criticisms to whatever specific plan is proposed, but there is a strong tendency at present to consider that in the main it will follow the pattern of the old World Court. It is conceded that the old Court must be incorporated into the new body in order to legalize the existing decisions established during its twenty years of operation.

The following section offers a brief survey of the Dumbarton Oaks machinery, how it is intended to operate, and the various fields of controversy which have developed. They primarily illustrate the criticism of the program as developed at Dumbarton Oaks based upon structure of the organization rather than upon the world organization idea itself. There are many other problems outside the proposed structure, which might conceivably interfere with the workings of any machinery established. These problems will be taken up briefly later in the volume. They would exist regardless of the type of organization, and cannot be construed as criticisms or weaknesses of the Proposals themselves.

THE GENERAL ASSEMBLY [1]

The General Assembly is the most democratic body of the United Nations. Each nation will have one vote. It will meet annually and more frequently if needed. The General Assembly will be the policy-making body. It will deal with the whole range of political, economic and social questions. It will study and make recommendations for the purpose of promoting co-operation in the economic and social fields and adjusting situations likely to impede the general welfare. It will be the world parliament where world problems will be debated annually. It will control the budget, and it is the history of parliamentary bodies that the control of the purse is one of the most effective weapons against tyranny. The General Assembly may establish new committees and create new autonomous agencies as they are needed. It is charged with coordinating these various agencies. The Economic and Social Council will be responsible to it.

[1] From "Proposals for the United Nations Charter," by Clark M. Eichelberger, Director, Commission to Study the Organization of Peace. p. 5-6. The Commission. New York. October, 1944. Reprinted by permission.

The General Assembly may also debate and make recommendations on general principles of international peace and security, including disarmament. It may also discuss any question relating to peace and security brought before it by any member or by the Security Council. It may make recommendations to the Security Council with regard to such problems. However, it cannot deal with a security problem which is pending before the Security Council. The small states may well feel that the Assembly should have the right to take a dispute out of the hands of the Security Council, if that body is not doing its job. There might be a revision of this provision by the larger conference.

The authority and scope of the General Assembly are stated in fairly precise terms. It profits by the evolution of the League of Nations Assembly and in a sense begins where the latter left off. The League Assembly started with comparatively vague authority but within ten years it had become the policy-making body of the League. Its power increased as its techniques of procedure developed and as the member states had the courage to use it, not only as a sounding-board but as a policy-making body.

The General Assembly will elect the non-permanent members of the Security Council, all the members of the Economic and Social Council, and will probably participate in the election of judges to the International Court of Justice.

Decisions on questions relating to international peace and security, election of members to the two councils, budget, etc., will be made by a two-thirds majority. Decisions on other questions will be made by a simple majority.

LIMITATIONS OF THE ASSEMBLY [2]

Within the organization the General Assembly, the only organ where all member nations are represented, has to depend on the *recommendation of the Security Council* before it can elect the Secretary General, admit new member nations, expel members, or suspend the exercise of right or privileges of membership

[2] From "Dumbarton Oaks." *World Federation Now,* 6:2. November, 1944. Reprinted by permission.

which, however, the Security Council can restore of its own accord. A two-thirds majority vote is suggested for these and other important decisions. The Assembly can "consider" principles of cooperation in the maintenance of peace and security including regulation of armament, and questions referred to it by members or the Council. However, if *action* is necessary, the questions are to be referred to the Security Council, and members are obligated to accept and carry out the decisions of the Council. *The Assembly may not of its own initiative make any recommendations in matters of peace and security with which the Security Council is already dealing.*

A BROADER POWER OF SUSPENSION [3]

Two features of the Dumbarton Oaks proposals have had insufficient consideration in the current discussion. Yet both are related to the voting procedure in the Security Council, and both may have a bearing upon the application of preventive or enforcement action.

These features relate to the suspension from membership and the expulsion from the organization. Paragraph 3 of Section B of Chapter V reads:

"The General Assembly should, upon recommendation of the Security Council, be empowered to suspend from the exercise of any rights or privileges of membership any member of the organization against which preventive or enforcement action shall have been taken by the Security Council. The exercise of the rights and privileges thus suspended may be restored by decision of the Security Council. The General Assembly should be empowered, upon recommendation of the Security Council, to expel from the organization any member of the organization which persistently violates the principles contained in the charter."

Expulsion, as well as suspension, should be pronounced by a two-thirds majority of those present and voting in the General Assembly. According to unofficial information about the results

[3] From "Procedure Criticized," letter by Leo Gross, Professor of International Law and Organization at Fletcher School of Law and Diplomacy, Tufts College; consultant to the United States Relief and Rehabilitation Administration. *The New York Times.* 94:4E. March 4, 1945. Reprinted by permission.

of the Crimea Conference, recommendations of the Security Council, as distinguished from its decisions, would not require a unanimous vote of the five states having permanent seats on the Council. Assuming this information to be correct, any member of the organization, even one of the Big Five, could be expelled by a majority vote in the Council and by a qualified majority in the General Assembly, if it persisted in the violation.

It follows that a big power which, in case of aggression or threat of aggression, by virtue of its veto right attempted to prevent the Security Council from taking the necessary preventive or enforcement action could be deprived of this right by the concurrent action of the Security Council and the General Assembly. It appears, therefore, that the veto power of the Big Five could only have a delaying effect.

This assumes, of course, that the Security Council has power to take such action against states which remain or are placed outside the organization. There seems to be ample evidence in the Dumbarton Oaks proposals that it is intended to arm the Security Council with such power.

As regards suspension it will be noted that, unlike expulsion, it presupposes not merely a violation of the principles of the charter but a violation which has caused the Security Council to take preventive or enforcement action against the member concerned. Such action can be taken only with the consent of the Big Five; if any one of them vetoes such action, no suspension could take place. As no such previous decision of the Security Council is necessary in case of expulsion, the suspension procedure appears more circumscribed than the expulsion procedure.

Both expulsion and suspension are in the nature of disciplinary measures. Clearly, suspension is the milder measure and the exercise of the rights thus suspended may be restored by the Security Council without the concurrence of the General Assembly.

It is therefore not readily seen why the General Assembly should be precluded to suspend a member for a violation for which it may pronounce its expulsion. It would seem as logical as it is politically advisable to confer upon the organization the power, in case of the violation of any principle of the charter, to pronounce, first, suspension and, next, expulsion if the member persisted in the violation. The required cooperation between the Security Council and the General Assembly should be deemed a sufficient guarantee for a judicious exercise of the powers which would be thus conferred.

The power to suspend is likely, in the long run, to give better results than the power to expel. The experience of the League of Nations points in this direction. The League had the power to expel; it lacked the power to suspend. This has often been felt to be a serious shortcoming of the Covenant.

The forthcoming United Nations Conference could perform an immensely useful task in revising the provision for suspension by divorcing it from the qualifying condition to which it is linked in the Dumbarton Oaks proposals.

If the power of suspension were thus strengthened it might be found expedient and, indeed, wise to omit altogether the provision for expulsion. Thoughtful students of international affairs have argued that the provision for expulsion can confer no visible benefit on the organization and that its application would weaken rather than strengthen the principle of universality.

These experts overlook perhaps the circumstance that in the Dumbarton Oaks proposals, as in the Covenant of the League of Nations, resort to expulsion offers the only possibility for overcoming the deadlock which would otherwise result from the power of the Big Five to veto any preventive or enforcement action directed against a breach of peace or an act of aggression committed by one of them. For this reason, within the framework of the charter of the future international organization, the provision for expulsion is both desirable and valuable.

But it would seem certainly more in keeping with the spirit and the ultimate objective of a comprehensive organization of the community of nations to strengthen the provision for suspension and dispense with the provision for expulsion. To confer power upon the organization to suspend recalcitrant members from the exercise of the rights and privileges of membership for violations of the principles of the charter would, it is believed, contribute more to the successful functioning of the future international organization than any other single measure which is at present under consideration.

As regards the practicability of the suggestion here made, it should be noted that if the big powers were willing to agree to the provision for expulsion in the Dumbarton Oaks proposals, there would seem to be no valid reason why they should refuse to accept the proposed revision of the provision for suspension. As pointed out, even as at present conceived their veto power lacks that absolute character which is commonly attributed to it. Far from materially changing the balanece between rights and obligations of membership, a broadened power of suspension would insure a more effective and harmonious functioning of the organization.

INADEQUACIES OF THE ASSEMBLY [4]

The purposes of the proposed organization of the United Nations, like those stated in the preamble of our own Constitution, include, in effect, establishing justice, securing tranquillity and promoting the general welfare. The defect in the Dumbarton Oaks Proposals is not in the ends sought but in a lack of efficient means to attain them. While the Security Council, intended to be dominated by the five permanent members, is given large powers to enforce peace, the exercise of what may be considered by many as totalitarian power may cause irritation and opposition; consequently, there is need of a body properly representative of the nations of the world to insure the support and cooperation necessary to make the Council's decisions effective.

The General Assembly, as proposed, is totally inadequate to the purpose. In it all the nations of the world are to have an equal vote, although of the forty-five nations listed twenty-three, a majority, represent but 7 1/3 per cent of the aggregate population, while thirty, two-thirds of the whole, represent but 10 per cent.

Evidently the thought behind this plan of equality of vote was that a proposal to make it more representative would result

    [4] From "Assembly Disapproved," letter by Clarence N. Goodwin, former justice of the Illinois Appellate Court. *The New York Times.* 94:8E. April 1, 1945. Reprinted by permission.

in the opposition of the smaller nations, but the result of the adoption of this principle made it impossible to confer upon the Assembly any power to participate in decisions and required limitations even on the right to discuss and recommend. There is, I suggest, no ground for belief that small nations would prefer equality of vote in an Assembly thus destitute of power to fair and just representation in one possessing power and influence in the affairs of the world. That they would prefer the latter seems not susceptible of rational denial.

The choice does not lie between equality of representation, which would give Luxembourg, with 300,000 people, the same representation as Russia, with 197,000,000 people, and representation based on power and population alone. In fixing a basis, consideration should also be given to a nation's enlightenment, its potential influence for world peace and its interest in maintaining it, its position during the present war, its devotion to liberty, its attachment to principles of representative government and opposition to totalitarian power, as well as other pertinent factors.

In making this suggestion I am following the position taken by Mr. Pinkney in our Constitutional Convention, where in place of equality of representation of states in the Senate or of representation on the basis of population alone, population was to be given partial consideration, and this was supported by Mr. Madison as a just compromise.

If the Assembly is thus constituted on a properly representative basis it will not be necessary to determine at the outset what powers, duties and responsibilities shall be given it. All that may be determined as need arises. But if the basis presented in the Proposals is adopted, that "fundamental" error will in all probability be "permanent." These two words I quote from the statement of Mr. Wilson in our Constitutional Convention of 1787 in opposition to equality of representation in the Senate. Once that insupportable principle is embedded in an international plan, generations of effort will not serve to remove it. On the other hand, inequalities in the representation accorded the different nations can be corrected from time to time without disregarding the principles upon which the initial apportionment is made.

Equality of representation in the Assembly has been vigorously attacked elsewhere and the suggestion made that an Assembly on a representative basis be given the powers now conferred on the Security Council and other instrumentalities. The logical answer is that, in view of the urgent need of agreement and the progress that has been made, practicality demands that any change in the structure be within the framework of the Proposals. That is exactly what is suggested here.

To put the foregoing in concrete form, but not as something to be accepted, it is suggested that each of the five great nations might be accorded, say, twenty delegates in the Assembly and the other nations be given representation of, say, one to fifteen on a basis in harmony with what is suggested here. This it is believed, would remove the fear that we may find ourselves with a Security Council in which a majority are chosen by the votes of nations representative of but an inconsiderable part of the world's population and power.

It may be suggested, however, that temporary members, chosen even by an Assembly thus constituted, would lack the advantage of definitely representing and being responsible to a nation or, as in the case of the Soviet Union, what is practically a group of nations, which will be enjoyed by the permanent members. This disadvantage will be overcome if the delegates in a fairly representative Assembly are given power, when they choose, to organize themselves in homogeneous groups, each empowered to select its own member of the Council.

Suppose, for instance, the Scandinavian countries, with the addition of perhaps Finland and other Baltic states; Canada, Australia, the Union of South Africa and New Zealand; the Mohammedan states; Mexico and the Central American republics; Brazil and sympathetic South American nations, and perhaps the Argentine, Chile, Uruguay and Paraguay were each accorded the right to choose a group representative on the Council, some, perhaps, with a seat in the Council but only half a vote. Obviously, the votes of members thus selected need not aggregate more than the six as now proposed. Members of the Council so selected would in no way menace its success, but would implement it and place behind it the power which would come from the feeling that its decisions truly represent the will of the world.

BIG THREE VOTING POWER [5]

Just because the Big Three's secret deal for multiple votes in the proposed League Assembly has shaken confidence in the San Francisco conference, friends of international organization should keep their shirts on. All is not lost by any means.

The shock to the smaller nations can be absorbed with less damage now than if this secret diplomacy had suddenly exploded at San Francisco. The present bitter reaction of the Allies, and of such American delegates as Senator Vandenberg, may clear the air and serve as an effective warning to the Big Three.

Maybe in the end this ill wind from Yalta will have blown more good. However destructive the secret method, the result is a useful reminder to all that the Dumbarton Oaks draft was only a tentative plan for revision by all the United Nations. Now the Big Three themselves have scrapped the Dumbarton provision for equal voting rights in the Assembly, and have recognized in the Yalta secret pact the authority of the San Francisco conference to decide. So it will be easier for the conference to challenge the closely related voting rights in the League Council also. Big Three control and one-power veto in the council is a basic issue because it, rather than the Assembly, has practically all of the authority.

There is also much to be gained by forcing advance public discussion of this representation question, which was one reason the United States refused to join the old League of Nations. Russia's refusal to accept one vote in the Assembly as against Britain's six—one each for the United Kingdom, the four dominions and India—is matched by similar objections in our Senate today. Though Britain can make a good case for separate votes for the four free dominions, India's foreign policy is controlled by London. So Churchill at Yalta had to agree to give Russia and the United States each three Assembly votes.

[5] From "Big Three Voting Power," editorial. *New York World-Telegram.* 77:10. March 31, 1945. Reprinted by permission.

But it is not that simple. Under such an apportionment, France, Holland, Belgium and other colonial powers will demand multiple votes. Noncolonial powers object that this system puts a premium upon imperialism, which the league is supposed to restrain. And 20 hemisphere nations in the new inter-American pact have just reasserted the equal voting rights of all sovereign nations regardless of size—which is the traditional United States policy.

Like other problems of international organizations, this is not an easy one. But it is far easier than having another world war. And that is what all of us must remember in the midst of these shocks from secret diplomacy and big power manipulation. The United Nations must stick together and work out machinery for world cooperation. That is the price of security.

As for ourselves, despite Yalta political deals, we have as much faith as ever in the United Nations' ability to agree on a just Golden Gate charter—if the Big Three allow the conference to function democratically.

THREE VOTES FOR RUSSIA [6]

The Soviet representatives at Yalta proposed that the White Russian and the Ukrainian republics be initial members of the proposed international organization. This was a question for the United Nations assembled at San Francisco to consider and decide.

In view of the importance which the Soviet government attached to this proposal, the American representatives at Yalta, having the utmost respect for the heroic part played by the people of these republics in their unyielding resistance to the common enemy and the fortitude with which they have borne great suffering in the prosecution of the war, agreed that the government of the United States would support such a Soviet proposal at San Francisco if made. No agreement was, however, made at Yalta on the question of the participation of these republics in the San Francisco conference.

[6] From "Stettinius Statement on Conference," newsstory. New York World-Telegram. 77:17. April 3, 1945. Reprinted by permission.

In the circumstances, the American representatives at Yalta believed that it was their duty to reserve the possibility of the United States having three votes in the general assembly. The Soviet and British representatives stated their willingness to support a proposal, if the United States should make it, to accord three votes in the assembly to the United States.

The President has decided that at the San Francisco conference the United States will not request additional votes for the government of the United States in the general assembly.

THE SECURITY COUNCIL [7]

The Security Council has three jobs: to settle disputes; to stop aggression; to provide for the regulation of armaments. Because of the necessity of constant vigilance the Security Council will be in continuous session. Since the American Secretary of State or the British Foreign Minister or any other foreign minister cannot be at the headquarters constantly, the men sitting on the Security Council will be high officials, probably with ambassadorial rank.

The Security Council will have eleven members. Four of the eleven seats will be occupied permanently by representatives of the United States, Great Britain, Russia and China. A fifth permanent seat is reserved for France. The six remaining seats are to be rotated among the smaller powers. A nation elected to the Security Council will sit for two years without the privilege of immediate re-election. Three seats will be filled each year. If a nation is not a member of the Security Council but its interests are involved, it shall sit with the Security Council while its interests are being discussed.

The Security Council is the executive security council for all the members of the Organization. Article I of Section B involves the most important delegation of sovereignty to be found in the proposed Charter. This article states: "In order to ensure prompt and effective action by the Organization, members of the

[7] From "Proposals for the United Nations Charter," by Clark M. Eichelberger, Director, Commission to Study the Organization of Peace. p. 6-7. The Commission. New York. October, 1944. Reprinted by permission.

Organization should by the Charter confer on the Security Council primary responsibility for the maintenance of international peace and security and should agree that in carrying out these duties under this responsibility it should act on their behalf. Furthermore, all members of the Organization will be obligated to accept the decisions of the Security Council and to carry them out."

OPERATION OF THE SECURITY MACHINERY [8]

You now can get a view of the machinery with which the world is likely to be run after this war. It is possible, too, to show you how this machinery will or will not function in case of threatened trouble.

There is to be a world organization with the official title of "United Nations," which this country will join if the Senate by two-thirds vote agrees. The heart of this organization is to be in its power to use force, if necessary, to prevent nations from threatening the peace. The extent of this power, and its meaning, can be shown only in relation to practical situations that may arise.

Here, then, is a quick picture of what might happen, once the United Nations is in action:

Trouble in Germany. Suppose that, in violation of the peace terms, Germans begin secretly rearming. The Security Council of the United Nations—United States, Britain, Russia, China, and eventually France, plus six rotating members—if empowered by the terms of the coming peace treaty, could order investigation. Assume that evidence of rearmament is found. The Council warns Germany, but Germany ignores the warning. Then the Council orders sanctions, involving full economic blockade. Germany resists. Finally, the Council decides on a military demonstration, and asks each one of the big powers to take part.

That would bring this country face to face with the question of use of her armed forces. If, in addition to joining the United Nations, she had authorized such use through a majority vote of

[8] From "Plan for World Security," newsstory. *The United States News.* p. 24-6. October 20, 1944. Reprinted by permission.

both houses of Congress, this country would take part in military action against Germany at once. If such use had not been authorized in advance, United States participation in that specific instance would have to await approval of Congress.

Trouble in Argentina. Or take another possible case, involving Argentina. Suppose that a Nazi-like military group is dominant in the Argentine Government. Elections are suspended, press and radio are censored, business and labor are regimented. Then Argentina starts fomenting revolutions in neighboring countries, to build up an anti-United States bloc. The United States, faced with this threat, appeals to the Security Council. Responding, the Council warns Argentina that she must abandon her Nazi-like ways, and leave other countries alone. Argentina ignores the warning, whereupon the Council orders an economic and naval blockade. The result is that the militaristic Argentine Government falls, and another one, willing to obey the Council, is formed.

That illustrates how the United Nations machinery might be used to deal with a totalitarian regime in one country before it got to the point of aggression.

Peru vs. Chile. A third example is what might happen in a dispute between two small countries. Suppose Peru and Chile disagree over fishing rights off the coast of South America. Peru asks Chile to submit the dispute to the International Court. Chile refuses. Peru then appeals to the Security Council. The Council turns the case over to the Court. The Court decides against Chile, but Chile refuses to abide by the discussion, and Peru again appeals to the Council. The Council then asks the United States, Mexico and Brazil to use armed force. On a demonstration by bombing planes, Chile agrees to obey the Court.

In such an instance, the mere demonstration of force would suffice. In all these three hypothetical cases, the United Nations machinery is assumed to be operating successfully. But in other cases it might not work.

United States vs. Nicaragua. Conceivably, the United States might be involved in a dispute which the United Nations could not settle. Imagine the following situation, as an example: The Nicaraguan Government is overturned, and the new regime seizes American-owned properties. The United States sends a detachment of marines to "restore order." The new Nicaraguan regime then appeals to the Security Council. But the United States votes against action by the Council, and effectively blocks any such action.

This illustration assumes that each member of the Big Five has power to veto action by the Council, even though it itself is accused of aggression. Actually, the voting powers in such cases have been left undecided in the plan announced.

Civil war in China. Another instance in which the peace machinery might be inadequate would be a civil war within one of the Big Five countries. Suppose civil war broke out in China, with the Chiang-Kai-shek regime on one side and the Communists on the other. (These groups actually have fought against each other in the past, and may again in the future.) Suppose, also that Russia were furnishing arms to the Communists, and the United States and Britain were furnishing arms to Chiang. In such a situation, unless all four of the big powers involved were willing, the United Nations peace machinery could not be applied. Not only would the civil war go on, but the other powers might be drawn in, and another world war might be the result.

POWERS OF THE SECURITY COUNCIL
REPRESENTATIVE [9]

The chief domestic issue which so far has grown out of the Dumbarton Oaks conferences is whether or not the American representative on the proposed World Security Council should be empowered to commit American military forces to action without, in each instance, the specific approval of Congress. This is the issue on which there was a lively but brief debate in the Senate a few weeks ago as a result of Secretary Hull's informative conferences with members of the Foreign Relations Committee. It is the one embodied in the last of the three blunt questions which Sen. Joseph H. Ball of Minnesota has addressed to all candidates for President, the Senate, and the House.

Actually, the issue is not domestic alone. It has to be settled here. It involves, in theory, a constitutional question centering

[9] From "The Practical Means of Peace," Ernest K. Lindley. *Newsweek.* 24: 49. October 23, 1944. Reprinted by permission.

on the power of Congress to declare war. But it is an international question also. Few, if any, nations will believe the United States means to collaborate in preserving the peace unless (1) it keeps in being the requisite forces and (2) at least a portion of these can be committed to action promptly by the Executive, without a debate and formal vote by Congress. The foreign offices of other nations have noted the signs that many of the ex-isolationists who have endorsed in principle American participation in an international organization to preserve peace are regrouping to oppose the practical means of making the principle effective.

To put this issue in a setting of reality, several points should be kept in mind:

1. The military forces which each participant might be called upon to provide would be prescribed in a separate master agreement. They would be agreed-upon quotas. The Executive, through the American representative on the Security Council, would not have the discretionary authority to commit forces beyond these quotas.

2. These quotas would be within the capacity of our permanent military establishment, which would, of course, have to be larger than it was between the two world wars. The pledge to make these forces available promptly would imply that they remain in being, ready for action. On the part of the United States, they probably would be chiefly naval and air units. They would be what might properly be called police forces.

3. When Germany and Japan have been defeated, and if they are kept disarmed, there will remain no nation, apart from the armed victors, capable, within the foreseeable time, of waging an important war. A relatively small part of the present wartime strength of the major Allies would be sufficient, if used promptly, to suppress any small or medium-sized threat to the peace.

4. To set these police forces into motion would require the vote of a majority of the eleven members of the Security Council, including the unanimous vote of the four Great Powers having permanent membership. The Dumbarton Oaks conferences left unsettled the procedure in the event one of the Great Powers serving as a permanent member should be charged with aggres-

sion or the threat of it. The British, Chinese, and American delegations said that the power thus charged should stand aside and let the others judge. The Russians objected. The Russian position is more frankly realistic, but the issue is theoretical. A decision that one of the powerful permanent members was guilty of aggression would mean that the effort to preserve the peace had collapsed. The military forces required to discipline it would be much greater than the agreed-upon quotas of the other nations. The world organization would then cease to be more than a means of forming a coalition to fight a war. No such situation could develop without ample opportunity for debate throughout the United States and for final decision of Congress on the question of war or peace.

The power of the Executive to use limited forces for police action without specific sanction by Congress has been established by many precedents stretching back to Jefferson. Now it is proposed to fix the President's powers in this respect. It is argued that through his representative on the Security Council, the Executive could maneuver the United States into a position where, if the Great Powers were to fall out, a major war would be unavoidable. He could do that if there were no world security organization. And who would venture to say that there would not be a greater risk of war within a generation, or sooner, if the victors of the present struggle did not try to perpetuate their alliance and to transform it into an organization for the enforcement of the peace?

UNIVERSITIES COMMITTEE ANALYSIS [10]

While the Groups are not entirely satisfied with the Dumbarton Oaks Proposals relating to security, and suggest many changes, those which express an opinion on the matter are unanimous in holding that the Proposals should be adopted even if no important modification of them is now obtainable. In their opinion the Proposals represent a significant first step toward the development of an international organization capable

[10] From "The Dumbarton Oaks Proposals: The Enforcement of Peace," summary of the first 41 reports received from cooperating groups. Universities Committee on Postwar International Problems. Released for publication, March 9, 1945. Reprinted by permission.

of maintaining peace and security against any aggressor. The alternative to them is recognized to be, not a better international organization, but none at all.

Nearly all the Groups agree that on balance the Proposals satisfy the conditions of probable effectiveness for the enforcement of peace in greater degree than the Covenant of the League of Nations, and the vast majority conclude that while imperfect, they meet these conditions to about as high a degree as can be expected under present world circumstances. The Proposals, the Groups recognize, do not offer any promise of success in putting down a breach of the peace by one of the "Big Three," but, they urge, this is out of the question for any international organization that would be acceptable today. Several Groups express themselves as greatly disappointed in the Dumbarton Oaks Proposals, regarding them as providing for what is in essence a great-power alliance which would maintain peace in the interest of these powers and which would depend for its effectiveness on their concerted good will, bought perhaps at a very high price. The overwhelming majority of the Groups, however, look at the Proposals from what they call the "evolutionary" rather than the "perfectionist" point of view, and they judge them to be a substantial and fairly satisfactory step forward toward an international organization capable of preserving a just peace from attacks from any quarter.

The Groups tend to assume that the action envisaged will not be taken against one of the "Big Three" and therefore their discussion is concerned with the question of the effectiveness of the organization, as described in the Proposals, in preventing or suppressing breaches of the peace by one of the other powers. They recognize that there is no possibility of the organization fulfilling this function against one of the three Great Powers, and that hence the question would be open to a more significant answer if it were modified as indicated.

The Groups point out that likelihood of decision to take action depends less on the machinery provided than on the existence of a serious will to use that machinery to prevent or suppress any breach of the peace. The Dumbarton Oaks Proposals, like the League Covenant, leave the decision to act or not to act primarily with the Great Powers. By their veto power they can prevent action, and by their influence they can, if united among themselves, compel action. A preponderant majority of the Groups express the view that under the plan envisaged in the Proposals there will be a greater approximation to certainty of decision than under the League Covenant. They base this conclusion on their belief that the present Great Powers have profited from the sad experiences of the last twenty-five years and will not again be so likely to fail to take preventive action in the face of a threat to the peace or suppressive action in the face of a breach of the peace. Further, the participation this time of the United States, they urge, will tend to make a decision to act more likely.

All Groups but one believe the Proposals give better guarantees as regards certainty that national forces will be provided upon call of the Security Council than did the League Covenant and the vast majority of them regard the Proposals as satisfactory in this respect. The setting up in advance of specific agreements as to the forces and facilities to be provided, together with the advance planning by the Military Staff Committee, would, the Groups believe, commit the nations concerned so thoroughly that they would be very likely to provide the contingents agreed upon when asked by the Security Council to do so. This would be particularly true of the Great Powers, from whom the largest contingents would come, because were they not willing to act, they would have prevented the call from being issued by the Security Council.

THE VOTING PROCEDURE EXPLAINED [11]

Text of supplemental voting procedure
decided upon at the Crimea Conference

CHAPTER VI.

C. VOTING:

1. Each member of the Security Council should have one vote.
2. Decisions of the Security Council on procedural matters should be made by an affirmative vote of seven members.

[11] Text of statement by Secretary of State Edward R. Stettinius, Jr. *New York Times.* 94:10. March 6, 1945. Reprinted by permission.

3. Decisions of the Security Council on all other matters should be made by an affirmative vote of seven members, including the concurring votes of the permanent members; provided that, in decisions under Chapter VIII, Section A, and under the second sentence of Paragraph I of Chapter VIII, Section C, a party to a dispute should abstain from voting.

The practical effect of these provisions, taken together, is that a difference is made, so far as voting is concerned, between the quasi-judicial function of the Security Council in promoting the pacific settlement of disputes and the political function of the council in taking action for the maintenance of peace and security.

Where the council is engaged in performing its quasi-judicial functions of promoting pacific settlement of disputes, no nation, large or small, should be above the law. This means that no nation, large or small, if a party to a dispute, would participate in the decisions of the Security Council on questions like the following:

(A) Whether a matter should be investigated;

(B) Whether the dispute or situation is of such a nature that its continuation is likely to threaten the peace;

(C) Whether the Council should call on the parties to settle a dispute by means of their own choice;

(D) Whether, if the dispute is referred to the Council, a recommendation should be made as to methods and procedures of settlement;

(E) Whether the Council should make such recommendations before the dispute is referred to it;

(F) What should be the nature of this recommendation;

(G) Whether the legal aspect of the dispute should be referred to the court for advice;

(H) Whether a regional agency should be asked to concern itself with the dispute; and

(I) Whether the dispute should be referred to the General Assembly.

Where the Council is engaged in performing its political functions of action for maintenance of peace and security, a difference is made between the permanent members of the Council and other nations for the practical reason that the permanent members of the Council must, as a matter of necessity, bear the principal responsibility for action. Unanimous agreement among the permanent members of the Council is therefore requisite. In such matters, therefore, the concurrence of all the permanent members would be required. Examples are:

(A) Determination of the existence of a threat or breach of the peace;

(B) Use of force or other enforcement measures;

(C) Approval of agreements for supply of armed forces;

(D) Matters relating to the regulation of armaments; and

(E) Matters concerning the suspension and expulsion of members, and the admission of new members.

SIGNIFICANCE OF VOTING PROCEDURE [12]

I wish at this time to comment to you briefly on the significance of the proposal on voting procedure. This procedure means that whenever any member of the council—including any permanent member—is a party to a dispute, that member cannot vote in any decision of the council involving peaceful settlement of that dispute.

Consequently, the council can examine the dispute thoroughly and the remaining members can make recommendations to all the parties to the dispute as to methods and procedures for settling it. They can refer the legal aspects of the dispute to the international court for advice. They can refer the dispute to the general assembly if they wish; and they can take any other appropriate steps short of enforcement measures to obtain a settlement of that dispute without the vote of the member of the security council involved in the dispute.

This means that all members of the security council when they are parties to a dispute will be on the same footing before this council. It means that no nation in the world will be denied the right to have a fair hearing of its case in the security council, and that the equal, democratic rights of all nations will be respected.

[12] From "Stettinius Offers Guide To Americas," newsstory. *The New York Times.* 94:9. March 6, 1945. Reprinted by permission.

If the dispute is not settled by such means, the major question before the council is whether force needs to be employed. In that event it is necessary that the vote of the permanent members of the council be unanimous. They are the nations which possess in sufficient degree the industrial and military strength to prevent aggression.

However, the decision of the council can be reached in such a case only by a majority of seven members, which means that the permanent members cannot alone decide to take action. It also means that the non-permanent members can prevent action.

ANALYSIS OF YALTA COMPROMISE [13]

The practical effect of the compromise is to make a distinction between what Secretary Stettinius calls "the quasi-judicial function of the Council in promoting the pacific settlement of disputes and the political function of the Council in taking action for the maintenance of peace and security." When questions of the first kind are involved—that is, when the issue is whether any particular situation threatening peace should be investigated, or what action (short of recourse to force) shall be taken in order to deal with such a situation—no nation which is a party to the dispute, whether that nation is great or small, will participate in the decisions of the Council, and these decisions shall be made by a majority of seven of its eleven members —the eleven consisting of the five permanent representatives of the Great Powers (Russia, Britain, China, France and the United States) and six representatives of the smaller powers. However, when the issue goes beyond pacific measures, and when the question is actually one of using force to prevent or restrain aggression, then a different voting procedure will be followed. In this case there must be unanimous agreement among the representatives of the five Great Powers before action can be taken. Each of these Great Powers, therefore, would have the right to veto action against itself.

Objection may be made that this arrangement proposes to put the five Great Powers in a favored position which the

[13] From "Yalta and San Francisco," editorial. *The New York Times.* 94: 20. March 6, 1945. Reprinted by permission.

smaller powers would not enjoy, and theoretically this objection is valid. But the reality of the situation must convince us that if a point is ever reached when one of the five Great Powers has to be coerced by force, then peace will have been lost anyway, beyond the possibility of salvage by any voting procedure that can possibly be devised, and a new world war will be in the making. The whole hope of maintaining peace rests, in the last analysis, upon the good faith of the Great Powers and their ability to get along together. If they cannot get along together, then no machinery of voting in the Council, however elaborate or however ingenious on paper, will suffice to keep the peace.

The Yalta compromise recognizes this essential fact. It recognizes that in any use of force to prevent or restrain aggression the five Great Powers must inevitably bear the principal responsibility for action, and that unanimity of opinion among these Powers is therefore indispensable to success. At the same time the Yalta compromise provides that not even the greatest of the Powers shall be above the law: any policies or actions on its part may at any time be questioned by a majority of seven of a Council in whose membership the small nations outnumber the large ones.

YALTA "HIDDEN" VETO [14]

There is an additional veto power that has been so consistently unmentioned by the official pronouncements on the voting procedure as to suggest that it is being expediently minimized.

This is the veto right that each big power has over every dispute in which it is not involved.

Under the terms of the Yalta compromise, any big power can block any one of the following steps, provided it is not one of the parties immediately concerned in the dispute under question:

1. Power to investigate any dispute or any situation which may lead to international friction or give rise to a dispute.

[14] From "Yalta 'Hidden' Veto," by Neal Stanford, staff correspondent. *The Christian Science Monitor.* 37:1. March 13, 1945.

2. Power to bring any such dispute or situation to the attention of the Assembly or Council.

3. Power to call upon parties to settle their dispute by negotiation, mediation, conciliation, arbitration, or judicial settlement.

4. Power to recommend appropriate procedures or methods of adjustment.

5. Power to refer justiciable disputes to the International Court of Justice.

6. Power to refer dispute to regional agency for settlement or decision.

Thus, while officials emphasized that a big power, party to a dispute, can veto the use of force against itself, they fail to point out that each big power has a veto over every other kind of dispute. And in those cases the veto power is not only over the use of force but extends to the very consideration of the dispute itself.

This veto power of each of the Big Five over disputes to which it is not a party stems directly from Paragraph 3 of Section C of Chapter VI—the voting procedure agreed on at Yalta, credit for which goes to President Roosevelt.

This reads: 3. Decisions of the Security Council on all other matters (other than procedural) should be made by an affirmative vote of seven members *including the concurring votes of the permanent members*; provided that, in decisions under Chapter VIII, Section A, and under the second sentence of Paragraph I of Chapter VIII, Section C, a party to a dispute should abstain from voting.

CLARIFICATION OF SECURITY VOTING [15]

Washington, March 24—Joseph C. Grew, Acting Secretary of State, affirmed today in a statement aimed at clarifying the question of voting procedure in the proposed International Security Council, that no one nation could prevent discussion of any dispute or situation that might arise.

It is only when the question arises as to what, if any, decision or action the Security Council should take, [said Secretary Grew] that the

[15] From "Grew Clarifies Security Voting," by Lansing Warren. *The New York Times*. 94:28. March 25, 1945. Reprinted by permission.

provisions covering voting procedure agreed upon at Yalta could come into action.

It is this Government's understanding that under these voting procedures there is nothing which could prevent any state from bringing to the attention of the Security Council any dispute or situation which it believes may give rise to a dispute.

And, furthermore, there is nothing in these provisions which could prevent any party to such dispute or situation from receiving a hearing before the Council and having the case discussed. Nor could any of the other members of the Council be prevented from making such observations on the matter as they wish to make.

The right of the General Assembly to consider and discuss any dispute or situation would remain, of course, at all times untrammeled.

The statement, to which was appended a full description of how the voting would be conducted under varying types of circumstances, brings into the foreground a basic conception of the new international organization which would leave wide latitude to the powers to devise the means of dealing with each and every particular situation.

It is provided in the Dumbarton Oaks charter . . . that the Security Council shall create its own rules of procedure. This discloses, in the conception of the framers of the charter, the express intention of primarily employing discussion and avoiding rigid regulations of conduct; of endeavoring to make the organization a medium for centering world moral opinion on a given dispute and providing effective and instantly operative machinery for action if the will for action undeniably exists.

The veto power of the permanent members which, in some situations is extended to the non-permanent members of the Council, under this interpretation becomes an instrument for maintaining that harmony among the chief holders of force which, according to all authorities on the question, is an essential for any combined international effort to maintain and develop peace. It goes back to the philosophy expressed by Cordell Hull, Secretary of State, in an address delivered on April 9, 1944, in which he stated:

Without an enduring understanding between these four nations (this country, the British Commonwealth, the Soviet Union and China) upon their fundamental purposes, interests and obligations to one another, all organizations to preserve peace are creations on paper and the path is wide open again for the rise of a new aggressor.

This essential understanding and unity of action among the four nations is not in substitution or derogation of unity among the United Nations. But it is basic to all organized international action, because upon its reality depends the possibility of enduring peace and free institutions rather than new coalitions and a new prewar period.

With this in mind as the foundation of the new world organization, the charter compromises sought to achieve flexibility to afford the maximum possibility of action and prevent the fixing of too rigid rules of application. The intention has been, it is understood from authoritative sources, to create a mechanism pledged to operate against all threats to peace and ready to recommend peaceful settlements of any and all such controversies.

The belief has been that the greater part of the business of the Council will consist in reaching means of settlement rather than with the use of force, which is provided as the last of a series of other measures and sanctions.

The machinery thus devised, in the estimate of its framers, therefore depends in the first place on the will for enforcement and is made stronger by the fact that the new organization will have at its disposal the means of enforcing that will. To that extent it is an advance on the conception of the old League of Nations, which required unanimity on all decisions of the kind and had not coercive authority at its disposal, relying on moral suasion and support of the individual powers.

The Yalta decisions, however, have endeavored further to limit the possibilities of the use of a veto, which has been reserved only for last extremities. As explained by Mr. Grew today, the voting procedure, as contrasted with League unanimity, has been defined as requiring an affirmative vote of seven out of eleven members for decisions on both "substantive and procedural" matters. Decisions on procedural matters would be made by the votes of any seven members.

As to a case where a permanent member was involved, Mr. Grew declared:

In decisions on enforcement measures the vote of seven must include the votes of all five permanent members, whether or not they are parties to a dispute. On questions involving the peaceful settlement of disputes, no party to the dispute, whether or not a permanent, may vote. In such decisions the vote of seven must include those permanent members which are not parties to the dispute.

This means that when a permanent member of the Security Council is involved in a dispute the representative of that state many not vote on matters involving a peaceful settlement of that dispute. In other words, that permanent member would have no "veto" in these matters. In this case, however, the remaining permanent members must concur in the total vote of seven by which the Security Council reaches its decisions. Any permanent member not a party to the dispute would thus have a veto, should it care to exercise it.

Further, if two of the permanent members of the Council are parties to a dispute, neither of them can vote and the decision must be made by the three remaining permanent members and four of the non-permanent members of the Council. If more than two permanent members are involved in a dispute the vote would require the concurrence of the remaining permanent members plus the number of non-permanent members necessary to make a total of seven.

Under such circumstances, if there are four members of the Council involved in the dispute—and, therefore, none of the four could vote— each of the remaining members of the Council, whether permanent or non-permanent, would have the same vote.

In the event a permanent member is not involved, the "affirmative vote of each of the five permanent members is required for the Council to take any decisions or action on that dispute."

JUSTICE UNDER THE YALTA FORMULA [16]

In some quarters the complaint is made that under the "Yalta formula" the Great Powers are proposing to establish . . . what would amount to a dictatorship by themselves of world affairs, with the Small Powers relegated to the position of mere pawns or helpless bystanders. . . .

It is true that under the "Yalta formula" each of the Great Powers retains power to veto *the use of force* against itself. But this arrangement merely recognizes the reality that if a point is ever reached when one of the five Great Powers must be coerced by force, then peace will have been lost anyway, beyond the possiblity of salvage by any voting procedure that can possibly be

[16] From "The Small Powers," editorial. *The New York Times.* 94:18. March 9, 1945. Reprinted by permission.

devised, and a new world war will be in the making. Meantime, long before this point is reached, let us note the very real degree of freedom and authority to initiate moves to prevent the outbreak of war which would be vested in the hands of the Small Powers.

The "Yalta formula" provides that all "procedural" matters shall be settled by an affirmative vote of seven in the proposed Security Council consisting of eleven members. In this Security Council the Small Powers will have a majority of six members; the Great Powers a minority of five. It is further provided that in all "procedural" matters a party to a dispute with a Small Power which is not a member of the council—if, let us say, the United States is involved in a dispute with Costa Rica—the line-up in the Security Council in voting on this question will be six Small Powers and only four Great Powers. And what authority will a Council so constituted have, in dealing with the matter in dispute? As summarized by Secretary Stettinius—

The Council can examine the dispute thoroughly and make recommendations to the parties involved regarding methods and proceedings for settling it. The Council can refer the legal aspects of the dispute to the new International Court for advice. It can refer the dispute to the General Assembly if it wishes. It can take any other appropriate steps to obtain a settlement, short of actual enforcement measures. Costa Rica, in short, can put the United States on the carpet, get a hearing for its case, and have the merits of that case voted on by a Council in which the Small Powers have a majority of six to four.

Moreover, let us note that when the "enforcement" stage itself is reached an affirmative vote of seven members of the Council is still necessary before action can be taken. The Great Powers will have only five votes. They must therefore have on their side the votes of at least two Small Powers. And therefore, by maintaining a unified front, the Small Powers themselves will have a veto power over any proposed enforcement action.

There is no warrant for describing a procedure of this kind as one which makes mere pawns of the Small Powers or relegates them to the position of helpless bystanders.

REVIEW OF OAKS CHANGES [17]

Although the Dumbarton Oaks agreement has, on the whole, weathered critical examination, a number of amendments will be offered at San Francisco and at least a few almost certainly will have to be adopted.

Senator Vandenberg wants to be sure that the world organization will have power to review and revise political settlements made during the present war. Under Dumbarton Oaks, it already has been given that power, and more. According to the agreement, any situation may be brought to the attention of the world organization. Whether the situation in question arose from a political settlement made during this war or from one made earlier would make no difference. But the Senator apparently wants the final charter of the world organization to be more explicit about this.

The voting procedure agreed upon at Yalta almost certainly will be opposed by some of the smaller nations. But there is little likelihood that it will be altered in any important way. Whether a great power has, or is denied, the right to veto action against itself is a question rather far removed from reality. Either way, a great power cannot be restrained or coerced without a major war, and the other great nations will not restrain or coerce it unless they consider the issue important enough to justify fighting a major war. It would seem honest intellectually to recognize this by permitting a great power to veto action against itself.

Sumner Welles has suggested that the proposed Big Five—the United States, Soviet Union, Britain, China, and France—be made a Big Six by giving Brazil a permanent seat on the world security council, with a corresponding increase in the total size of the council from eleven to thirteen members. Some of the other Latin-American nations probably will be less interested in that than in making sure that one or two of the temporary seats on the council are always filled from the Western Hemisphere.

[17] From "Dumbarton Oaks," by Ernest K. Lindley. *Washington Post.* March 21, 1945. Reprinted in the *Congressional Record.* (Current) A1470. March 21, 1945.

The San Francisco Conference clearly will have to go into the question of regional security arrangements more thoroughly than was done at Dumbarton Oaks. Regional arrangements were specifically authorized at Dumbarton Oaks. But the tendency there was to heap the responsibility for keeping the peace on the world organization instead of decentralizing it. Under Dumbarton Oaks the nations of the Western Hemisphere could not act to preserve the peace within the hemisphere without the prior authorization of the world security council. This discovery came as a shock to many during the discussions at Mexico City which led to the Act of Chapultepec.

Regional agreements and all special alliances must be consistent with the purposes and principles of the world security organization as the Act of Chapultepec certainly is. If the close neighbors of a threatening aggressor can deal with him effectively, so much the better. The world organization would want to be sure that they were, in fact, dealing with a threat to the peace and not ganging up on an innocent party. But this safeguard might be established without requiring a prior authorization from the world security organization before a regional group could act. The close neighbors usually know what is going on sooner than more distant observers do. In most cases, what should cause concern to the world organization is not regional action to curb an aggressor, but failure by the regional group to act promptly and effectively.

SMALL NATIONS' FEARS OF VOTE INEQUALITY [18]

A major issue troubling the small nations concerns the voting procedure of the Supreme Council. Many fear that under the Yalta proposal—which requires a unanimous vote of the Big Five to take military or economic action against aggressors—their interests might not be protected adequately. A speech of British Foreign Secretary Anthony Eden before the Scottish

[18] From "The Nation: As Nations Gather," editorial. *The New York Times*. 94:2E. March 25, 1945. Reprinted by permission.

Conservative party's conference in Glasgow appeared to be aimed at answering this objection. Mr. Eden, declared,

It is against all traditions of our policy to allow unity among the great powers to become a means to bully the smaller. There can be no freedom in the world unless the smaller states can be joined with the great powers in their common interest.

That the United States, Britain, Russia and China will make strenuous efforts to obtain approval of the program substantially as it stands was indicated by one of them last week. The Russian radio declared in a broadcast that attempts were being made under the guise of a "sincere regard for the small countries" to "return the future organization of security to the evil days of the League of Nations. [Small countries in the League] had formal equal rights. This made it possible for [them], on the instructions of a large aggressor, to disrupt important measures intended for the insurance of peace and security."

NEED OF MAJOR POWER VOTE HARMONY [19]

Washington, March 16—The State Department emphasized the importance of unity among the great powers in replying to a question from newspaper correspondents today concerning the voting formula reached at Yalta for the Dumbarton Oaks peace plan.

The question was in several parts, as follows:

Apparently under the Yalta voting formula each great power not only has a veto on the forceful settlement of disputes to which it is a party, but also a veto on the peaceful settlement of disputes to which it is not a party. If the department agrees this is so, will it explain why in official explanations the first veto power has been emphasized and the second minimized? Does this complete veto that each power has in some form over every dispute that arises express America's official desire?

In reply, the department said:

The department has never attempted to emphasize or minimize any aspect of the voting procedure.

In cases brought before the Council, under Chapter VIII-A (for investigation of disputes) and the second sentence of Paragraph 1 of Chapter VIII-C (concerning regional adjustments) of the Dumbarton

[19] From "Big Powers' Unity Is Declared Vital," newsstory. *The New York Times.* 94:10. March 17, 1945. Reprinted by permission.

Oaks proposal, decisions of the Council require unanimity of the permanent members as well as a total majority of seven members, with the proviso that no party to the dispute will be entitled to vote.

Such recommendations and other decisions of the Council are bound to have the greatest weight when they are made by a unanimous vote of the permanent members of the Council not party to the dispute and the concurrence of the required number of other members necessary for the majority of seven.

The department feels that in particular the unity of policy and attitude among the permanent members on matters concerning the organization would be one of the strongest means of making the organization effective in its operation.

INTERNATIONAL COURT OF JUSTICE [20]

An International Court of Justice is to be established. It will either be virtually the present World Court, using its Statute with any necessary revisions, or a new Court, using the present Statute as the basis for a new one. Opinion seems to be that the present Court will be used because it has issued some valuable decisions and certain international bodies, such as the International Labor Organization, are in the habit of using it.

The Court is brought into closer relationship with the United Nations than it was with the League of Nations because the Statute is to be part of the United Nations Charter. All members of the Organization will be automatically members of the Court. Arrangements will be made for non-member states to use it or join it.

It has not yet been decided whether the Statute will obligate the nations to accept the compulsory jurisdiction of the Court in legal disputes.

THE PERMANENT COURT OF INTERNATIONAL JUSTICE [21]

The idea of a world court has long enjoyed the support of the United States and the American contribution to the setting

[20] From "Proposals for the United Nations Charter," by Clark M. Eichelberger, Director, Commission to Study the Organization of Peace. p. 7-8. The Commission. New York. October, 1944. Reprinted by permission.

[21] From "Problem XVII, Peaceful Settlement of International Disputes," analysis by Leland M. Goodrich, Executive Secretary, and Charles A. Baylis, Secretary, Universities Committee on Postwar International Problems. September, 1944. p. 13-14. Reprinted by permission.

up of the Permanent Court of International Justice was substantial. Nevertheless, we have not formally adhered to the Statute of the Court, largely because of the fact that the question of American adherence became mixed up with that of our relation to the League of Nations.

According to its Statute, the Court consists of fifteen judges (at first eleven judges and four deputy judges) elected for terms of nine years by the Council and Assembly acting concurrently. Not more than one national from any state can be a judge at any one time. The Court is open to all states, whether parties to its Statute or not. Its jurisdiction extends to all cases which the parties refer to it. In addition, provision is made for the optional acceptance of the Court's compulsory jurisdiction "in all or any of the classes of legal disputes concerning: (a) the interpretation of a treaty; (b) any question of international law; (c) the existence of any fact which, if established, would constitute a breach of an international obligation; (d) the nature or extent of the reparation to be made for the breach of an international obligation."

Where the compulsory jurisdiction of the Court is accepted, either party may by application to the Court bring the dispute before the Court for judgment, and the Court is final judge of any question of jurisdiction which may be raised. Article 38 of the Statute provides that The Court shall apply to

1. International conventions, whether general or particular, establishing rules expressly recognized by the contesting states;

2. International custom, as evidence of a general practice accepted as law;

3. The general principles of law recognized by civilized nations;

4. Subject to the provisions of Article 59, judicial decisions and the teachings of the most highly qualified publicists of the various nations, as subsidiary means for the determination of rules of law.

It is highly probable that the Permanent Court will be continued as an important part of the postwar general international organization or that a court of a similar nature will be set up. It is also highly probable that the United States will be willing in principle to join in support of such a court. The chief question which is likely to cause serious debate is that of the conditions on which we are to accept the jurisdiction of such a tribunal.

DRAFTING THE WORLD COURT STATUTE [22]

The main task . . . will be the decision as to whether the statute will be a modified form of the existing statute of the Permanent Court of International Justice at the Hague or whether it will be an entirely new statute, using the old statute as a basis.

State Department experts have for some time been examining the Permanent Court statute, and discussing suggestions made by our leading jurists and organizations such as the American Bar Association. It is understood that they feel that with some amendments the statute offers a tested and workable instrument permitting rapid creation of the court.

The principal amendment our legal specialists would suggest is a revision of the statute to eliminate all reference to the League of Nations, with which the World Court was affiliated, and to substitute the United Nations organization. It is contended, too, that an essential amendment would be to introduce into the statute a provision for its own amendment.

An unofficial committee, on which the United States was not represented, met some time ago in London, attended by members of the British Commonwealth and some of the Governments in exile. This committee, . . . recommended alterations in the method of selecting judges, who were elected by the Permanent Court simultaneously for nine years. The proposed change would have them elected by a meeting of the representatives of the member Governments.

One feature of the present statute was the absence of any provision for enforcement of its decisions other than the agree-

[22] From "To Draft Statute for World Court," newsstory. *The New York Times*. 94:16. March 28, 1945. Reprinted by permission.

ment of the parties to a dispute to accept its rulings. Some modification of this situation may be suggested to the jurists when
they assemble here, since under the Dumbarton Oaks charter, it
may be conceived that failure to accept court decisions on certain
matters would be construed as threats to peace and subject to
sanctions by the Security Council.

VANDENBERG AMENDMENTS TO IMPLEMENT JUSTICE [23]

Washington, April 1—The text of Senator Vandenberg's
memorandum to the State Department proposing eight amendments to the Dumbarton Oaks proposals is understood to be as
follows:

I. In this preliminary memorandum I wish to present certain
specific amendments to the Dumbarton Oaks framework. I believe they are essential for three reasons:

(a) Permanent peace is impossible if the new league is a
straightjacket which attempts to freeze the status quo (as largely
dictated by military expediency in the course of war) regardless
of justice.

(b) The total lack of any reference to "justice" as a league
criterion (except in the World Court Section) minimizes the
moral authority of an enterprise which finally must depend far
more upon moral authority than upon force.

(c) Senate ratification will be seriously jeopardized by our
failure to disarm the critics who will magnify the flaws I seek to
correct.

The art of peace is not to identify peace with a static condition. That assures war. Peace requires instrumentalities which,
on the one hand, prevent violent and evil change while, on the
other hand, they facilitate such changes as will effect a more just
and equitable arrangement of the world. We must be practical.

We must avoid attempted miracles. But we need not go to
the other extreme of setting up a league with a mandate to sus-
tain, by force if need be, any status irrespective of judgment as to
whether it is just or unjust.

[23] From "The Text of Senator Vandenberg's Oaks Memorandum," The New
York Times. 94:11. April 2, 1945. Reprinted by permission.

That becomes particularly objectionable in the light of the veto power to be given the permanent members of the Council. The small states, the ones most greatly in need of protection, deserve to be reassured that our pursuit of "security" will have some regard for morality and justice and not merely seek to make "secure" whatever it is that the great powers have acquired or may hereafter acquire at the possible expense of weaker nations. In a word, our League needs a "soul."

The first amendment I propose is as follows: Amend Chapter 1 by adding a newly numbered paragraph (among defined objectives)—

To establish justice and to promote respect for human rights and fundamental freedoms.

The first phrase is taken from the preamble of our own Constitution. The second phrase is taken from Dumbarton Oaks itself in respect to the objectives of the Economic and Social Council, I see no reason why this Economic and Social Council should be the only branch of the League interested in "the creation of conditions of stability and well-being."

There is no assumption in this latter section that the world which will emerge from this war ought to be preserved "as is." Any such assumption elsewhere would be fatal.

I could support this thesis with many exhibits indicating the widespread wish for some such declaration as I propose. Merely as examples, I refer to the statement by the Inter-American Juridical Committee, sitting permanently at Rio de Janeiro, demanding that "the promotion of justice in international relations" should be thus recognized. I refer to the Pope's Christmas message of 1944:

The peace settlement should not give different countenance to any injustice.

I refer to the statement of our own Federated Churches. I refer to the memorandum of suggestions from the Netherlands Government from which I quote:

A statement, duly embodied in the proposals where its absence is very striking, to the effect that some standard of justice will always be observed, would go a long way toward dissipating anxieties, and it appears difficult to see why, if the thing is self-evident, there could be any objection to making such a statement.

The second amendment I propose is as follows:

Strike out the following sentence from Chapter 5, Section B, Paragraph 1:

The General Assembly should not on its own initiative make recommendations on any matter relating to the maintenance of international peace and security which is being dealt with by the Security Council.

It seems to be quite in order to constitute the Security Council as the sole organ of action in the maintenance of peace and security, because "action" requires the prompt and continuous functioning of a relatively small body.

But the broad base of the assembly qualifies it to be the conscience of mankind and that conscience should not be stilled at the behest of a council dominated by a few great powers. Here again the concept of justice is involved. So is the voice of justice.

At most the voice of the Assembly can do no more than recommend. The Security Council should not be permitted to still this voice of the Assembly at its own will and to oust it of all jurisdiction even to discuss the fate and destiny of which all the United Nations are a part.

The third amendment I propose is as follows: Amend Chapter 5, Section B, Paragraph 6 so as to read:

The General Assembly should initiate studies and make recommendations for the purpose of promoting international cooperation in political, social economic and social fields; *for establishing justice* and for adjusting situations likely to impair the general welfare, *or to violate the principles of the United Nations as declared by them on Jan.* 1, 1942. [This puts Atlantic Charter into the Dumbarton Oaks Charter. The italicized words are Senator Vandenberg's changes.]

Somewhere in this league there must be a free forum in which to discuss the states' aspirations and the ideals for which this war has been waged and the condition of their subsequent health. The General Assembly will be the "town meeting" of the world. It is the logical forum for these discussions.

To ignore or to repress these discussions would be to cynically deny the freedoms for which we fought. To authorize them by direct recognition is to practice what we preached in the Atlantic Charter. Unless we intend consciously to desert the principles of the United Nations we will thus implement them in a post-war world which was promised their benediction.

The fourth amendment I propose is as follows: Amend Chapter 5, Section C, Paragraph 2, by adding the world "justice" between "international" and "peace." This simply brings this broader concept of the authority of the assembly under the two-thirds voting rule. But it again emphasizes our devotion to justice as a primary element in the planning of a permanent peace.

The fifth amendment I propose is similar, but with reference to the Council. Amend Chapter 6, Section B, Paragraph 1, to insert the word "justice" between the words "international" and "peace."

The sixth amendment I propose is as follows: In chapter 2, Section A, Paragraph 1 (which states that "the Security Council should be empowered to investigate any dispute or any situation which may lead to international friction or give rise to a dispute . . ."), eliminate the words "be empowered to." This makes it obligatory upon the Council to "investigate any dispute" which threatens "international peace and security." It denies to the Council the easy expedient of ignoring a probem which it prefers not to face.

The seventh amendment I propose is as follows: Add a new paragraph to Chapter 8, Section A,

If the Security Council finds that any situation which it shall investigate involves injustice to peoples concerned it shall recommend appropriate measures of adjustment which may include revision of treaties and of prior international decisions.

This is a direct escape clause from "injustice." It involves only the power to recommend. It may be implicit in the general powers already created but it should be spelled out to avoid all misunderstanding. Otherwise the league is a straightjacket. Otherwise there is no pacific hope ahead for any peoples who consider themselves aggrieved.

The door to progress is slammed shut for keeps—except by war. We would thus invite the very thing we seek to avoid.

For example, it is one thing to accept a dictated boundary for Country X under the pressure of immediate expediency. It is quite a different thing to accept such a boundary as a permanent limitation, underwritten in the basis of world peace, never again to be changed except by international rebellion which we shall agree to help suppress.

With every emphasis at my command, I urge the indispensability of this amendment. Without it, we attempt to police a rigid world. Without it, we deny the progress of legitimate change except through the armed conflict which we pretend to strive to eliminate. Without it we fly in the face of all history and experience and tradition, including our own. Without it, we are at the mercy of critics who may use our error to destroy all our works.

The eighth amendment I propose is as follows: Add to Chapter 8, Section B, Paragraph 1, a new paragraph reading as follows:

The Security Council shall not act, nor shall any member be called upon to act, to perpetuate a status which has been created in disregard of recommendations of the Security Council under Section A, or a status the adjustment of which has been recommended by the General Assembly or by the Security Council.

This might be more aptly phrased. The sole purpose is to assure that the military or economic might of the League and of its members will not be blindly put behind either (a) a postwar status which the General Assembly or the Security Council judge to be unjust, or (b) a new status which comes about through a permanent member of the Council vetoing measures of restraint against it.

Something of this nature seems to be required, particularly as a result of the new voting rule which permits one of the great powers to freeze a status which has been condemned but which the League is powerless to correct.

I am not presently prepared to offer an amendment dealing with "the aggressor problem," as it affects one of the major powers, each of which can immunize itself against sanctions, under the new voting proposal.

IMPLEMENTING THE WORLD COURT [24]

At San Francisco the little nations will protest that they should have greater voting power than proposed at Dumbarton Oaks and Yalta. Another group of critics will press for an increased factor of justice and law in relation to enforcement of peace to mitigate the dominance of the Vigilance Committee of great powers in the proposed Security Council.

Both protests can be met by reducing the power of the Security Council, transferring its quasi-judicial function of stigmatizing an aggressor to the International Court.

This brings us to that mystic word "justiciable." Mr. Dulles expounded "justiciable disputes" . . . as those "which can be determined in accordance with a pre-existing body of law." But the law need not be written law and the justiciability of aggression has been admitted in many times and places. For example, there is no written interstate law in the American Union but all interstate disputes, boundary disputes, aggression and every other kind of dispute go to the Supreme Court. In fact, a non-justiciable dispute is one which the parties are not willing or pledged to refer to a court. A non-justiciable type of dispute becomes justiciable by the simple willingness or pledge of the parties to take it to court and abide by the findings.

If the great powers will pledge that they will respond in court to complaints of aggression against themselves—a noble gesture of reassurance to the little nations—aggression becomes justiciable. This could be extended to all disputes of any nature whatever, but for enforcement of peace, the extension of the court's jurisdiction to include complaints of aggression (made by either the aggrieved party or a bystander or the council) is enough to introduce justice into the machinery. The council then becomes sheriff of the court to uphold its jurisdiction, prevent its being flouted, collect penalties and costs. In its reduced capacity, the little nations will be less envious of its authority.

The American delegate to the council will be within a framework of law and court decisions and can vote without separate

[24] From "Implementing World Court," letter by Richard S. Childs. *The New York Times.* 94:18. March 9, 1945. Reprinted by permission.

referrals to Congress. The American people will respond to a call to arms to support the court more readily than to support the "quasi-judicial" function of a shifting group of political Foreign Ministers constituting the council. Furthermore, a nation, even a big one, will accept the finding of a court against itself with less resentment, less backbiting, less loss of self-respect, than a decision made by a group of other nations in the council.

Mr. Dulles in his recent letter here admits the need of changes to bind the Security Council to "standards of justice rather than mere expediency." Senator Vandenberg has just complained that Dumbarton Oaks "except in its brief world court chapter, does not once mention 'justice' as a guiding objective." Senator Taft as long ago as August, 1943, and repeatedly since, has urged "covenants to join in the use of force against any nation determined to be an aggressor by the decision of some international tribunal."

The Netherlands asks that "the charter should incorporate some statement to the effect that some standard of justice will always be observed as the basis upon which decisions will be taken" and suggests "an independent body of eminent men" to decide "whether decisions are in conformity with generally accepted principles of justice and equity." Uruguay asks that the court "should hear all differences of an international character without any exception whatever." Brazil "deems expedient . . . that the Security Council shall refer [disputes] to the International Court or to an international court of arbitration."

The Catholic Asociation for International Peace complains: "The council is apparently its own court of arbitration, yet in its representation it is the most partial body conceivable." The Federal Council of the Churches of Christ in America exclaims: "Reliance is placed primarily on force unrelated to any explicitly agreed upon principles of justice."

The tide of such comment is rising. The San Francisco conference can by a simple provision in procedure require any nation to answer in court accusations of the use or threat of force and abide by the verdict, subject to enforcement by the council. The five great powers will be exempted from coercion through their veto power, but as they cannot be coerced anyway, the best we can do at such a point is to leave them in the morally untenable position of flouting a court which they had agreed to respect.

THE ECONOMIC AND SOCIAL COUNCIL [25]

The Economic and Social Council will be composed of eighteen seats. There will be no distinction between great powers and small powers. Here a number of so-called "middle class powers," such as Canada, the Netherlands, and Brazil, while not considered great powers in the security sense and not entitled to permanent seats on the Security Council, will have an opportunity to play important roles. Some of these nations are of great industrial importance; some have large colonial empires; others have important merchant fleets.

The Economic and Social Council will deal with such matters as food and agriculture, currency stabilization, economic cooperation, international finance, regulation of civil aviation, human rights and public health. It will receive and discuss reports of the agencies brought into relationship with the organization, and will help the Assembly to coordinate their activities. It will be a connecting link between the General Assembly and these agencies.

The Economic and Social Council will assist the General Assembly in working out a coordinated budget for the United Nations Organization and possibly for its autonomous agencies. It will set up an economic commission, a social commission and other commissions. These commissions will be composed of experts, thus bringing together the most outstanding individuals in their respective fields.

It may be generally forgotten that shortly before the outbreak of World War II, the League of Nations had before it the "Bruce Report" which recommended the segregation of the non-political activities of the League in a separate division. The plan for the Economic and Social Council together with the various commissions may be said to continue the development which the war interrupted.

[25] From "Proposals for the United Nations Charter," by Clark M. Eichelberger, Director, Commission to Study the Organization of Peace. p. 12-13. The Commission. New York. October, 1944. Reprinted by permission.

The Economic and Social Council may assist the Security Council at its request, presumably in the matter of quarantining the aggressor by denying him the benefits of social and economic cooperation.

THE BRETTON WOODS PROPOSAL [26]

If we are to measure up to the task of peace with the same stature as we have measured up to the task of war, we must see that the institutions of peace rest firmly on the solid foundations of international political and economic cooperation. The cornerstone for international political cooperation is the Dumbarton Oaks proposal for a permanent United Nations. International political relations will be friendly and constructive, however, only if solutions are found to the difficult economic problems we face today. The cornerstone for international economic cooperation is the Bretton Woods proposal for an International Monetary Fund and an International Bank for Reconstruction and Development.

These proposals for an International Fund and International Bank are concrete evidence that the economic objectives of the United States agree with those of the United Nations. They illustrate our unity of purpose and interest in the economic field. What we need and what they need correspond—expanded production, employment, exchange, and consumption—in other words, more goods produced, more jobs, more trade, and a higher standard of living for us all. To the people of the United States this means real peacetime employment for those who will be returning from the war and for those at home whose wartime work has ended. It also means orders and profits to our industries and fair prices to our farmers. We shall need prosperous markets in the world to insure our own prosperity, and we shall need the goods the world can sell us. For all these purposes, as well as for a peace that will endure, we need the partnership of the United Nations. . . .

[26] Message of President Franklin D. Roosevelt to the Congress of the United States on the Bretton Woods Proposals, released to the press by the White House February 12, 1945. Reprinted in *The Department of State Bulletin*. 12:220-2. February 18, 1945.

We all know, however, that a prosperous world economy must be built on more than foreign investment. Exchange rates must be stabilized, and the channels of trade opened up throughout the world. A large foreign trade after victory will generate production and therefore wealth. It will also make possible the servicing of foreign investments. . . .

It is time for the United States to take the lead in establishing the principle of economic cooperation as the foundation for expanded world trade. We propose to do this not by setting up a super-government but by international negotiation and agreement, directed to the improvement of the monetary institutions of the world and of the laws that govern trade. . . .

A good start has been made. The United Nations Monetary Conference at Bretton Woods has taken a long step forward on a matter of great practical importance to us all. The Conference submitted a plan to create an International Monetary Fund which will put an end to monetary chaos. . . .

There are other problems which we will be called upon to solve. . . . These will include the establishment of the Food and Agriculture Organization of the United Nations, broadening the Trade Agreements Act of 1934, international agreement for the reduction of trade barriers, the control of cartels and the orderly marketing of world surpluses of certain commodities, a revision of the Export-Import Bank, and an international oil agreement, as well as proposals in the field of civil aviation, shipping, and radio and wire communications. . . . They are all parts of a consistent whole. That whole is our hope for a secure fruitful world, a world in which plain people in all countries can work at tasks which they do well, exchange in peace the products of their labor, and work out their several destinies in security and peace; a world in which governments, as their major contribution to the common welfare, are highly and effectively resolved to work together in practical affairs and to guide all their actions by the knowledge that any policy or act that has effects abroad must be considered in the light of those effects.

The point in history at which we stand is full of promise and danger. The world will either move toward unity and widely shared prosperity or it will move apart into necessarily competing economic blocs. We have a chance, we citizens of the United States, to use our influence in favor of a more united and cooperating world.

NEED FOR INTELLIGENT TARIFF
POLICY AFTER THE WAR [27]

A free flow of commerce between the several states of this country is one of the cornerstones upon which our national existence and well-being have rested. A free flow of commerce among all nations is precisely as essential to the security and prosperity of the world. . . .

After this war there will be the need for a healthy trading industry just as there will be the opportunity for trade and industry to go on to new heights of production and of distribution of commodities or goods. . . .

In the relatively short time that our reciprocal tariff agreements were in effect before the war, we began to realize that the abolition of artificial trade barriers could accomplish much for our international trade. Our Lend-Lease operations, too, have been striking evidence of the effectiveness of hurdling such barriers and of the desirability of knocking them permanently down.

We must plan for an intelligent postwar American trade and tariff policy. We must also prepare for and encourage international understandings and agreements which will open the markets of the world to all on a fair competitive basis, and which will give all nations fair and equitable access to the raw materials of the world. . . .

An expanding volume of world trade offers the greatest hope for a peaceful and prosperous world. One of the surest ways to achieve the full-scale employment here at home—something that we are all seeking—is to open up world markets. This does not mean the exploitation of one country by another. The most advanced countries economically are those that trade the most. The restoration of the economy of Europe, Asia and other parts of the world after the war will offer a tremendous

[27] From an address by Leo T. Crowley, Foreign Economic Administrator, before the Commerce and Industry Association, New York, January 17, 1944.

challenge to American production and an expanding market for American products. Industrial development and construction and reconstruction in China, Russia and in other countries will open up vast new markets. Such construction and reconstruction will help to lay the sound economic foundations for a secure peace. It will also raise the standard of living abroad and enlarge the capacity of the peoples abroad to buy what we have to sell.

UNITED STATES—RUSSIAN RIFT [28]

Moscow thinks that the United States is over-emphasizing the importance of the San Francisco Conference. The Russians want to see an international security organization established, and they are prepared to support the draft charter they helped create at Dumbarton Oaks.

But they are reported not looking on this proposed security organization as their first line of defense, and they do not think it means much unless it is backed up by much more positive acts, such as agreements to disarm Germany and arrangements to settle territorial questions, which will not be under discussion at the San Francisco Conference.

As a corollary to this point, the Russians . . . believe the United States is minimizing the importance of reaching other international agreements particularly in the economic field. Several specific cases are put forward in support of this contention.

The first is that while the United States is talking more than any other nation about the necessity of creating machinery of international collaboration, we are not, in the Russian view, showing much desire to implement that collaboration in the economic field.

BILL OF HUMAN RIGHTS PROPOSAL [29]

President Roosevelt today expressed sympathy and interest in proposals for three commissions to be set up in the world organ-

[28] From "Russian Relations Cause Uneasiness In Capital Circles," by James B. Reston. *The New York Times.* 94:17. April 3, 1945. Reprinted by permission.

[29] From "International Bill of Rights To Be Offered at World Peace Parley," newsstory. *The New York Times.* 94:13. March 21, 1945. Reprinted by permission.

ization by the San Francisco Conference, to deal with the questions of human rights, migrations and statelessness.

The committee's proposals center on three principal permanent commissions to be included in the world organization.

The first is a committee to frame a world decision of human rights, which all nations will insure to all persons living within their boundaries, and which will deal constantly with problems in this connection as they arise.

The second commission, to deal with migrations, would concern itself with the vast question of transfers of populations which will come as a result of the war settlements, and will endeavor to facilitate unavoidable migrations as much as possible. The commission's aim also would be to eliminate, as much as possible, the necessity for migrations from the countries of origin.

The third commission would deal with the problem of statelessness, which affects not only Jews in many countries of Europe but peoples of various countries who will have no nationality status. The international commission would aim not only to provide these stateless persons with a status but to insure protection of their rights.

The final report which the committee will prepare for the peace conference will deal with problems of the peace settlement, the questions of indemnities and reparations and the punishment of war criminals.

Chapter V

REGIONAL ORGANIZATION

One of the new concepts arising from the World War II, which is almost as strong as that of a security organization itself, is Regionalism. Actually, it isn't a new concept by any means. It is simply the agreement of nations in particular areas of the world to work together to find a solution to their common problems.

It is recognized, for example, that the United States and the Latin American countries are vitally concerned with certain questions of policy and practice, which are of almost no interest to Europe. Similarly, we cannot get overly interested, here, in the final determination as to whether the Dardanelles are placed under international protection, together with Gibraltar and Suez, or whether they are left in control of a single nation. Yet such problems are important, naturally. Accordingly, practically all nations are agreed, first, that a world organization should be established; and, second, that exceedingly strong emphasis should be placed upon regional organization within the framework of the international organization. Many of these regional units, as contemplated, would overlap. Some would be political, others economic. Some would be racial or cultural alignments, others mere business partnerships.

It is agreed, however, that regardless of the type, the international organization should have final authority to decide whether the regional group should exist and the extent of its powers in any field. In other words, no regional group should be allowed to assume the responsibilities of the world organization, unless such responsibilities are so delegated. This is necessary to prevent the development of such regional groups, in effect, into super-states which might enormously increase the dangers of a third world war.

Although it is part of the framework of the Dumbarton Oaks Proposals, very little is explained as to the nature, extent, or powers of such regional organization. A number of practical organizations have been developed, the foremost of which, and one which will undoubtedly be exceedingly important in the world organization itself, is the organization of the American nations created under the Act of Chapultepec. While the Americas have taken the lead in setting up a working organization, the greatest agitation for such groupings comes from Europe, where the proposed methods of organization range from bilateral agreements to an actual European federation including Britain and Russia and their colonies. Each country seems to have its own favorite regional plan. Norway expects to participate in two, at least: one, economic in general authority, to include Sweden, Iceland, Belgium, the Netherlands, Denmark and Finland; the other, economic and political, to be made up of merchant powers on the Atlantic, including Britain, the Netherlands, France, and the United States, among others. The Netherlands would expect to participate in still another: a Pacific organization, economic and political, on the basis of her East Indian colonies. Of course, if a colonial commission or some such group were set up in the West Indies, the Netherlands would probably expect a place on that council.

Britain presents the greatest problem in any regional organization. Her status as a European nation as her location would justify ignores the Empire. Yet it is inconceivable that Britain can be represented, at least very effectively, on all of the regional councils. Yet if the Empire is included, Britain would have a major voice in every single regional council established, with the possible exception of the Western Hemisphere. And even there, it may be likely that Canada and the West Indies will become a part of the regional organization established under the Act of Chapultepec.

There are certain weaknesses of the regional philosophy. But the primary purpose here is to explain the concept itself and how it is working out up to this moment. Until the world organization is set up, naturally, no present regional structure will be considered as final.

REGIONALISM [1]

One of the most satisfactory sections of the Charter is that which deals with regionalism. Very sensibly, it provides that the Security Council should encourage the settlement of local disputes through regional arrangements either on the initiative of the states concerned or at the request of the Security Council. This is a clear recognition of the fact that some difficulties can be better settled as neighborhood quarrels than by the entire world organization. The Security Council can also utilize regional agencies for enforcement action.

But here is a very important limitation, ". . . no enforcement action should be taken under regional arrangements or by regional agencies without the authorization of the Security Council." This clearly avoids a system in which one nation in a region could use the big stick to have its way without reference to the Security Council. In the enforcement of peace the Security Council is paramount.

THE PROBLEM OF REGIONALISM [2]

Among the United Nations conference problems at San Francisco one of the most important will be regionalism. How can separate groups of nations be fitted into the general security organization? An effective solution of this could be the strongest base for an international league; mishandling could easily wreck the whole works.

This is vaguely recognized by a brief provision in the Dumbarton blueprint.

[1] From "Proposals for the United Nations Charter," by Clark M. Eichelberger, Director, Commission to Study the Organization of Peace. p. 11. The Commission. New York. October, 1944. Reprinted by permission.

[2] From "A European Council Versus Blocs," editorial. *New York World-Telegram.* 77:10. March 24, 1945. Reprinted by permission.

Recent developments point up the problem. Britain is trying to tighten the political and economic unity of its empire group. The recent Inter-American Conference at Mexico City set up a hemisphere security system for mutual protection against aggression.

Arab nations are reaching regional agreements for the Near East. France—after making a Russian alliance—is negotiating with Belgium, the Netherlands and Luxembourg for regional security pacts. Russia wants a federation of Balkan and Danubian countries under her influence.

Whether there shall be regionalism is not the question. There always has been. The question is whether regionalism shall take the form of separate spheres of influence and conflicting blocs under big power domination, or an association of free and equal nations for mutual security and prosperity. The former is the old European war-breeding method. The latter is the inter-American system, which never has encouraged foreign domination or caused world war.

The Golden Gate conference problem is to convert regionalism generally into a constructive basis for international organization.

THE ROLE OF STRONG REGIONAL GROUPS [3]

There should be a much more definite regional organization . . . than that suggested at Dumbarton Oaks.

Three years ago Mr. Gibson and I proposed that regional organization should be the foundation of the whole machinery and that three regional groups should be established—the Western Hemisphere, Europe and Asia. A year later Mr. Churchill publicly supported this idea.

In the Western Hemisphere the long development of the Pan American Union pointed in that direction and the recent agreement at Mexico City advances it one step further. The

[3] From "Hoover Asks Pacts Be Open to Change," by Herbert Hoover, former President of the United States. Article III in a series of four articles copyrighted by the North American Newspaper Alliance. *The New York Times.* 94:11. March 27, 1945. Reprinted by permission.

success of the nebulous "Concert of Europe" in preventing world war for nearly a century pointed in that direction for Europe, and the practical problems which developed in the League of Nations abundantly confirmed the need for that form of organization.

Such regional councils should embrace all United Nations areas and should deal in the first instance with all controversies that might lead to war. If they fail to secure settlement by pacific methods, then, and only then, should the world security council intervene.

If regional organization were established at once, it would bring six powerful benefits:

First, it would give the smaller nations a greater voice, for they should be more largely represented in the regional councils and could well be given equal standing;

Second, policies which would prevent conflict are different in the three great areas and need separate organization;

Third, these regional organizations would relieve the security council of many problems and controversies before they reached it;

Fourth, such an organization would relieve the whole mechanism of much of its present color of a military alliance of a few great powers;

Fifth, regional organization at once lessens the pressure for military alliances;

Sixth, such a regional organization would greatly relieve the anxieties of the American people and probably most nations lest they be constantly involved in secondary problems all over the earth.

There is no reason why the proposed economic, social and political rights councils should not also be regionalized for the better handling of problems peculiar to those regions. Their top world councils would be the more free for coordination of the three great areas. It might also be worth consideration that the World Court be organized with three regional courts which would act as courts of first instance in questions involving nations in that region alone.

Some objection has been raised that there would be some implied rivalry of interest between regions which would be thus emphasized. The contrary is the truth, for such decentralization would make cooperation the more easy.

REGIONAL VERSUS INTERNATIONAL ORGANIZATION [4]

Should the Atlantic nations, after ample consideration, come to the conclusion that peace in the Atlantic is an objective not inspired through any theoretical idealism, or by any altruistic motive, but required by and in conformity with their own self-interest, we might reasonably hope to witness the establishment of the "Pax Atlantica," of a durable peace in the Atlantic. Personally, I am convinced that such a regional organization for the countries living on the Atlantic corresponds with their self-interest. Therefore, I believe that such an organization is viable. But let me add in the same breath that I do not believe that any organization which does not take into account this most important element of self-interest will have any chance to survive a serious crisis.

For that very reason, I do not believe in any scheme or project which tends to create a European Federation. . . .

Any solution of the European problem with Great Britain and Russia is no longer a European solution, Britain and Russia being not only European, but world powers. A solution of the European problem without Russia and Britain would inevitably result in German hegemony over all the other European countries. A strictly continental European solution is decidedly not possible. . . .

As for Europe, many plans have been advanced of regional federation of certain Pacific countries, especially of territories which in the past had not reached independence or self-government. Personally, I feel convinced that such a union or federation of Pacific countries has no more chance to succeed than a

[4] Excerpts from an address by Alexander Loudon, Netherlands Ambassador to the United States, before the Daughters of the American Revolution, Cincinnati, April 17, 1943.

European federation. Any attempt to weld these territories into one single unit would be artificial, and would, therefore fail. For countries and people are not inanimate, but living organisms, in which nothing endures which does not result from natural growth. Therefore, I believe that the United Nations will be wise to build after the war upon the historic foundations which have been laid during centuries of evolution. . . .

It may prove opportune after the war to transform the Pacific War Council into a permanent Pacific Peace Council. But this is of secondary importance. What should be realized by every country with Pacific interests is, that there again, as in the Atlantic, their united might will prove to be a definite safeguard against aggression. In the Pacific, the problem which confronts us is relatively easier to solve than in Europe. For there is but one aggressor nation in the Pacific: Japan. Once Japan is defeated—and let no one believe that this is going to be an easy task—the vital interest of all the other Pacific nations will be to maintain peace in that region. The basis for successful cooperation in the Pacific is available, and therefore it should not prove beyond the power of the Pacific nations to establish a just and durable peace in the Pacific, in other words the "Pax Pacifica."

I realize, of course, that in many Pacific countries there is one faction which may complicate the problem. I refer to the native populations which will certainly not remain static. But I am convinced that, at least as far as the Netherlands is concerned, the change in relationship between Holland and Indonesia will be carried out in a spirit of harmony and mutual understanding. The people of Indonesia know the pledges that have been given them by the Queen and her Government, and they know also that these pledges will be carried out in good faith. . . .

We realize that such a policy can only be carried out in close cooperation with other countries whose vital interests are similar to our own. Such a similarity of interests does not exist between all the countries of the world nor does it exist even between the nations of Continental Europe. Therefore, we do not believe that a universal institution as the ill-fated League of Nations or a strictly Continental European organization will solve the problems of our country's future security. On the other hand, we do believe that the peaceful countries bordering on the Atlantic and the Pacific Oceans are all faced with analogous problems regarding their security, and therefore could establish a solid and durable organization to maintain peace and to banish aggression from the Atlantic and Pacific regions. . . .

Contacts will certainly have to be established between these regional security groups to discuss questions of inter-regional character. . . . It may be that some kind of world-embracing institution to promote cooperative regionalism will have to be created to this effect.

In the system of regional collective security which I have endeavored to sketch, each of the United Nations will in the future become a guardian of the peace. But to fulfil this sacred duty, the guardians of peace will have to be on the spot when trouble starts. Therefore, each of the United Nations should substantially contribute his share in the common task to maintain peace in that region where his vital interests are involved and, therefore, where his action will be of the greatest benefit to all. But, should it become apparent that a conflict tends to develop which does not seem likely to be settled by regional mediation or intervention, then all the other United Nations, although not directly affected, will have to be ready to act, and through their united military power they should and they will be in a position to quell local conflicts, before these have assumed dangerous proportions.

Such a system could, in my opinion, create the means to maintain peace in the world.

UNITED EUROPE OR CHAOS [5]

In the absence of a concerted plan, individual countries are making one-sided decisions that will confront the world with insuperable "accomplished facts." Despairing of Europe's future, one of its nations, Czechoslovakia, has already accepted the

[5] From "Why Not the United States of Europe?" by Count Richard Coudenhove-Kalergi, founder and president of the Pan-European Union, director of the research seminar for European Federation at New York University. *The American Mercury.* 58:417-23. April 1944. Reprinted by permission.

protection of the Soviet Union; smaller democracies play with the idea of joining the British Commonwealth; power politics in its most cynical forms are gaining sway.

It is becoming more obvious every day that Europe is threatened with a partition into Russian and British spheres of control. The speech of General Smuts, the activities of Beneš, civil war in Yugoslavia, revision of the Stalin Constitution to facilitate association of non-Soviet areas—these are just a few of the clear symptoms of European division. If this tendency is not arrested swiftly, no prophetic gifts are needed to predict that Europe will first become the scene of permanent Russo-British friction and rivalry, and soon thereafter, the theatre of World War III. . . .

Because Britain and the United States of America are uncertain and confused about the desirable European order, Marshal Stalin is free to carry on his own policy. He knows precisely what he wants. His inspired press has come out sharply against a United States of Europe, as hostile to the Soviets. Russia is ready to back the national sovereignties of individual countries to perpetuate rivalries within Europe and to keep the continent as a whole as weak as possible. At the same time it has provided the framework of a Soviet-controlled federation within which these fragmented countries can seek sanctuary.

The Russian policy can be readily justified from a purely Russian standpoint. Having suffered terribly through centuries of history from invasions by Swedes, Poles, French, now Germans, she wishes to see no nation of Europe strong enough to attack her. Her new leaders visualize a strong and united Soviet nation facing a weak and disunited Europe. The logic of this purpose, if fulfilled, is clear: should Europe fail to unite, its smaller Eastern and Central states, at least, will be at Russia's mercy.

Does the Kremlin plan to integrate Eastern Europe, or even the whole continent, into the all-Soviet federation? Does it intend to absorb some and transform others into a *cordon sanitaire* against the Atlantic Powers? Probably Stalin himself does not know the exact answers. Much will depend on the evolution within the European states after their liberation; more will depend on British and American policies. I believe that Russia's vital preoccupation in Europe is not conquest but security—security through balance of power and European disunion. On this policy Russia will insist as long as no better and more constructive system is found to assure her peace.

Britain's situation with regard to Europe is not unsimilar to Russia's. Britain, too, has been threatened again and again by continental nations. It has been saved again and again by national disunion on the continent. Many Englishmen are therefore afraid of the idea of European Union. On the other hand, Britain has paid dearly for the chronic wars on the continent. The idea of a United States of Europe to guarantee peace and assure European prosperity therefore appeals to wide sections of British opinion, both sentimentally and as a matter of sound statesmanship.

The difficulties start with the question whether or not Great Britain should become a member of the United States of Europe. The idea of England being in any way directed by a majority of continental nations is repugnant to British nationalists. While ready to consider some kind of European League of Nations that would leave their sovereignty intact, they are against submitting to anything like a federal government of Europe. Moreover, they fear that British entry into a European Union would lead to the dismemberment of their world-wide empire, since Canada, Australia, New Zealand and South Africa would be unwilling to bind their future to the European continent. . . .

There is every reason to expect that Britain would favor European union, if it did not stand alone in this. Without forthright American support, it has little left but reliance on old-style spheres of influence. . . .

No one in Europe wishes to return to the prewar political anarchy, and the idea of federation is to the fore. Even the half-hope of union held out by Soviet hegemony has a powerful appeal, despite the knowledge that Russia is politically a dictatorship. The mind of Europe contemplates two very different examples of federation—one is the Soviet Union, the other the United States of America.

Every honest European knows that the appeal of the American example is immeasurably stronger. . . . Yet if they cannot have a democratic United States of Europe, they may in sheer despair accept a Soviet Europe. Even that would seem preferable to a Third World War. The tragedy of the continent today is that while Russia is throwing its full weight behind a Europe on its own model, America has failed to declare itself clearly in favor of a Europe that is both united and free—a United States of Europe. . . . Willkie, in *One World,* opposes the re-creation of small European countries "as economic and military units" but favors their survival as "political units." Political identity, that is to say, within a framework of economic and military unity for the continent as a whole. . . .

Neither Russia nor Britain belongs in the United States of Europe. The presence of either would weigh it against the other. The presence of both is unthinkable because it would create a gigantic Russo-British-European-Asiatic bloc isolating and encircling the United States. The only practical scheme is therefore a Federation of Europe without Russia and Britain, but under the common sponsorship of these two nations and the United States of America.

There is no contradiction whatsoever between a European union and the idea of world organization. No sound world organization can be based on European disunion. A united Europe would be a regional part of whatever world body is set up, just like the USSR, China, Pan-America and the British Commonwealth. Pending the emergence of a world organization, the United States of Europe would have to be guaranteed against foreign invasion or a new German threat by the combined pledges of the Big Three. Backed by such a guarantee, the continent could drastically limit its armaments. Europe, in effect, would be transformed into a peaceful and neutral Federation, living between Russia and Britain—just as peaceful and neutral Switzerland has lived so long between Germany, France and Italy.

THE LEAGUE OF AMERICAN STATES [6]

Mexico City, March 3—The Inter-American Conference created today what Woodrow Wilson conceived thirty-one years

[6] From "American Nations Form an Alliance to Protect Peace," by James B. Reston. *The New York Times,* 94:1. March 4, 1945. Reprinted by permission.

ago—a League of American States, each pledged to protect the territorial integrity and political independence of the others against aggression from any quarter. . . .

The guarantee was incorporated in "the Act of Chapultepec," which obligates the American nations to combine their force against any aggressors that interfere with the war effort by attacking the territorial integrity and political independence of one of its neighbors, and it was adopted unanimously by all twenty nations in the Inter-American Organization Committee of the conference. Adoption in this form is tantamount to acceptance by the conference itself. . . .

In long range, the Act of Chapultepec marked the end of a century-old tradition that the power of the United States should be kept north of the Rio Grande and that no American state should interfere in the external affairs of another "for any reason whatsoever."

The act as adopted this morning fulfilled in detail previous published reports of its main points. It did not commit United States force to support the present boundaries indefinitely, but instead provided that the frontiers be protected first under the wartime powers of the President for the duration of the war, and then that a treaty among the American states be drafted to extend the guarantee into the postwar period and present it to the United States Senate for ratification.

Emphasizing the principle that the security and solidarity of the hemisphere are threatened just as much by an American as by a non-American aggressor, the act obligates the American states to consult with one another whenever an act of aggression has been committed or appears about to be committed; to agree on the measures to be taken against the aggressor, and to use, in conformance with their constitutional processes, armed force if necessary to prevent or repel the aggression.

The American states have never before combined in this manner to take action against an aggressor state in this hemisphere. The United States, through the unilateral Monroe Doctrine, obligated itself to take action against the intervention of any non-American power in this hemisphere, and the other American states joined with us at the second meeting of the

Ministers of Foreign Affairs at Havana in 1940 to say that an act of aggression against the territorial integrity and political independence of an American state by a non-American state was considered an act of aggression against all.

But never before have they combined to guarantee the boundaries of the hemisphere against an American aggressor. Indeed, they have often emphasized that no American state should interfere in the "external affairs" of another American state for any reason whatever.

THE ACT OF CHAPULTEPEC [7]

Declaration on reciprocal assistance and American solidarity by the Governments represented at the Inter-American Conference on War and Peace.

Whereas:

1. The peoples of the Americas, animated by a profound love of justice, remain sincerely devoted to the principles of international law;

2. It is their desire that such principles, notwithstanding the present difficult circumstances, may prevail with greater force in future international relations;

3. The Inter-American Conferences have repeatedly proclaimed certain fundamental principles, but these must be reaffirmed and proclaimed at a time when the juridical bases of the community of nations are being established;

4. The new situation in the world makes more imperative than ever the union and solidarity of the American peoples, for the defense of their rights and the maintenance of international peace;

5. The American states have been incorporating in their international law, since 1890, by means of conventions, resolutions and declarations, the following principles:

(A) The proscription of territorial conquest and the non-recognition of all acquisition made by force. (First International Conference of American States, 1890.)

[7] Text of Act Creating Hemisphere Security Apparatus. *The New York Times*. 94:25. March 4, 1945. Reprinted by permission.

(B) The condemnation of intervention by a state in the internal or external affairs of another. (Seventh International Conference of American States, 1933, and Inter-American Conference for the Maintenance of Peace, 1936.)

(C) The recognition that every war or threat of war affects directly or indirectly all civilized peoples and endangers the great principles of liberty and justice which constitute the American ideal and the standard of its international policy. (Inter-American Conference for the Maintenance of Peace, 1936.)

(D) The procedure of mutual consultation in order to find means of peaceful cooperation in the event of war or threat of war between American countries. (Inter-American Conference for the Maintenance of Peace, 1936.)

(E) The recognition that every act susceptible of disturbing the peace of America affects each and every one of them and justifies the initiation of the procedure of consultation. (Inter-American Conference for the Maintenance of Peace, 1936.)

(F) That any difference or dispute between the American nations, whatever its nature or origin, shall be settled by the methods of conciliation, or unrestricted arbitration, or through the operation of international justice. (Inter-American Conference for the Maintenance of Peace, 1936.)

(G) The recognition that respect for the personality, sovereignty and independence of each American state constitutes the essence of international order sustained by continental solidarity, which historically has ben expressed and sustained by declarations and treaties in force. (Ninth International Conference of American States, 1938.)

(H) The affirmation that respect for and the faithful observance of treaties constitutes the indispensable rule for the development of peaceful relations between states, and treaties can only be revised by agreement of the contracting parties. (Declaration of American Principles, Eigth International Conference of American States, 1938.)

(I) That in case the peace, security or territorial integrity of any American republic is threatened by acts of any nature that may impair them, they proclaim their common concern and their determination to make effective their solidarity, coordinating their respective sovereign will by means of the procedure of consultation, using the measures which in each case the circumstances may make advisable. (Declaration of Lima, Eighth International Conference of American States, 1938.)

(J) That any attempt on the part of a non-American state against the integrity or inviolability of the territory, the sovereignty or the political independence of an American state shall be considered as an act of aggression against all the American states. (Declaration of the Second Meeting of the Ministers of Foreign Affairs, Havana, 1940.)

6. The furtherance of these principles, which the American states have practiced in order to secure peace and solidarity between the nations of the continent, constitutes an effective means of contributing to the general system of world security and of facilitating its establishment;

7. The security and solidarity of the continent are affected to the same extent by an act of aggression against any of the American states by a non-American state, as by an American state against one or more American states.

PART I. DECLARATION: First—That all sovereign states are juridically equal amongst themselves.

Second—That every state has the right to the respect of its individuality and independence, on the part of the other members of the international community.

Third—That every attack of a state against the integrity or the inviolability of territory, or against the sovereignty or political independence of an American state, shall, conformably to Part III hereof, be considered as an act of aggression against the other states which sign this declaration. In any case, invasion by armed forces of one state into the territory of another, trespassing boundaries established by treaty and marked in accordance therewith, shall constitute an act of aggression.

Fourth—That in case that acts of aggression occur or there may be reasons to believe that an aggression is being prepared by any other state against the integrity or political independence of an American state, the states signatory to this declaration will consult amongst themselves in order to agree upon measures they think that it may be advisable to take.

Fifth—That during the war and until treaty arrangements recommended in Part II hereof, the signatories of this declaration recognize such threats and acts of aggression as indicated in Paragraphs Third and Fourth above, constitute an interference with the war effort of the United Nations calling for such procedures, within the scope of their general constitutional and war powers, as may be found necessary, including:

Recall of chiefs of diplomatic missions;

Breaking of diplomatic relations;

Breaking of consular relations;

Breaking of postal, telegraphic, telephonic, radio-telephonic relations;

Interruption of economic, commercial and financial relations;

Use of armed force to prevent or repel aggression.

Sixth—That the principles and procedure contained in this declaration shall become effective immediately, inasmuch as any act of aggression or threat of aggression during the present state of war interferes with the war effort of the United Nations to obtain victory. Henceforth, and with the view that the principles and procedure herein stipulated shall conform with the institutional principles of each republic, the respective governments shall take the necessary steps to perfect this instrument in order that it shall be in force at all times.

PART II. RECOMMENDATION: The Inter-American Conference on Problems of War and Peace recommends:

That for the purpose of meeting threats of acts of aggression against any American republic following the establishment of peace, the governments of the American republics should consider the conclusion, in accordance with their constitutional processes, of a treaty establishing procedures whereby such threats or acts may be met by:

The use, by all or some of the signatories of said treaty thereto, of any one or more of the following measures:

Recall of chiefs of diplomatic missions;

Breaking of diplomatic relations;

Breaking of consular relations;

Breaking of postal, telegraphic, telephonic, radio-telephonic relations;

Interruption of economic, commercial and financial relations; use of armed force to prevent or repel aggression.

PART III. This declaration and recommendation provide for a regional arrangement for dealing with matters relating to the maintenance of international peace and security as are appropriate for regional action in the Western Hemisphere and said arrangements and the activities and procedures referred to therein shall be consistent with the purposes and principles of the general international organization when formed.

This declaration and recommendation shall be known by the name of Act of Chapultepec.

ACT OF CHAPULTEPEC: EDITORIAL OPINION [8]

The treaty adopted . . . by the Inter-American Conference in Mexico City and christened the Act of Chapultepec, institutionalizes the principle of collective security on a regional scale. By making counter-action to aggression the joint responsibility of all the nations of the Western Hemisphere, the Act, if effectively applied, should serve as a mighty check on a potential aggressor. That it was created as a specific warning to fascist Argentina's bellicose intentions, there can be no doubt. While its immediate practical effect is to recognize the reality of United States military power in this part of the world and to legalize American intervention if the peace of the Americas is threatened south of the Rio Grande, it does not preclude genuine collective action by the other American nations after industrialization has made them militarily stronger than they are now. Even at the present time the combined power of Brazil, Uruguay and Chile, for instance, would probably be sufficient to halt possible Argentine aggression without aid from the United States. Finally, the Act does not contravene the international-security scheme envisaged by the Dumbarton Oaks plan. On the contrary, it supplements that plan. One of the major weaknesses of the old League of Nations was the failure of its Covenant to provide for regional guarantees

[8] From "The Act of Chapultepec," editorial. *The New Republic.* 112:349. March 12, 1945. Reprinted by permission.

against aggression, to be enforced, and for all practical purposes enforceable, only by those powers geographically close to the theatre of war. Indeed, this line of criticism of the old League was the chief argument in favor of regionalism by many Latin American international lawyers.

INTER-AMERICAN SECURITY [9]

The Act of Chapultepec, which calls for regional, or inter-American, security within the proposed world organization, is based upon the idea that "all sovereign states are juridically equal among themselves." That is the language of the opening paragraph.

At Yalta, the Big Three—Russia, Britain and the United States—acted alone. And while they "resolved upon the earliest possible establishment with our allies of a general international organization to maintain peace and security," they retained for themselves—and for France and China if they make it the Big Five—a veto over the use of force. And the use of force, of course, is the key to future peace and security.

Here in Mexico City everybody is strong for hemisphere defense as an American proposition. An attack against the territory, sovereignty or political independence of an American state will be considered as an act of aggression against them all. And they all plan to do something about it, each according to ability.

But there is no room in this plan for any American Big Three or Big Five. Under the Dumbarton Oaks formula, indorsed at Yalta, any one of the Big Five might commit an aggression and then veto any action against itself. Under the Act of Chapultepec, in the event of aggression, the rest of the Americas "will consult amongst themselves in order to agree upon measures . . . to take."

That is why sentiment here is overwhemingly in favor of a regional arrangement whereby the Western Hemisphere can look after its own peace. Unless the rest of the world is threatened, no one with whom I have talked down here wants Europe to take a hand. European methods and American methods differ.

[9] From "Yalta and Americas," column by Wm. Philip Simms. *New York World-Telegram.* 77:23. March 7, 1945. Reprinted by permission.

Sentiment is also against too much power in the hands of the Big Five in the security council. However delegates would feel better about it if Latin America had one of the number. They think it would be more equitable if Europe had only two votes, each carrying veto power, leaving one to Asia (China), one to North America and one to South America (Brazil.)

Although the Act of Chapultepec stipulates that the "arrangements, activities and procedures referred to therein shall be consistent with the purposes and principles of the general international organization when formed," Latin-American delegates will go to San Francisco determined not to permit any material change.

INTER-AMERICAN DEVELOPMENT COMMISSION [10]

This conference is building upon a strong foundation—cooperation, equality and opportunity—which we together have laid through the years. Inter-American cooperation has been tested in peace and in war, and today is preparing for the readjustment period ahead of us.

The Inter-American Development Commission, and the twenty-one individual country commissions, constitute one of the invaluable mechanisms which the Americas have created for mutually beneficial cooperation. The delegates to this conference have an important function in preparing for the future as well as aiding the wartime mobilization of hemisphere resources. This conference and the commissions provide a particularly effective channel for the direct participation by private business in hemisphere economic progress.

AUSTRALIAN-NEW ZEALAND CONFERENCE [11]

I claim now, some ten months after the Australian-New Zealand Conference, that any fair-minded student of Australia's external policy will admit that the Australian-New Zealand Agree-

[10] Message by Franklin D. Roosevelt to the First Conference of Inter-American Development Commission, May 9, 1944.

[11] Excerpts from a statement by the Australian Minister for External Affairs, Herbert V. Evatt, Canberra, Australia, November 29, 1944. Reprinted in *United Nations Review*. 5:4-6. January 15, 1945. Reprinted by permission.

ment helped us to declare objectives which were important to both countries. The Agreement stated in a comprehensive way primary considerations governing the foreign policy of Australia in those matters in which we have a common or identical interest with New Zealand, and they comprise a very important content of our external relations. It is wrong to regard the Canberra Agreement as a final or fixed definition of our interests and objectives. Success has attended the agreement in certain important respects which will gradually be unfolded in the next twelve months.

Discussions opened at Wellington on November 1 and ended on November 6 with the adoption of a series of agreed conclusions on four main subjects. These were:

> World Security Organization;
> Participation in Armistice arrangements;
> Welfare of South Pacific territories, and
> International Economic Relations

A main part of the background of the Wellington talks was formed by the international discussions at Dumbarton Oaks on world security, concluded not long before. The Wellington conference had before it the actual draft text of the organization which issued from discussion at Dumbarton Oaks.

Attention was given to the general principles implied in the proposals and the conference was able to agree on matters which the two governments felt should form part of the broad planning for general international organization, of which the two objects will be, first, to maintain peace and security and second, to promote human welfare.

It would be wrong to contend that Australia and New Zealand can have an exclusive concern with the future of any part of the Pacific region in particular. Without the continued interest and active participation of the United States as well as the United Kingdom in arrangements for welfare and security there is no hope of stability and harmonious developments in this area.

The Australian-New Zealand Agreement contemplates international arrangements for future security and welfare in the South-West Pacific, arrived at on a basis of discussion and consultation between all powers concerned. All these matters are treated in agreement as matters for settlement through consultation between all governments concerned. One thing we have consistently claimed is that in this region, which is more directly vital to us than to any other nation, and where our destiny lies, these things should be determined only after full prior consultation with us. No democratic leader would take or has taken exception to this claim.

We feel a special responsibility for non-self-governing territories in the region in which we live, and in neighboring regions. We feel that great constructive work can and should be done by governments responsible for territories in the South Seas and in the South-East Asia region to provide for mutual assistance, exchange of information and collaboration in particular problems such as health, transport, economic development and native welfare.

We endeavored to give a lead in this matter of regional collaboration by proposing in the Australian-New Zealand Agreement establishment of a commission to advise the various governments responsible for territories in the Pacific islands. On the present occasion we decided, so far as our two governments were concerned, that the South Seas Commission should consist of representatives of all governments and administrations in the region and that there should be a permanent secretariat as well as research and functional bodies established by the governments on the advice of the Commission. We considered that provision should be made for associating with the work of the Commission existing research and functional bodies, and that in order to provide a suitable forum for discussion of Pacific islands problems there should be held regularly a South Seas Conference which might comprise nominees of governments represented on the Commission, and of international organizations concerned with welfare problems, for example, the I.L.O. and the Food and Agriculture Organization. We would think it appropriate that among these nominees there should be representatives of scientific bodies, missionary bodies and native peoples. We also considered that wherever practicable native peoples should be enabled to take part in the work of the Commission and its agencies.

We are hopeful that there will be early action to set up a South Seas Commission in 1945. Since there are three other governments with territorial interests in the area concerned, Australia and New Zealand are about to consult with other governments as to the Constitution and establishments of the Commission.

The Wellington talks also covered economic policy and economic relations. Stress can be laid on the endorsement by the Conference of the view on employment policy put forward by Australia and New Zealand on various recent occasions in the course of international discussions. Therefore Australia and New Zealand have agreed to press strongly for an international agreement by which member states will bind themselves to pursue domestic policies aimed at full employment, and which will provide for use of existing organizations, such as the I.L.O. or, if necessary, establishment of new agencies for exchange of information and consultation with each other on employment policy.

PATTERN FOR COLONIAL COOPERATION [12]

At a time when it becomes increasingly apparent that future international cooperation will take the form of nations organized in regional groups on the basis of mutual necessity, but welded into the framework of a larger association of nations to safeguard peace, it is interesting to note that one area of the world, at least, offers a preview of the possible structure of the postwar order. With the creation of the Anglo-American Caribbean Commission in 1942, practical international planning for dependent territories was inaugurated in the Western Hemisphere. Early in the war, Britain and the United States realized they would have to meet not only the menace of enemy submarines operating virtually at will in strategic Caribbean waters, but also the ideological challenge of Axis propagandists, who emphasized the "accumulated social, economic and political shortcomings of centuries" in an effort to undermine the morale of the peoples living around that sea. The Anglo-American reply was startling

[12] From "Anglo-American Caribbean Commission—Pattern for Colonial Co-operation," by Olive Holmes, research associate, Foreign Policy Association. *Foreign Policy Reports*. 20:238-47. December 15, 1944. Reprinted by permission.

in its simplicity. The two governments demonstrated, by concrete measures, that when several powers have a direct concern in a backward area through territorial, economic or strategic commitments, it is possible to adjust common problems on a regional basis, with the object of assuring colonial communities a greater measure of prosperity and stability. . . .

The growing realization that advanced nations have responsibilities for the welfare of colonial territories, expressed by public opinion and embodied in national policies during the inter-war period, was brought into sharp focus in the early months of the war by vital considerations of security. On September 3, 1940 the governments of the United States and Britain announced the conclusion of an agreement whereby the United States received 99-year leases on sites to construct naval air bases in the British West Indies in exchange for fifty "overage" destroyers. The practical implementation of the agreement involved far-reaching adjustments on the part of both the islanders and the American newcomers. Military and naval cooperation in the Caribbean made the necessity for continuing and expanding this relationship apparent.

Shortly after the acquisition of the base sites, President Roosevelt appointed a commission to carry out an extensive survey of the social and economic problems of the Caribbean area. The commission pointed out the advisability of the Caribbean dependencies working together as a unit, both in meeting the emergency and in carrying out broad-scale research activities in agriculture, labor and social services. Out of this recommendation grew a plan for an international commission in this area.

On March 9, 1942 a modest communique was issued in London and Washington announcing the creation of the Anglo-American Caribbean Commission, "for the purpose of encouraging and strengthening social and economic cooperation between the United States of America and its possessions and bases in the area . . . and the United Kingdom and the British colonies in the same area." Both governments stressed the advisory nature of the body. The Commission's status was made entirely clear: it was to be a body appointed by and responsible to the executive branch of the component governments, with authority to act in an advisory capacity in the closest possible relationship with other interested agencies in both governments. In addition, it was instructed to "bear in mind the desirability of close cooperation in social and economic matters between all regions adjacent to the Caribbean." It was to concern itself "primarily with matters pertaining to labor, agriculture, housing, health, education, social welfare, finance, economics, and related subjects," and to advise its respective governments on these matters. . . .

At first, one element lacking in the picture of regional collaboration was a program formulated by the dependent peoples of the Caribbean themselves for their own development. A step toward genuine representative democracy for the area was the establishment of a standing West Indian Conference, designed to act as a clearing house for the discussion and formulation of plans for cooperation. The first session of that Conference, in Barbados in March 1944, was the nearest thing to a democratic regional assembly that has yet been convened. . . .

The Conference is to be a standing body with a central secretariat (not yet established), and sessions will probably be convened once a year. There will be no carry-over of representatives from one session to the next. The Conference, as yet purely advisory in character, enjoys no executive powers unless such powers are specifically entrusted to it by the governments. The question of voting powers and weight of representation is thus left open. Non-member governments may be invited to send representatives in the capacity of observers. . . .

With the establishment of the West Indian Conferences, the mold of the Anglo-American Caribbean Commission seems now to have been set. It is—according to the British Colonial Secretary—an organization functioning at the governmental, the technical and the popular levels, with the three-fold objective of assuring "real partnership" between home government and dependency, of assembling the various parts of the region in order to "enable them to find some solution of problems which are as common to Puerto Rico or inded to Cuba and Haiti as to Jamaica," and of fitting "the Caribbean area as a whole into the world, so that (it) can survive and prosper." . . .

The prospect of including other interested nations in the Commission leads naturally to the larger question of whether the machinery so laboriously erected in the Caribbean is to be applied for the benefit of dependent peoples all over the world through the establishment of regional international commissions. It is possible to find the same problems here that characterize the world's other backward areas. The hope that the Caribbean experiment may be the model for international collaboration elsewhere was given stimulus by the British Colonial Secretary in a significant statement to Parliament, to the effect that Britain would welcome the establishment of commissions for certain regions—bodies which would comprise not only the states that possess colonial territories there, but also states which have a major strategic or economic interest in the given area. Implied in the Secretary's blueprint, too, is the creation of an all-embracing international colonial council, perhaps under the aegis of the proposed United Nations organization, to which the regional commissions would be responsible. This is a new tendency in world colonial policy—and the logical development of the ideas which set the Caribbean Commission in motion. But realization of these proposals will depend in the final analysis on the determination of the colonial powers to achieve international collaboration in the interest of dependent peoples.

BRITISH COLONIAL COMMISSIONS [13]

We must recognize that this idea of regional international machinery is still a novel one to some people, and that it does not yet command universal acceptance. . . .

The beauty of the new idea of Regional Commissions is that the members who are going to sit around a table and to pool their experience will be representatives of nations who have themselves colonial possessions in the areas in question, and they for that very reason will be in a position to tackle these questions on an entirely practical basis. . . .

This idea . . . of constructing machinery to link together existing territories for certain purposes where joint action is obviously desirable, is really nothing new in the British Colonial Empire.

[13] From a statement by Viscount Cranborne, Secretary of State for Dominion Affairs, before the British House of Lords, January 26, 1944. Quoted in *War and Peace Aims,* special supplement Number IV. p. 64-5. November, 1944. Reprinted by permission.

It has already for some time been the recognized practice, of which there are notable examples. . . . First of all, there is the East African Governors' Conference. . . . Through this organization the Governments of Kenya, Tanganyika, Uganda and Zanzibar are able at present to discuss and cooperate over matters of common concern. Naturally, under the impact of the war, that machinery has been expanded, so that today questions of defense, production and supply are being dealt with centrally and efficiently by the East African Governors' Conference. . . . The final responsibility still rests with the government of each individual territory. . . . Any development must be examined in the light of the consideration that in this particular area we are dealing with territories in different stages of constitutional development and with different racial composition. What will be the form which the further evolution of the machinery in this area will take it is not for me to say today. . . . But at any rate there is in that area a rudimentary regional organization in being. . . .

In the West African Colonies regional grouping is already developed to a very considerable extent. . . . Even before the war the West Governors' Conference was beginning to function, and it was doing valuable work. During the war . . . a further step was taken. The Governors' Conference was superseded to some extent by the organization created by the Resident Minister . . . Lord Swinton. Originally Lord Swinton's organization was limited to questions which were related to the coordination and stimulation of the war effort. More recently through the Civil Members Committee of the West African War Council, the Resident Minister has extended his activities to cover all important matters which are of common concern to the British West African Governments. Thus, the fullest use is being made of the organization by the West African Governments whose own responsibility again remains unaffected. . . .

The functions of this new organization . . . over [the] spheres of administration, security, material development, welfare services, etc. . . . The success of this Swinton Organization has been extremely striking . . . and in my view there is no doubt that the cooperation which has been created during the war will be maintained and, I believe, extended in some form or other when hostilities are over.

I give . . . one other example in Africa of this collaborative machinery. . . . In 1931 His Majesty's Government here in this country, in response to an approach by the Southern Rhodesian Government, expressed their full appreciation of the cooperation between the Governments of Southern Rhodesia and Northern Rhodesia on all matters of policy of common interest. In pursuance of this policy inter-territorial conferences between the two Governments named and the Government of Nyasaland have been held since 1935, with most useful results. Further, as a special war measure a step has been taken to establish a Secretariat, which deals centrally with certain matters affecting the war effort of the three territories. Here again of course, the independent position and responsibility of the three governments remains unimpaired. They built up this machinery for the purpose of consultation and collaboration.

I will give your Lordship one last example from another part of the world, the Caribbean. . . . Not long after the outbreak of war it was found desirable to appoint a comptroller of Development and Welfare for the West Indies. The object was to enable economic and sound development to proceed as evenly as possible in spite of the disturbance of the war. . . . In the Caribbean, as elsewhere, trade was seriously dislocated, and every effort had to be made to maintain the economic life of the area and to make the fullest use, for the purposes of the United Nations, of local productive capacity. . . . This organization has achieved a very great measure of success. It has proved to be an innovation of the greatest value. . . .

What is now being suggested is a development of an already existing machinery. . . . One must suit one's machinery to the special circumstances of the area. On that basis I should have thought there was no limit to the advantages to be obtained by cooperation and collaboration. That, at any rate, is the view of His Majesty's Government, and it has seemed to them, in the light of their own Colonial experience, that it is a principle which, now that it has been tried out on a small scale, might well be extended to the international field with advantage both to all Colonial Powers and to the world at large. . . .

We have already one example of such collaboration on a small scale in the Caribbean. . . . The Anglo-American Commission . . . was set up . . . on a consultative basis with representatives of the two countries concerned. . . .

The Commission is an attempt by ourselves and the United States to cooperate in the solution of some of the problems in the Caribbean region; . . . it does not cover them all, but it does make a start on the solution of some of them. . . . The Commission has no executive authority, and there is no interference with sovereignty. . . . Both the United States and ourselves retain our own responsibility, and the position of the Colonial Governments remains unaffected. It is just an experiment in practical collaboration.

In the view of the Government, its success provides justification for proposing an extension of just such similar machinery to appropriate areas throughout the world. . . . This idea of regional commissions, as I have said, is an entirely new conception in the international field. It will require very careful consideration by other governments, both Dominion governments and foreign governments, who have colonial responsibilities. . . .

General Smuts, with his unrivalled experience of world affairs, has given this conception his full blessing and . . . within this last week it has had further important public support from the Australian and New Zealand Governments. In the Report of the Conference between the two countries held at Canberra they have jointly adumbrated a scheme for just such an organization for the South Pacific. . . . In particular we warmly welcome their declaration with regard to a Regional Commission, and we should be very ready to discuss these ideas with them at the meeting of the Dominion Prime Ministers which, as your Lordships know, it is hoped to hold at an early date. . . .

His Majesty's Government would be very ready that the sphere of the machinery of these Commissions should include such questions as public health, education and housing. . . . In addition, I imagine also that the Commissions would concern themselves with questions such as communications, which play so great a part in the development of backward areas. . . . We . . . agree that it would be important to give to the people of Colonial territories an opportunity to be associated with such work. . . .

The policy of His Majesty's Government with regard to
Colonial territories is in no way negative. . . . The development
of regional organizations is already going on in the Colonial
Empire itself. We certainly wish to see that development extended and that both the British Dominions overseas and foreign
Colonial Powers should be associated with those wider developments. . . .

THE NEW PAN-ARABISM [14]

Although the official declarations of the Crimean Conference
did not mention the Middle East, some of the ticklish problems
of this area are known to have been discussed. Silence presumably indicates that no agreement was reached. It underlies the
explosive character of the existing situation which will certainly
be a testing ground of the future relations among the great
powers. The meetings between Messrs. Churchill and Roosevelt and a number of Arab potentates are additional proof of the
importance of the Middle East in world politics.

With the exception of still French-controlled Syria and Lebanon, the whole Middle East has been a British sphere of influence, both political and economic. But in the course of the
present war, outside challenges to Great Britain's exclusive domination have made themselves felt. While Axis intrigues have
been successfully eliminated, the Soviet Union and the United
States, both Britain's allies, have actively entered the field. The
oil resources of Iran and Arabia are serving as cracks through
which Russian and American influence is penetrating. While
the United States is not yet known to have exerted political pressure on any of the Middle Eastern countries to protect American
oil interests, the Soviet Union did intervene last fall in Iran's
internal affairs after the Iranian government had turned down
a Russian request for concessions in the northern part of the
country.

The British, faced with the Soviet-American intrusion into
what they consider their sphere of interest, appear to be meeting
it with a technique of contemporary diplomacy now generally

[14] From "The New Pan-Arabism," by Heinz Eulau, assistant editor of the
New Republic. The New Republic. 112:357-8. March 12, 1945. Reprinted by
permission.

accepted. It consists in the ability of one of the "Big Three" to confront the other two with a *fait accompli* and then ask for its recognition. The Soviet Union used this technique in building an Eastern European regional system under its hegemony. The United States is busy strengthening the ties of the Pan-American regional system at the Mexico City Conference. Great Britain is evidently sponsoring the new Pan-Arab movement which is about to be institutionalized in the establishment of a league of Arab states.

The idea of a Pan-Arab union is an old one. What is new is its British sponsorship. Although the Arab countries, with the exception of Lebanon and Palestine, are united in the Islamic religion, earlier efforts at union failed because this common ground was insufficient to bridge the many cultural and economic differences among them, the conflicting claims for leadership and those national antagonisms which the British, at an earlier date, exploited for their "divide and rule" policy. The new Pan-Arab movement, in spite of unquestionably indigenous roots, is clearly a power-politics solution, occasioned by Great Britain's need for common action with the Arab states as whose "good neighbor" and spokesman she will confront the Soviet Union and the United States when Middle Eastern questions are discussed at future meetings of the "Big Three."

FORMATION OF THE ARAB LEAGUE [15]

Cairo, Egypt, March 22—The Arab League conference here adopted the final draft of its constitution with its signature here tonight by six of the member states. . . .

This is the final step in establishing the Arab League and it lacks only the formal approval of the governments concerned to become fully operative. The states that signed today are Egypt, Iraq, Lebanon, Saudi Arabia, Syria and Trans-Jordan. . . .

The Arab League's constitution, it is understood, consists of twenty-one articles. It states that the league's aim is to promote cooperation among members states, particularly in matters of

[15] From "Charter Adopted by Arab League," by Sam Pope Brewer, *The New York Times.* 94:8. March 23, 1945. Reprinted by permission.

culture, trade and communications, and to settle questions of passports and nationality among its members.

Membership is open to all independent Arab states signing the charter. Others are eligible as they achieve their independence. The league's council is to meet regularly in March and October of each year in Cairo and may be summoned whenever any member wishes consultation.

The charter provides for consultation in case of aggression against any member and provides that, if members accept arbitration of a dispute, the league's decision must be final and binding. It forbids the use of force to settle disputes.

The members of the league are free to conclude such treaties and alliances as they wish but they are to deposit copies with the league's council. They are free to withdraw at any time and may be expelled by the unanimous vote of the other members.

CHAPTER VI

PROBLEMS OF INTERNATIONAL ORGANIZATION

INTRODUCTION

Probably the most important factor bearing on the success or failure of the world organization outlined in the Dumbarton Oaks Proposals is the ability of the major powers to cooperate, not only at this time, but in all the years to come. It is well recognized by the leaders of the United Nations, including those of the Big Three, that no organization can succeed unless the Big Three participate on a common basis of agreement. It is asserted that unless the Big Three can settle their difference now, there is little prospect of their getting together when the fighting is done and the pressing necessity for unity is behind them.

Accordingly, it seems pertinent to review the major conflicts between the major powers, which might conceivably bar the establishment and maintenance of a successful organization for peace. It is difficult to provide a thorough analysis of the factors involved. Much has been written, criticizing various acts of each of the major powers in recent months. From several sources abroad, it appears that as much criticism of British and American actions circulates in the Soviet Union as criticism of Russia circulates in this country and in Britain. How much effect this criticism may have upon the public in each country cannot be estimated. Nor can it be determined exactly to what degree the criticism represents even a sizable body of official opinion in any nation.

Furthermore, the importance of the major criticisms may be wholly disproportionate to the problems with which we are concerned here. It is probable that the conflict which shows up in harsh detail today, and is seemingly insurmountable may tomorrow be completely resolved—and the entire feeling of distrust dissipated with no ill effects. Again, it is probable that issues barely realized today may tomorrow actually become insurmountable for one reason or another. For this reason, an attempt is made here to indicate the nature of the criticisms of British and Soviet policy which, to us, conflict with our own policy. They are presented only as potential problems which, if unsolved prior to the end of hostilities, might and probably would make any organization the nations of the world devise unworkable from the very beginning.

Generally speaking, the major conflicts outlined in the following pages are as follows:

With regard to Britain, we in the United States are critical of her "imperialistic" doctrine and her determination upon the maintenance of the Empire at all costs. Our public agitation for dissolution of the Empire and public criticism of the governing of the Empire, is the basis of conflict.

We do not concern ourselves unduly with Britain's affairs on the Continent. We profess an interest, but if Britain wishes to maintain, establish or revise the existing (or prewar) spheres of influences, we seem perfectly willing to permit such actions. The colonial question is practically our only criticism, or rather the foundation of all Anglo-American conflict.

With regard to Russia, we are critical of their expansion in Eastern Europe, their apparent refusal to abide by the terms of the Moscow Conference and other Big Three agreements, not forgetting the Atlantic Charter. Specifically, we fear Russia's absorption of the small countries of Eastern Europe, countries to whom we have guaranteed a reestablishment of national, representative government. Further, we, as well as the British, are critical of Russia's actions regarding Rumania and Bulgaria without first consulting our governments. In the main, our criticism of the Soviet Union lies in her strong-arm tactics, in disregard of the wishes of her Allies, and even in negation of her own pledged word.

There are other conflicts, primarily based upon British and Soviet insistence upon reestablishment of the balance-of-power philosophy of international relations, and their apparent determination to make bilateral treaties independent of any world organization set up. Also there are conflicts which are based upon economic policies of the two nations. Their relative importance, however, cannot yet be determined.

THREAT OF POSTWAR CONFLICT [1]

In discussions of the future peace it is usually assumed that the chief protection against a new war will be cooperation among the three great powers, codified in some security pact like that outlined at Dumbarton Oaks. But, whatever treaty is ratified, it is far from certain that these powers will in fact and for a long period pursue harmonious policies. In particular there is danger that Britain and the United States, with their respective economic spheres of influence, will drift apart. And this peril lies mainly not in political faults like American isolationism or British imperialism, or in weakness of miltary guarantees against aggression, but in the realm of economic policy. At least, that is where it is likely to arise. And having arisen there, it can lead the world to a disaster which formal political or military commitments can do little to avert. . . .

Against the background of their experience and their resolution, it is easy to understand the British fear of American postwar economic policy—or lack of policy. They have formally pledged, through governmental declaration, to maintain high employment. They have ambitious plans for other means of improving the standarrd of living—broadened social security, housing, health service, education, nutrition and community life. At the same time they know that in order to survive at all they will have to export far more than before the war. They are confident of managing their end of this job, in one way or another. But they are acutely conscious that the United States is an immensely more important factor in the world economy than they are. We are richer in natural resources, capital, labor power and productive efficiency in many industries. If we choose to try to compete them out of world markets, we can cause them

[1] From "America and Britain after Victory," by George Soule, economist and author. *The New Republic*. 112:321-3. March 5, 1945. Reprinted by permission.

great damage. If we manage our own affairs so badly that we have another depression like that which preceded the war, we shall inevitably drag the whole world down with us. If, on the other hand, we contrive to consume as much as we can produce, maintain full employment at home and remain prosperous, their task will be relatively easy.

Their observation of our history and our political institutions does not give them much confidence that we shall not upset the apple cart. They watch eagerly for signs of intelligence and economic competence here, but they fear that our resources of reflection and control are not able to coordinate our great and muscular economic body, with its immensely energetic but spasmodic activity. We may turn out to be a giant with the mind of a child, devastating through mere inadvertence and immaturity.

ANGLO-SOVIET FRICTION [2]

To understand a country's attitude toward the outer world, one must place himself in its position and try to think on its terms (without losing one's own judgment). How would we feel in this country if Argentina had an army of six million men with sufficient industry to equip it? What does the outer world look like from the Russian point of view after Germany and Japan will be eliminated? It is generally assumed that Britain will come out of this war as a second-rate power, and the Soviets will be the foremost power of Europe. This is a complete misunderstanding of the realities, as the Russians see them.

In the first place, Russia will emerge with a decimated population. Experts agree that the Russian population of 180,000,000 (before 1939) is a greatly exaggerated figure. Taking into account the colossal bloodletting of World War I, two bloody revolutions, a murderous civil war, two major periods of famine, the liquidation of millions of kulaks, the ruthless mass-purges, plus the fact that during such periods of upheaval the infantile

[2] From "Is a Third World War Inevitable," by Dr. Melchior Palyi, advisor to a number of U. S. corporations on international economic matters, economist and lecturer. *American Business*. 14:10-12. October, 1944. Reprinted by permission.

death rate rises and the birth rate declines, and adding to it the spread of birth control methods under Bolshevism—Russia's population in 1939 couldn't have been more than 160,000,000, and possibly less. This war may have cost another 10,000,000 lives and another wave of reduced birth rate.

Loss of manpower is the No. 1 problem of the Soviet regime. The more so since Britain's casualties are negligible, and those of western Europe small, in comparison, to say nothing about the Dominions and the United States. . . .

The most serious aspect of the population situation, from the Russian viewpoint, is the fact that Britain has virtually the whole of Europe on her side. Communists are a small minority everywhere and their philosophy antagonizes the property-mindedness of the majority. The fact that Russia is identical with Bolshevism arouses national suspicions and idiosyncracies. Religious feelings are antagonized, too, by the atheism of the Communists, and religion is a factor especially in the Latin countries.

Some 250,000,000 people from Portugal to Finland, and from Norway to Turkey, either actually are or prefer to be allies of Britain.

Every European nation, small and great, prefers British domination, which is mild and doesn't interfere with internal affairs, to the hardfisted Muscovites. This holds for the Germans, too, most of whom will be under British control; for the Arabs, and for the present regime in China.

Probably as much as 60 per cent of Russia's industrial capacity has been destroyed or damaged in this war and so was a large sector of her agriculture. Given the bureaucratic clumsiness of the Communist organization and the easy-going nature of the Russians, it will take many years to rehabilitate the Ukraine and other areas. By contrast, British industry has suffered comparatively little; its military potential has been vastly expanded. After the war, Britain will also control, directly or otherwise, nine-tenths of the Continent's industries (outside Russia) in addition to the greatly increased manufacturing capacity of the Empire.

A most important fact is, as the Russians see it, the access of the British to the industrial resources of the United States.

There is little doubt that, in the case of conflict, Britain can always get supplies from America, to say nothing of potential military aid. Indeed, the world is inclined to believe that American aid to Britain is available in a quasi-automatic fashion, and Moscow has to take that into consideration when weighing the respective forces.

Russia is not only far from the goal of self-sufficiency, but is also very vulnerable from a geographic point of view. . . . Against the British, if such a conflict should arise, . . . Britain's world-wide tentacles . . . could be applied all around against the Russian land mass. With roads and railroads built up in Turkey, Mesopotamia, Persia, India, and China, and with air supremacy, a British system of alliances might be a deadly danger to a country with such widespread frontiers, few of them protected by natural barriers. This vulnerability is further enhanced by the fact that vital Russian resources are in easy reach of any enemy. The vital oil sources in the Baku area, e.g., could be wiped out in the first twenty-four hours of a war.

Lastly, there is a psychological element to be kept in mind. All the wartime cooperation and all the assurances of friendship could not possibly have obliterated Bolshevist suspicions against capitalistic and semicapitalistic countries. The Soviet philosophy is one of revolution against capitalism, and no social hierarchy within the collectivist system can change that. The mere fact that large sectors of public opinion in both England and the United States are bitterly opposed either to Bolshevism in general or to Soviet expansion in particular, helps to keep the flame of Russian suspicions burning.

The British, in turn, cannot be free of suspicion of the Soviet aims in view of the obvious expansionistic tendencies. Neither do they feel really strong. They don't have the degree of control over their own people that would give them the freedom of diplomatic and military action. True, they might count on allies against Russia (in case of conflict), but a system of alliances is a slow-moving machine and unreliable at times; some of the second-rate powers might try to play their own balance-of-power politics, while others may be in the throes of internal turmoils. Britain certainly counts on American aid in case of war, but she cannot be sure of it.

Perhaps the greatest weakness of Britain is financial. It is a commonplace that Britain is "broke," but the implications are not always understood. The Soviets may wipe out the savings of their population or may strangulate their consumption. Lowering of living standards is much more difficult in a country like England, where a peace-at-any-price situation may prevail. From the British long-run point of view, this inherent weakness of their position necessitates preparation by far-reaching alliances which, in turn, irritate the Soviets, just as the expansionist moves of the latter are an irritant to all of Europe.

It is in the light of these mutual fears and respective interests that British as well as Russian postwar policies have to be appraised. The idea of the London Foreign Office was to organize Europe in confederations. A central European bloc under Polish leadership would mean a reliable fortress protecting England. But the Russians refuse to tolerate any sort of blocs in Central Europe or in the Balkans, and made that point clear beyond doubt. They won the point, and Europe will be divided as it ever has been. Stalin can use the Romanian-Hungarian antagonism to hold down both. Similarly, the Tito-Mikailovitch conflict serves to perpetuate the antagonism between Croats and Serbs. It is characteristic of Beneš, who was a leading advocate of a Union, and who actually organized one with the Poles in London, that he dropped any such idea after his "alliance" with Stalin.

An even more effective irritant is the Russian territorial expansion. It amounts to the restoration of Stalin's booty in Hitler's robberies, adding to it East Prussia and the Bulgarian Black Sea ports. What hurts British feelings is the fact that this Soviet policy is based on unilateral decisions without even consulting the Allies; that it openly violates all Russian treaties with its neighbors, and the Atlantic Charter; and that it creates explosive tensions in Central Europe.

Moscow appears determined to control Central Europe either by forcing upon them Quisling governments as in Poland, or by imposing treaties of "mutual assistance" which permit unilateral military occupation. The Stalin-Beneš treaty of 1943 is the pattern for this sort of arrangements which, presumably, will cover Romania, Bulgaria, and Hungary as well. . . .

Given the discrepancy of objectives, the resulting tensions, the growing areas of conflict, and the mutual suspicions—what are the prospects of a durable peace between Britain and Russia? . . . All frictions could be straightened out. Aud they have to be straightened out if we want to see the establishment of a permanent peace.

TURKISH-RUSSIAN RELATIONS [3]

News that Russia was dissatisfied with the terms of her non-aggression pact with Turkey and desires a new treaty more in keeping with "present conditions" is as startling in Washington and London as in Ankara. Perhaps more so; for Turkey has long been uneasy over her relations with the Soviet Union. Since the beginning of the war, and especially since the defeat and realignment of Rumania and Bulgaria, the Turks have known that their guardianship of the Straits, Russia's only door into the Mediterranean, was bound to be one of the questions coming up for review in the settlements to be agreed on after the war.

In the three-day conference following the Big Three meeting in Teheran, President Inonu resisted the pressure of Mr. Roosevelt and Mr. Churchill to enter the war, on the ground that Turkey could not fight without much more military equipment than the Allies were ready to supply. It is doubtful if she would have abandoned her stubborn neutrality after Yalta had not this action been the price of admission to San Francisco, also, presumably, to representation in subsequent negotiations concerning the future status of the Dardanelles.

This was one subject that did not come up at Yalta. Turkish-Russian relations were not mentioned in the Crimean conversations. There was no discussion of the Dardanelles. It seems to have been carefully avoided, in fact, perhaps on the theory that it would open up the matter of the existing conventions and

[3] From "Abroad: Russian Demands on Turkey Upset U. S. and Britain," by Anne O'Hare McCormick, *The New York Times.* 94:16. March 24, 1945. Reprinted by permission.

might even lead to questions on the other gates of the Mediterranean under British control, Gibraltar and the Suez.

The picture of the Big Three throwing every issue on the
table at their meetings and arguing it out to a decision is undoubtedly a false one. From all accounts, they bring up as few
disputable points as possible, leaving any that can be postponed
to the "final settlement" that will come after—maybe long after
—the end of hostilities.

That Moscow's sudden demand for an "improved" understanding with Turkey is an unexpected move is apparent in the
puzzled surprise in British and American official circles. It re-
news the speculation, put to rest by the Yalta agreements for
consultation and joint action, as to whether Russia means to
regulate relations with all her border states in her own way.
Following events in Rumania and the stalemate in the attempt
to "broaden" the Provisional Government of Poland, it at least
suggests a difference in interpretation of the various issues on
which the three powers are pledged to act together.

The pressure for a new arrangement with Turkey is in a
somewhat different category from Moscow's other moves. Assuming that it aims at a change in the control of the Straits, this
is so clearly an international question that if any issues are reserved for a general settlement, this is certainly one of them.
Other powers besides Russia and Turkey have a vital interest in
this question.

President Roosevelt has often expressed the view that all
such waterways should be open to all nations. There is at present a simmering dispute in Egypt, sure to boil up as the present
treaty nears an end, over the future ownership of the Suez Canal.
The British have very decided ideas on strengthening the control
of Gibraltar. The internationalization of the Kiel Canal is part
of the Allied plan to curb any attempt to restore the military
power of Germany.

The question of straits is related to the question of bases.
It has been generally believed that all such questions would be
studied and discussed in relation to an international security
system. The President's main concern at Yalta was to get the
framework of this world security system set up before the war

ends. At his insistence the date for the San Francisco Conference was fixed as early as possible. It is reported that he wanted the meeting held in March, with the objective of capitalizing at once on the agreement reached at Yalta, and the approval of the fact of agreement evoked in this country. No doubt he was also anxious to get all the unilateral decisions incorporated into some multilateral pattern of decision, or at least to start in motion the machinery for corporate decision.

It is not by accident that the American Government, now as in 1918, is more eager than other great powers to get this machinery started. In both crises our war leaders recognized that the American stake in security and world order is paramount because we stand to gain least out of war and most out of peace. Our position between the two great oceans gives us what Russia always seeks, while our continental solidarity makes us less vulnerable at home than Britain can be in her scattered empire. We don't seek territory because we don't need it; we have no reason to change our frontiers if we could. Our prime interest is to maintain this favored position. Twice in a man's lifetime we have fought for this, and two Presidents have taken the initiative in setting up a system designed to protect it.

This time it is important that the people realize that it is primarily to the interest of the United States to overcome the obstacles that once before deflected us from our purpose and involved us in disaster.

THE FRANCO-RUSSIAN PACT [4]

Our Paris dispatches say that a fundamental factor in the reluctance thus far of the Provisional French Government to take a more active part in sponsoring the San Francisco Conference is General de Gaulle's desire to make sure that the Franco-Russian pact shall operate independently of the new world security system. In General de Gaulle's eyes this assurance is said to be essential to the protection of France against a renewal of German aggression.

[4] From "France and the League," editorial. *The New York Times.* 94:16. March 24, 1945. Reprinted by permission.

That there is some conflict between the Franco-Russian pact in its present form, on one side, and the Dumbarton Oaks-San Francisco plan in its present form, on the other side, is evident from an examination of the two texts:

The Franco-Russian pact provides that during the lifetime of this treaty (a period covering the next twenty years) France and Russia will themselves undertake "all measures necessary to eliminate any new threat on the part of Germany." That is, these two nations are made the sole judges of when the time has come to take enforcement action in the interest of peace, under their regional agreement. But the Dumbarton Oaks-San Francisco plan provides (Chapter VIII, Section C) that "no enforcement action should be taken under regional agreements or by regional agencies without the authorization of the Security Council" of the new league of nations. Such authorization would require the approval not only of France and Russia but also of Britain, the United States, China and at least two of the six smaller nations which will be represented on the Security Council. How is some conflict of authority, or at the very least some confusion of purpose and some risk of misunderstanding, to be avoided unless one plan or the other is amended? And if this is true, which plan—Franco-Russian or Dumbarton Oaks-San Francisco—should be amended?

One factor in the situation which is not yet clear, and which is of great importance, is the position of Russia in the matter. Does Marshall Stalin fully share General de Gaulle's belief that at this point and in this respect the Franco-Russian pact should have preeminence over the general security system? But even if de Gaulle obtains Stalin's agreement in this matter, there are good friends of France who must wonder why he should seek it. Surely, great as Russia's future power seems certain to be, there is an even larger measure of security for France in any enforcement action against Germany which finds the immense resources of the United States and Britain thrown into the action contemporaneously with the power of France and Russia. And surely the machinery of the proposed new league of nations is far better devised than that of the old League for prompt decisions in matters of this kind.

Is there not, in fact, some danger that if General de Gaulle continues to press hard for bilateral rather than multilateral guarantees, and achieves his purpose, he will lead France into a position of comparative isolation, rather than place her where she belongs, in the center of the Great Powers, in a general security organization?

THE NEED FOR CLEAR UNDERSTANDING [5]

American interests in the Mediterranean are certainly secondary to British. Yet it is of serious consequence to us that the Mediterranean littoral should be controlled by states friendly to our freedom of commerce through the Mediterranean and Suez Canal. We want to see an Italy and a Greece that cannot be used by a warlike Germany for its own purposes. We have only to recall the narrow margin by which the Suez Canal and its approaches were saved less than three years ago. Had Britain finally failed to throw back the Axis legions, their lifeline, the Suez Canal and the route to the east might have been gone. Our own operation in North Africa would have been far more difficult, our entire attack upon Japan in the Pacific indefinitely postponed and the war might have been lost.

If America had been plunged into any such imminent peril as these two of our allies were, our attitude of seeking safety first would have been equally insistent. Thus Russia may have been far too peremptory in her decision about the Polish boundary. Yet if we thought the approaches to the Panama Canal were threatened we should take whatever prompt action we thought essential. We are, and not unnaturally, most intolerant of anybody butting into what we feel are our affairs.

Suppose we remind ourselves again that America has her Monroe Doctrine and her Good Neighbor Policy toward the score of nations from the Rio Grande south to the tip of Tierra del Fuego. We can hardly complain if Russia and Britain desire

[5] From "Poland and Big Three," letter by Thomas W. Lamont, chairman of J. P. Morgan & Co., Inc.; representative of the Treasury on the American Commission to Negotiate Peace, Paris, 1919. *The New York Times*. 94:8E. March 18, 1945. Reprinted by permission.

to be surrounded by friendly neighbors so as to prevent a possible new Germany from having readier means of access and attack.

I sometimes wonder whether in the field of international politics we Americans are not still living largely in an age of innocence. We declaim upon the virtues of democracy, and are inclined to thank God that we are not as other men are. But do we fully understand that as yet our strength has been largely economic? Feeling the oats of our powerful economic situation, we assume that we have the right to lay down the law generally in idealistic but not always workable terms. We demand that the European states, that have endured frightful suffering and are still in the midst of the mess, promptly live up to our American ideals.

The difficulty, however, is that our allies, the United Nations, and we ourselves are at present embarked upon a sea of troubles and are pursuing our perilous enterprises of winning the war and the peace in a craft that is not too steady and has many leaks. That is the reason why it is dangerous for us, with all our immense economic strength, to throw our weight about the boat and with our offhand orders create near-panic among our fellow-passengers, thus giving them perhaps the impression that, as twenty-five years ago, we shall be content to stand aside and fulfill our part in international cooperation simply by word of mouth, by precept rather than by example.

In this imperfect world there can be no complete solution of these postwar problems, no way to satisfy all the needs and aspirations of the widely disparate nations that inhabit this globe. The best that we can hope to do is to arrive at solutions that over the years are as nearly workable as possible.

DEMAND FOR MID-COUNCIL ROLE: CANADA [6]

Ottawa, March 20—The position of secondary states in the world security organization was raised by Prime Minister W. L. Mackenzie King in Parliament today when he moved a resolu-

[6] "Canada Supports Security Program," by P. J. Philip. *The New York Times*, 94:13. March 21, 1945. Reprinted by permission.

tion aimed to obtain the widest possible support by Parliament to the delegation that will attend the San Francisco conference.

Exception, he said, could hardly be taken to the extending of special prerogatives to the great powers, on which the major responsibility for keeping the peace must rest. That is a correct application of the functional idea to international organization and the position accorded to a state should correspond with the functions that it was able and ready to discharge, he added.

But, the Prime Minister continued, if this principle were granted it would seem right that its further application to secondary states should be both logical and appropriate. The contribution of states other than the great powers to the success of the security organizations will vary very greatly, in his opinion. It would be in the general interest, he said, to accept the guiding principle that power and responsibility should be made to coincide as far as possible.

If this can be done, the result will be to narrow the gap between the great powers and other nations while maintaining the principle of the sovereign equality of all member states, he added. It will mean that the smallest and least powerful members will not bear the same responsibilities as countries like Australia, the Netherlands and Brazil.

"It is the view of the Government," Mr. Mackenzie King said, "that the constitutional position within the organization of important secondary states should be clarified and that the delegation from Canada should exert the utmost effort to assure due recognition of their relative standing among the nations of the world." This declaration was cheered by members of all parties in the House of Commons.

As the proposals stood, Mr. Mackenzie King continued, all states other than the great powers would have the same constitutional position in the organization. No regard would be paid to their national significance, to their record in resisting aggression or to their potential contribution to the maintenance of peace. It is surely desirable, he added, that, among the states that are to be elected members of the security council there should be several that could make a valuable contribution to the maintenance of security.

The proposal that all members should bind themselves to carry out diplomatic, economic and military sanctions at the request of the security council raises another difficult question for Canada and other secondary states, Mr. Mackenzie King said. As the proposals stand, their acceptance will in no way commit Canada to send forces beyond Canadian territory at the call of the security council. If any such commitment were sought it would be embodied in a later agreement freely negotiated by the Government of Canada and coming into effect only after it had been approved by Parliament, he added.

It would seem desirable, Mr. Mackenzie King said, to develop some procedure whereby states not represented on the security council would not be called on to undertake serious enforcement action without the opportunity of participating in the council's proceedings or without agreeing separately to join in executing its decisions. The cooperation of states not represented on the council and especially of those bordering on an offending state would be essential and what would be a probable practice might well be made the formal rule, he added.

DEMAND FOR MID-COUNCIL ROLE: AUSTRALIA [7]

London, April 2—Australia wants recognition as "a middle power" in the world security council, which will be established at San Francisco, and will press at the conference there for amendments to give more power to the economic and social council suggested in the Dumbarton Oaks agreement, H. V. Evatt, Australian Minister for External Affairs, said today.

Australia is the second dominion to seek status as "a middle power." Canada is the other. One of the proposals which are expected to be made at San Francisco is that a fixed proportion of non-permanent members of the security council should be drawn from "the middle powers." This suggestion is reported to have received considerable support at a recent unofficial British Commonwealth relations meeting here.

[7] From "Australia To Seek Mid-Council Role," newsstory. *The New York Times.* 94:3. April 3, 1945. Reprinted by permission.

Mr. Evatt described as "most inaccurate and misleading" some suggestions made in the United States that Britain would have multiple representation in the assembly of the world organization through the votes of the dominions.

The suggestion that the United States and Soviet Union should have three representatives each in the proposed international assembly, whereas the United Kingdom will retain one only, has already led to serious misconceptions about the position of the United Kingdom and the other members of the British Commonwealth, [he said, adding that Britain and the four dominions] will be separate, distinct, equal autonomous members of the organization.

He cited the position of Australia and New Zealand, which have already concluded a regional defense compact in the southwestern Pacific, as a case where regional interests extend "over and above the more general interests that they share in common with other peace-loving states." The two dominions, he said, have declared that while maintenance of peace is a world responsibility the defense of the southwest Pacific should rest on "special arrangements" by Australia, New Zealand and other Pacific powers.

Australia's war record has demonstrated her capacity to make a substantial contribution to the planning of measures for future security, he said.

Because of her resources and geographical position Australia must rank among those nations who have been termed middle powers. [Mr. Evatt described these countries as] powers which while not great powers command considerably greater strength than the majority of small powers.

In a system of world security the cooperation of all nations is essential but it is plain that some will have to take a more active part than others, either because of the number of their fighting men, their resources or their geographical position.

Discussing the economic aspects of the world organization, Mr. Evatt said that Chapter Nine of the Dumbarton Oaks tentative agreement setting up an economic and social council required an amendment to give the council the power to take adequate action in any grave international social or economic emergency. It should also have the power to coordinate the policies of other social and economic agencies and its activities should be directed by "a binding statement of principles," he said.

As now proposed the council was little more than a discussion group on economics, "a weak organization having very little influence over the work of the general international organization," he went on.

He said that lasting security could be obtained only through higher standards of living and full employment throughout the world. In the Australian view, unless full employment were an objective of each nation and the basis of international economic collaboration, the separate objectives of the specialized organizations could not be attained, Mr. Evatt said.

COLONIAL TRUSTEESHIP [8]

During the early years after the close of the first world war there was a widespread outburst of Oriental nationalism.

Those years marked an Egyptian revolt, a bitterly contested rising of the Syrian people, the elimination by the Persians of all vestiges of foreign domination, the first of the Iraqi rebellions, the attack by Afghanistan upon British forces in India, extensive nationalist agitation in India and in Burma, as well as in the Netherlands East Indies, and long-continued hostilities between the new Turkey and the Allied nations.

Immediately after the end of this second world war a far more powerful surge toward freedom among the peoples of the East will be inevitable. Compared to the forces which it will unleash, the outbreak of the 1920's will be trivial.

The symptoms are unmistakable.

During the period between the wars nationalist leaders in most of the colonial areas have steadily gained popular support. There has been a constantly growing demand for self-government. The clamor for liberty has taken on the tinge of a religious fanaticism. Many of the dependent peoples are fully aware that they are strongly supported by public opinion in the Western democracies.

[8] From "Welles Asks World Trusteeship to Administer Colonial Areas," by Sumner Welles, former Under Secretary of State. *New York Herald-Tribune.* 104:21. March 28, 1945. Reprinted by permission.

The grant of immediate independence to the Philippine people has established the needed and welcome precedent.

Recognition of China as one of the major powers has lent impetus to the movement to abolish Western imperialism. The Chinese government is strongly supporting this trend.

The prestige of the Western powers during the second world war has suffered a blow in the Far East which will make it wholly impossible for the Oriental peoples ever again to regard themselves as "subservient races." However much the peoples of Burma and Malaya, of the Netherlands East Indies and of the Philippines may have suffered at the hands of the Japanese invaders, they will not forget Japan's initial successes, nor the story of the fall of Rangoon, of Singapore and of Hong Kong.

To the leaders of the nationalist movements the period immediately after the close of the present war will present the opportunity they have sought to press their demands for liberty.

In the Near East the republics of Syria and of the Lebanon will not acquiesce in any continuation of an exclusive French influence. Egypt has already announced her intention to secure the abolition of all semblance of British control. The creation of a Pan-Arab federation, even though initially favored by Great Britain, is bound to result in joint resistance by the Arab states to any attempt on the part of the European powers to continue their present hegemony.

India has long been seething. With the liberation of Burma, of the Malay Peninsula and of the Netherlands East Indies, the demand for autonomy or independence among those hundreds of millions of peoples will be overpowering.

To the Oriental mind, the Atlantic Charter unequivocally promises an end to imperialism. They have seen the major powers at Yalta jointly pledge to the peoples of the liberated countries of Europe the untrammeled right to choose their own governments. They can see no reason why the peoples of the Orient who are fitted for self-government should not at once be accorded the same right. They are unable to comprehend how the terms of the Atlantic Charter, which are clearly universal in their scope, can logically be interpreted as applying only to the West and not to the East.

Some of the colonial powers, notably the Netherlands, have already announced the constructive steps which they will take to prepare for the whirlwind which is looming.

The French provisional government, however, seems not as yet to realize that if a peaceful world is to be achieved the old colonial order of exploitation and of repression must be discarded.

If the United Nations Conference at San Francisco fails to deal with this great problem in the same spirit in which this war for freedom has been waged, Gandhi's prophesy that unless the peoples of the East obtain their fundamental liberties, another and a bloodier war will be inevitable, will bid fair to be realized.

Any hope that peace can be maintained in the postwar period in the Near East and in the Far East will be illusory unless the United Nations find a solution which will give the Oriental peoples the firm assurance that they can obtain their freedom as soon as they are ready to enjoy it.

The peoples of the Orient are not going to be satisfied this time with unimplemented promises. Nor will some of them submit for more than a very brief time longer to any form of alien control.

There is only one practical method by which the international organization can safeguard the world against a general and violent upheaval in the East.

That method involves the creation within the international organization of an international trusteeship, to which every colonial power will be directly responsible, and which must assert final authority over all dependent peoples. At the conclusion of the war, all presently dependent peoples recognized by the international organization as being fitted for self-government should be immediately intrusted with that right. Where alien governments control dependent peoples who are not yet ready for the enjoyment of autonomy, those colonial powers should demonstrate to the international trusteeship that they are administering such regions for the benefit of the native inhabitants and that they are preparing their wards for autonomy or independence.

The international organization should for all future time establish these principles; that all peoples, like all individuals, possess the inherent right to freedom under law, and that until such freedom can be enjoyed, the powers administering dependent peoples shall be held responsible by the public opinion of the world, through the international organization, for the manner in which they discharge their obligations as trustees.

BRITISH OPPOSITION TO TRUSTEESHIP [9]

From the mutual desire of the three colonial powers in the Commonwealth, there will likely come a common policy opposed to the American idea of an international trusteeship for colonies.

Col. Oliver Stanley, Colonial Secretary, made the British position clear in a recent speech here. Britain's responsibility for her colonies, he declared, cannot be shared, and any division of responsibility would be impracticable as well as against the wishes of the colonial people themselves.

Fearful of any future aggression against the mandated islands on the northern approaches to Australia, where the Japanese in this war were within a figurative stone's throw of landing, Australian members have protested publicly against the possibility of international guardianship. And South Africa, rather than looking for such control, has indicated it would like to bring into the Union the protectorates at present administered by Colonel Stanley's department in London.

Whereas the Americans and the Indians have suggested that the United States participate in the Indian Government during the transition period after the war until the dominion status promised by Britain is achieved, Britain clearly has shown she intends to solve this problem by her own means and with her own resources.

TENSION ON COLONIAL QUESTION [10]

In the Dumbarton Oaks meeting the colonial problem was not on the agenda. The British Government wished the prepara-

[9] From "Colonial Trustees Opposed by British," Sydney Gruson. *The New York Times.* 94:6. March 30, 1945. Reprinted by permission.

[10] From "France's Joining Big Four Envisaged," by Pertinax. *The New York Times.* 94:12. March 21, 1945. Reprinted by permission.

tory work to be restricted to matters having an immediate bearing on the maintenance of peace.

It insisted that colonial affairs were a subsidiary subject and had better be left over. In Yalta the gap was filled in. A new chapter is therefore to be added to the Dumbarton Oaks proposals, the rough draft of the charter.

Only the structure of a system of international control or cooperation will be outlined. All reference to particular colonies will be ruled out. The time has come for the "inviting powers" to write that missing chapter.

Britain and America must attempt to reconcile their views. France more or less agrees with the British thesis, but she wants to share in the debate otherwise than by proxy.

In the colonial debate, Britain and America stand rather far apart. American diplomacy thinks in terms of "international trusteeship" and British diplomacy in terms of "international partnership." International trusteeship means that the community of nations has a responsibility for dependent peoples in Asia, Africa and Oceania and that the sovereignty of the colonial powers may be interfered with. International partnership means that the system of consultation and free cooperation first put to the test when the Anglo-American Caribbean Commission set to its task in 1939 is to become of general application.

The pattern now tried in the Caribbean area would be improved and strengthened. Delegates of the International Labor Office would in all probability play a part. But no international body would be allowed to intervene in the internal management of a colony.

Under the American scheme, the British, French, Netherlands, Belgian and Portuguese empires might ultimately pass under some form of international authority. A lengthy process indeed. At the beginning (the point was cleared up in Yalta), only the mandated territories of 1919 and the territories taken from the enemy on the termination of this war would be affected. Nevertheless, sooner or later the general trend could not help asserting itself. Under the British-sponsored plan, the various colonial empires have the prospect of a new lease on life provided that they part with what still remains of the old tenets of colonialism, which their rulers of today are ready to do.

This forthcoming colonial discussion is loaded with explosive material. It can easily lead to mutual recriminations, to invidious comparisons of past records concerning the treatment of subject populations. The colonial nations, so sorely tried during this war, are sure to do their utmost to retain in full their sovereignty in overseas territories.

EXCERPTS

We Czechoslovaks cannot help seeing that full understanding between London, Moscow, Washington and Paris will alone make a third German war impossible.—*Edvard Beneš, President of Czechoslovakia, in address to the City of London Livery Companies, London,* February 29, 1944.

The London Daily Express said editorially: "Imperial preference is the mainstay of our empire trade. That policy is only in its infancy. It should be developed even more toward empire economic unity or empire free trade."

Supporters of the Empire preference policy plan maintain that it is dictated by the war-spurred development of trade between the Americas and by indications that Russia plans to bring the Balkans within the Soviet economic sphere.—*From "British Empire to Stand as Unit at Security Parley, newsstory. New York World-Telegram. 77:31. March 14, 1945.*

We must be consulted, we must participate in the actual making of decisions and not only be presented with accomplished facts. We do not ask for small states the right to veto decisions or to paralyze any international organization. We are prepared to let the great powers play the leading role they have the right to play. But we insist on the sovereign equality of all states in that sense that our cause should be heard from the very beginning, that we should have the right to take care of our interests and, by participating in decisions, have the possibility of exerting our influence.—*From an address by King Haakon of Norway before the Foreign Press Association, London, June 7, 1944. Quoted in War & Peace Aims, special supplement to the United Nations Review, number 4, p. 96. Reprinted by permission.*

His Majesty's Government are convinced that the administration of the British Colonies must continue to be the sole responsibility of Great Britain. The policy of His Majesty's Government is to plan for the fullest possible political, economic and social development of the Colonies within the British Empire, and in close cooperation with neighboring and friendly nations. —*Winston Churchill, British Prime Minister, March* 17, 1943, *in House of Commons.*

BIBLIOGRAPHY

An asterick (*) preceding a reference indicates that the article or a part of it has been reprinted in this book.

BOOKS AND PAMPHLETS

Adler, M. J.; Friedrich, C. J.; and Waymack, W. W. Challenge of the four freedoms. (no. 232) 29p. University of Chicago Round Table. Chicago. 1942.

America speaks for unity in war and peace; a symposium. 14p. Committee to Study the Organization of Peace. New York. 1945.

*American membership in a general international organization: constitutional difficulties. (Problem 16) 27p. Universities Committee on Post-War International Problems. Boston. 1944.

America's peace aims. (Pamphlet no. 28) 48p. Catholic Association for International Peace. Washington. 1941.

Angell, Norman; Gottschalk, Louis; and Schuman, Frederick. United nations. (no. 222) 29p. University of Chicago Round Table. Chicago. 1942.

Arbitration and the world court. (Pamphlet series no. 23) Catholic Association for International Peace. Washington.

Baker, Ray Stannard. Woodrow Wilson and the world settlement. 2v. Doubleday. New York. 1922.

Bishops' statement on international order. Issued N. 16, '44, by the Catholic Bishops of the U.S. National Catholic Welfare Conference. Washington.

Burton, Margaret E. The assembly of the League of Nations. 441p. Univ. of Chicago Press. Chicago. 1941.

Butler, Harold B. The lost peace: a personal impression. 246p. Harcourt, Brace. New York. 1942.

Carr, E. H. Conditions of peace. 282p. Macmillan. New York. 1942.

Chase, Stuart. The road we are traveling: 1914-1942. 106p. Twentieth Century Fund. New York. 1942.

Chase, Stuart; Ezekiel, Mordecai; and Yntema, T. O. Economic requisites of a durable peace. (no. 231) 29p. University of Chicago Round Table. Chicago. 1942.

Cole, G. D. H. Europe, Russia and the future. 233p. Macmillan. New York. 1942.

Colegrove, Kenneth W. The American senate and world peace. 209p. Vanguard Press. New York. 1944.

Commercial policy in the interwar period; international proposals and national policies. (League of Nations Doc. 1942: II. A. 6) Columbia University Press. New York.

*Commission to Study the Organization of Peace. Preliminary report and monographs. The Commission. New York. November 1942.

Commission to Study the Organization of Peace. Second report and papers: The transitional period. The Commission. New York. February 1942.

Commission to Study the Organization of Peace. Third report. The United Nations and the organization of peace. p. 203-385. The Commission. New York. February 1943.

*Commission to Study the Organization of Peace. Fourth Report. Fundamentals of the international organization: general statement; I. Security and world organization; II. The economic organization of welfare. 40p. The Commission. New York. November 1943.

Commission to Study the Organization of Peace. The United Nations and non-self-governing peoples; a plan for trusteeship. 8p. The Commission. New York. December 1944.

Condliffe, J. B. Agenda for a postwar world. 232p. Norton. New York. 1942.

*Condliffe, J. B. Problems of economic reconstruction. 44p. Commission to Study the Organization of Peace. New York. 1944.

Conwell-Evans, T. P. The League Council in action. Oxford Univ. Press, London.

Corbett, P. E. Post-war worlds. (Institute of Pacific Relations, Inquiry series). 211p. American Council of the Institute. New York. 1942.

Corwin, E. S. The constitution and world organization. (Princeton studies in American civilization) 64p. Princeton Univ. Press. Princeton. 1944.

Corwin, E. S. National supremacy. Henry Holt. New York. 1913.

Craven, A. O.; Ezekiel, Mordecai; and Herring, Hubert. How united are the Americas? (no. 202) 27p. University of Chicago Round Table. Chicago. 1942.

Davis, Harriet Eager, ed. Pioneers in world order; an American appraisal of the League of Nations. 272p. Columbia Univ. Press. New York. 1944.

Dean, Vera Micheles. Struggle for world order. (Headline Books no. 32) 96p. Foreign Policy Association. New York. 1941.

De Roussy de Sales, Raoul J. J. Making of tomorrow. 338p. Reynal and Hitchcock. New York. 1942.

*Dickinson, John. Peace, realism, and the balance of power, address before the midwinter meeting of the Maryland State Bar Association, Ja. 20, '45.

Doman, Nicholas. The coming age of world control; the transition to an organized world society. 301p. Harper. New York. 1942.

*Dumbarton Oaks proposals; a comparison with the League of Nations Covenant. 4p. United Nations Educational Campaign. New York. 1945.

Dumbarton Oaks proposals; the enforcement of peace. (Problem 18) 39p. Universities Committee on Post-War International Problems. Boston. 1944.

*Dumbarton Oaks proposals; the enforcement of peace; summary of the first 41 reports received from cooperating groups. Universities Committee on Post-War International Problems. Boston. 1945. mimeo.

*Eagleton, Clyde. Aggression and war. (Preliminary report and monographs) p. 29-39. Commission to Study the Organization of Peace. New York.

Eagleton, Clyde. Fundamental principles and problems of post-war reconstruction. 21p. American Council on Public Affairs. Washington. 1942.

*Eichelberger, Clark M. Proposals for the United Nations charter. 32p. Commission to Study the Organization of Peace. New York. 1944.

Eichelberger, Clark M. Time has come for action. 32p. Commission to Study the Organization of Peace. New York. August 1944.

Fox, W. T. R. The super-powers: the United States, Britain and the Soviet Union—their responsibility for peace. (Yale University International Studies) 184p. Harcourt, Brace. New York. 1944.

Friedrich, Carl and Edgerton, R. B. War: the causes, effects and control of international violence. (Problems in American Life series Unit no. 11) National Education Associations. Washington. n.d.

Fry, Varian. Bricks without mortar; the story of international cooperation. (Headline books no. 16) 96p. Foreign Policy Association. New York. 1938.

Fry, Varian. Peace that failed; how Europe sowed the seeds of war. (Headline book no. 21) 96p. Foreign Policy Association. New York. 1939.

*Fulbright, J. W. New delegation of sovereignty. 60p. (Program no. 19) World Wide Broadcasting Foundation. New York.

*Goodrich, L. M. and Baylis, A. C. Peaceful settlement of international disputes. (Problem 17) 34p. Universities Committee on Post-War International Problems. Boston. 1944.

Hambro, C. J. How to win the peace. 384p. J. B. Lippincott. Philadelphia. 1942.

Hocking, W. E. Colonies and dependent areas. (Problem 9) 33p. Universities Committee on Post-war International Problems. Boston. 1943.

*Hoover, Herbert. Series of four articles prepared for the North American Newspaper Alliance. March 25-28, 1945.

Hoover, Herbert and Gibson, Hugh. The problems of a lasting peace. 295p. Doubleday, Doran. Garden City, N.Y. 1942.

Hudson, Manley, O. The Permanent Court of International Justice. 1920-1942; a treatise. 807p. Macmillan. New York. 1943.

Hula, Erich. Pan-Americanism: its utopian and realistic elements. 22p. American Council on Public Affairs. Washington. 1942.

International economic collaboration. (Problem 6) 16p. Universities Committee on Post-War International Problems. Boston. 1943.

Jennings, William Ivor. A federation for western Europe. 208p. Macmillan. New York. 1940.

Johnsen, Julia E. The "eight points" of post-war world organization. (Reference Shelf, v. 15, no. 5.) 126p. H. W. Wilson Co., New York. 1942.
Bibliography

Kirk, G. L. and Sharp, W. R. Uniting today for tomorrow. (Headline books no. 37). 96p. Foreign Policy Association. New York. 1942.

Lasswell, H. D. and Cummings, H. H. Public opinion in war and peace. (Problems in American Life unit no. 14) 68p. National Association of Secondary School Principals. Washington. 1943.

*Lauterbach, Albert. The changing nature of war. (Preliminary report and monographs) Commission to Study the Organization of Peace. New York. November 1942.

*Lerner, Max; Lerner, Edna; and Abraham, H. J. International organization after the war. (Problems in American Life unit no. 15) 56p. National Association of Secondary School Principals. Washington. 1943.

Logan, R. W. The operation of the mandate system in Africa, 1919-1927. 50p. Foundation Publishers. Washington. 1942.

Lorwin, Lewis L. Economic consequences of the second world war. 510p. Random House. New York. 1941.

MacCormac, John. America and world mastery; the future of the United States, Canada and the Britishh Empire. 338p. Duell, Sloan and Pearce. New York. 1942.

Millspaugh, Arthur C. Peace plans and American choices: the pros and cons of world order. 107p. Brookings Institution. Washington. 1942.

Myers, Denys P. Handbook of the League of Nations. 338p. World Peace Foundation. Boston. 1935.

Nash, P. C. An adventure in world order. 139p. Beacon Press. Boston. 1944.

O'Donnell, Charles, ed. World society. (Pamphlet no. 29) 48p. Catholic Association for International Peace. Washington. 1941.

Peace agenda for the United Nations. (Pamphlet no. 32) 40p. Catholic Association for International Peace. Washington. 1943.

Peffer, Nathaniel. Basis for peace in the Far East. 277p. Harper. New York. 1942.

Phelps, E. M. ed. University debaters' annual: 1942-43. Blueprints for a better world. p.273-319. H. W. Wilson Company. New York. 1943.

Phelps, E. M. ed. University debaters' annual: 1942-43. Federal world government. p.193-240. H. W. Wilson Co. New York. 1943.

Proposed methods and agencies for international economic collaboration; should America participate in them? (Problem 8) 22p. Universities Committee on Post-War International Problems. Boston. 1943.

Public looks at world organization. (National Opinion Research Center, report no. 19) University of Denver. Denver. 1944.

Questions and answers on the Dumbarton Oaks proposals. (Publication 2218, Conference series 58) U.S. Department of State. Washington.

Rappard, W. E. The quest for peace since the world war. 516p. Harvard Univ. Press. Cambridge. 1940.

Riches, C. A. Majority rule in international organization. 322p. Johns Hopkins Univ. Press. Baltimore. 1940.

*Shotwell, James T. Radio broadcast transcribed by World Wide Broadcasting Foundation. New York. Program No. 19.

Should the governments of the United Nations at this time formulate and announce a "common strategy for peace"? (Problem 1) 8p. Universities Committee on Post-War International Problems. Boston. 1943.

Should there be an international organization for general security against military aggression; and Should the United States participate in such an organization? (Problems 4 and 5) 19p., 14p. Universities Committee on Post-War International Problems. Boston. 1943.

Straight, Michael. Make this the last war. 417p. Harcourt, Brace. New York. 1943.

Sweetser, Arthur. League of Nations. American Council on Public Affairs. Washington.

*Thomas, Norman. Something better than Dumbarton Oaks, broadcast over CBS, Mr. 10, 1945.

Torpats, John. Economic basis for world peace. 222p. John Felsberg. New York. 1941.

Toward new horizons, the world beyond the war. Office of War Information. Washington.
Speeches by Wallace, Welles, Perkins, and Winant.

United Nations agreements and documents. (Bulletin no. 7) Commission to Study the Organization of Peace. New York. 1942.

*War and peace aims. Extracts from statements of United Nations leaders. United Nations Information Office. New York.
Special supplements: No. 2. 118p. December 1, 1943; No. 3. 127p. April 30, 1944; No. 4. 124p. October 31, 1944.

Welles, Sumner. The time for decision. Harper. New York. 1942.

Whitton, John B. ed. The second chance; America and the peace. Princeton Univ. Press. Princeton. 1944.

Woodrow Wilson Foundation. Official documents issued during the two world wars. 8p. The Foundation. New York. 1944.

PERIODICALS

*American Business. 14:10-12. O. '44. Is a third world war inevitable? Melchior Palyi.

American Mercury. 55:536. N. '42. The American plan for a reorganized world. Kingsbury Smith.

*American Mercury. 58:417-23. Ap. '44. Why not the U.S. of Europe? Count Richard Coudenhove-Kalergi.

American Mercury. 59:148-56. Ag. '44. The government's blueprint for peace. Flora Lewis.

American Mercury. 60:135-42. F. '45. America's plan for the colonial world.

American Mercury. 60:198-203. F. '45. A Mercury survey of opinion leaders. Edward L. Bernays.

American Political Science Review. 37:862-72. O. '43. Distribution of powers between an international government and the governments of national states. Arnold Brecht.

American Political Science Review. 37:872-87. O. '43. International administration: lessons from the experience of the League of Nations. E. F. Ranshofen-Wertheimer.

American Political Science Review. 37:903-9. O. '43. Small states and a new league, from the viewpoint of Norway. E. I. Hambro.

American Political Science Review. 38:235-48. Ap. '44. Leadership of the U.S. in the postwar world. C. A. Berdahl.

American Political Science Review. 38:931. O. '44. American foreign relations within an organized world framework. Walter R. Sharp.

American Scholar. Summer, 1942. p. 275. International utopias. Zechariah Chaffee, Jr.

Annals of the American Academy. 228:47-51. Jl. '43. International cooperation or World war III. W. M. Agar.

Annals of the American Academy. 228:58-64. Jl. '43. The northern European countries after this war. E. I. Hambro.

*Annals of the American Academy. 228:40-6. Jl. '43. A more perfect united nations—how and when? Claude Pepper.

Annals of the American Academy. 234:61-9. Jl. '44. The small European nations after the war. Frans Van Cauwelaert.

Atlantic. 174:46-52. D. '44. Pacification for peace. Walter Lippmann.

Canadian Forum. 24:173-4. N. '44. United nations, ltd; Dumbarton Oaks plan.

Catholic World. 160:464. F. '45. European federation. G. H. Leibholz.

Christian Century. 61:1281-2. N. 8, '44. American action in the new league; should power to declare war be delegated?

Christian Century. 61:1374-7. N. 29, '44. Amend Dumbarton Oaks!

*Christian Science Monitor. 37:1. Mr. 13, '45. Yalta "hidden" veto. Neal Stanford.

Collier's. 115:11+. Ja. 6, '45. Questions for the Big Three. George Creel.

Collier's. 115:11+. Ap. 21, '45. The cost of lasting peace. Harold E. Stassen.

Commercial and Financial Chronicle. 160:2743. D. 21, '43. Amendment to Dumbarton Oaks plan by Canada.

Commonweal. 41:27. O. 27, '44. Dumbarton Oaks; proposed world organization.

Congressional Digest. 22:193-224. Ag. '43. Should the United States join in reconstituting the League of Nations?

Congressional Digest. 23:192. Je. '44. U.S. of Europe?

Congressional Digest. 22:202. 1943. Legal steps requisite to U.S. membership in an international organization.

*Congressional Record. 90:A1470. Mr. 21, '45. Reprinting of article "Dumbarton Oaks," by Ernest K. Lindley, from *Washington Post*, Mr. 21, '45.

Contemporary Review. 166:321-5. D. '44. Dumbarton Oaks scheme. Viscount Cecil.

Current History. ns. 7:89-94. Ag. '44. Role of the small nations. S. B. Fay.

Current History. ns. 7:501-8 D. '44 Dumbarton Oaks agreements; statements by Cordell Hull and E R. Stettinius, Jr., and text of proposals for establishment of a general international organization.

Department of State Bulletin. 7:210-20. Mr. 7, '42. The problem of economic peace after the war. Leo Pasvolsky.
Issued monthly by the U.S. Department of State. Washington, D.C. Contains excerpts from speeches, statements, press releases by officials of the Department of State; texts of official documents; news of current developments, etc.

*Department of State Bulletin. 11:265. O 8, '44. Washington conversations on international organization. Franklin D. Roosevelt.

*Department of State Bulletin. 12:220-2. F. 18, '45. Text of message of President Roosevelt to Congress on Bretton Woods Proposals.

*Department of State Bulletin. 12:253-5. F. 18, '45. A general peace and security organization: analysis of its major functions. Andrew W. Cordier.

Empire Review. 75:58-63. Feb. '42. World order or world ruin. Jerrold Douglas.

Foreign Policy Bulletin. 23:1-2. O. 13, '44. Acts not words will be test of Dumbarton Oaks blueprint. V. M. Dean.

Foreign Policy Reports. 19:209-11. O. 15, '43. International organization and the U.S. J. P. Chamberlain and H. L. May.

Foreign Policy Reports 20:219-20. N. 15, '44. Europe's search for a security organization. O. K. D. Ringwood and W. N. Hadsel.

*Foreign Policy Reports. 20:238-47. D. 15, '44. Anglo-American Caribbean commission—pattern for colonial cooperation. Olive Holmes.

Fortnightly. 161(ns. 155):290-5. My. '44. Mr. Cordell Hull's seventeen points. F. Whyte.

Fortune. 29:94-5. Ja. '44. The British Empire and the U.S.; editorial

*Fortune. 29:94+. Mr. '44. The Fortune survey

*Fortune. 31:156-60+. Mr. '45. Make your own world. Susanne K. Langer.

International Conciliation. 369:394-423. Ap. '41. The economic organization of peace. Eugene Staley.

International Conciliation. 397:140-9. F. '44. League of Nations and associated agencies; United States reverses thinking and policy on organized international cooperation. Arthur Sweetser.

International Conciliation. 407:2-3. Ja. '45. Statement adopted by trustees of Carnegie Endowment for International Peace, D. 11, '44.

International Conciliation. 409:129-77. Mr. '45. The National study conference on the churches and a just and durable peace. Reports on meetings, Nov. 28, '44, and Ja. 16-19, '45.

International Conciliation. 409, Sec. II:203-10. Mr. '45. Miscellaneous material on international organization: Report on the Crimea conference, Dumbarton Oaks proposals for economic and social cooperation, etc. Leo Paslovsky.

International Labour Review. 45:420. Ap. '42. Anglo-American agreement implementing the Atlantic charter.

International Postwar Problems. 1:465-97. S. '43. Labor's stake in the organization of the postwar world. Oscar Jaszi.

International Postwar Problems. 1:163-76. Mr. '44. Labor and American foreign policy. John L. Childs.

International Postwar Problems. 1:281-92. Mr. '44. Labor's postwar programs in free and axis-dominated countries. Survey.

*Life. 16:102-4+. Ap. 17, '44. America's world purpose. W. E. Hocking.

Life. 17:30-1. O. 23, '44 United nations; tentative proposals for new international peace organization.

Look. 9:26-7. Ap. 3, '45. How can we keep the peace? Tom Connally (marginal notes by A. K. Vandenberg).

*Nation. 159:451. O. 21, '44. Great power hegemony; editorial.

New Europe.
Issued nearly every month in New York under subsidy by London Polish Government. Contains articles bearing on problems of small nations, particularly East and East Central Europe.

New Republic. 110:261-3. F. 28, '44. How to unite the world: Professor Mitrany advocates functional international agencies rather than federation.

*New Republic. 111:510-11. O. 23, '44. The Dumbarton Oaks plan; editorial.

New Republic. 111:679-80. N. 27, '44. British bloc in Europe.

New Republic. 112:319-20. Mr. 5, '45. The Mexico City conference; editorial.

*New Republic. 112:321-3. Mr. 5, '45. America and Britain after victory. George Soule.

*New Republic. 112:349. Mr. 12, '45. The Act of Chapultepec; editorial.

*New Republic. 112:350-1. Mr. 12, '45. America and Dumbarton Oaks; editorial.

*New Republic. 112:357-8. Mr. 12, '45. The new pan-Arabism. Heinz Eulau.

New York Herald Tribune. 104:1+. Mr. 9, '45. Vandenberg demands big three set up true Polish coalition. Jack Steele.

New York Herald Tribune. 104:10. Mr. 9, '45. Mexico parley seen helpful to San Francisco.

New York Herald Tribune. 104:10. Mr. 11, '45. Stettinius back, stressing need for world unity. Leo Cullinane.

*New York Herald Tribune. 104:21. Mr. 28, '45. Welles asks world trusteeship to administer colonial areas. Sumner Welles.

*New York Times. 93:12. O. 10, '44. Texts of statements on Dumbarton Oaks and documents giving tentative security plans.

*New York Times. 94:1+. Mr. 4, '45. American nations form an alliance to protect peace. James B. Reston.

New York Times. 94:E2. Mr. 4, '45. For hemisphere security; editorial.

New York Times. 94:E3. Mr. 4, '45. We're all on our way to a new league now. E. L. James.

*New York Times. 94:E4. Mr. 4, '45. Procedure criticized; letter. Leo Gross.

New York Times. 94:E5. Mr. 4, '45. Rumanian crisis provides a test of Russian policy. John MacCormac.

New York Times. 94:23. Mr. 4, '45. Americas in doubt on Oaks program. Camille M. Cianfarra.

*New York Times. 94:25. Mr. 4, '45. Text of Act of Chapultepec.

*New York Times. 94:8. Mr. 6, '45. Meeting in Mexico asks Oaks changes.

*New York Times. 94:9. Mr. 6, '45. Stettinius offers guide to Americas.

*New York Times. 94:10. Mr. 6, '45. Text of statement by Secretary of State Edward R. Stettinius, Jr.

*New York Times. 94:20. Mr. 6, '45. Yalta and San Francisco; editorial.

New York Times. 94:20. Mr. 7, '45. Beginning of the question period for the big three. Anne O'Hare McCormick.

New York Times. 94:20. Mr. 7, '45. Yalta vote formula upheld; letter. J. F. Dulles.

New York Times. 94:11. Mr. 8, '45. Stassen gives plan for unity in peace.

New York Times. 94:22. Mr. 8, '45. Alliances and league; editorial.

New York Times. 94:12. Mr. 9, '45. Partial texts and summaries of resolutions adopted at Mexico City .

*New York Times. 94:18. Mr. 9, '45. Implementing world court; letter. R. S. Childs.

*New York Times. 94:18. Mr. 9, '45. The small powers; editorial.

New York Times. 94:16. Mr. 10, '45. Pan-American conference; editorial.

New York Times. 94:14. Mr. 15, '45. Voting plan is questioned; letter. H. S. Quigley.

New York Times. 94:22. Mr. 15, '45. High world court suggested; letter. J. W. Ryan.

New York Times. 94:9. Mr. 16, '45 Churchill upholds vote method.

*New York Times. 94:10. Mr. 16, '45. Oaks amendments offered by Paris. Harold Callender.

*New York Times. 94:14. Mr. 16, '45. The great powers; editorial.

*New York Times. 94:10. Mr. 17, '45. Big powers' unity is declared vital.

New York Times. 94:E3. Mr. 18, '45. Paul-Boncour advises the smaller nations. E. L. James.

*New York Times. 94:E3. Mr. 18, '45. Hurdles for the San Francisco Conference. Lansing Warren.

*New York Times. 94:E8. Mr. 18, '45. Poland and big three; letter. T. W. Lamont.

New York Times. 94:1+. Mr. 19, '45. Vandenberg gives peace review idea. Lansing Warren.

*New York Times. 94:12. Mr. 21, '45. France's joining big four envisaged. Pertinax.

*New York Times. 94:13. Mr. 21, '45. Canada supports security program. P. J. Philip.

*New York Times. 94:13. Mr. 21, '45. International bill of rights to be offered at world peace parley.

New York Times. 94:1+. Mr. 22, '45. Eden bars "bullying" by big powers. Clifton Daniel.

New York Times. 94:17. Mr. 22, '45. France strong for security. Harold Callender.

*New York Times. 94:17. Mr. 22, '45. Canadians agree on parley plans. R. J. Philip.

*New York Times. 94:8. Mr. 23, '45. Charter adopted by Arab league. S. P. Brewer.

*New York Times. 94:16. Mr. 24, '45. Abroad: Russian demands on Turkey upset U.S. and Britain. Anne O'Hare McCormick.

*New York Times. 94:16. Mr. 24, '45. France and the league; editorial.

*New York Times. 94:2E. Mr. 25, '45. The nation: as nations gather; editorial.

New York Times. 94:8E. Mr. 25, '45. Vote power analyzed; letter. Herbert F. Judd.

*New York Times. 94:28. Mr. 25, '45. Grew clarifies security voting. Lansing Warren.

*New York Times. 94:11. Mr. 27, '45. Hoover asks pacts be open to change. Herbert Hoover (Third in series of four articles specially prepared for the North American Newspaper Alliance).

*New York Times. 94:16. Mr. 28, '45. To draft statute for world court.

*New York Times. 94:6. Mr. 30, '45. Colonial trustees opposed by British. Sidney Gruson.

*New York Times. 94:8E. Ap. 1, '45. Assembly disapproved; letter. C. N. Goodwin.

*New York Times. 94:11. Ap. 2, '45. The text of Senator Vandenberg's Oaks memorandum.

*New York Times. 94:3. Ap. 3, '45. Australia to seek mid-council role.

*New York Times. 94:17. Ap. 3, '45. Russian relations cause uneasiness in capitol circles. James B. Reston.

New York Times Magazine. p. 9. O. 17, '43. Power adequate to enforce peace. J. A. Fulbright.

New York Times Magazine. p. 9. S. 24, '44. The large role of the small nations. Paul Van Zeeland.

New York Times Magazine. p. 5+. F. 11, '45. Hour is late, we must not fail; task of building new international machinery on a global scale. R. B. Fosdick.

New York World-Telegram. 77:14. Mr. 6, '45. The San Francisco setup; editorial.

*New York World-Telegram. 77:23. Mr. 7, '45. Yalta and Americas. W. P. Simms.

New York World-Telegram. 77:9. Mr. 8, '45. Stassen denounces avid nationalism as medieval idea.

New York World-Telegram. 77:23. Mr. 14, '45. Colonial Asia. W. P. Simms.

*New York World-Telegram. 77:31. Mr. 14, '45. British empire to stand as unit at security parley.

New York World-Telegram. 77:10. Mr. 15, '45. Churchill defines a point about Yalta.

New York World-Telegram. 77:14. Mr. 20, '45. The test of Yalta; editorial.

New York World-Telegram. 77:18. Mr. 22; 77:22. Mr. 23, '45. Bases of U.S. and British accord. Lord Kemsley.

New York World-Telegram. 77:22. Mr. 23, '45. Eden has the answer; editorial.

*New York World-Telegram. 77:10. Mr. 24, '45. A European council versus blocs; editorial.

*New York World-Telegram. 77:10. Mr. 24, '45. World peace hope seen in big three. Scrutator.

*New York World-Telegram. 77:10. Mr. 31, '45. Big three voting power; editorial.

*New York World-Telegram. 77:17. Ap. 3, '45. Stettinius' statement on conference.

Newsweek. 23:37. Je. 12, '44. Mr. Hull doesn't like to be scolded; liberty and the small nations. E. K. Lindley.

*Newsweek. 24:49. O. 23, '44. The practical means of peace. Ernest K. Lindley.

Newsweek. 24:38+. D. 25, '44. Britain and Russia now striving to build own security system.

Nineteenth Century. 136:193-200. N. '44. New league. F. A. Voight.

Nineteenth Century. 137:43-8. Ja. '45 Old and new security league. T. P. Conwell-Evans.

Pacific Affairs. 14:141-53. Je. '41. After four years—victory for nations or for democracy in European and Asiatic wars? Owen Lattimore.

PM. 5:2. Mr. 18, '45. PM's poll of U.S. senators indicate battle of peace far from won. J. A. Wechsler, Elizabeth Donahue, and J. T. Moutoux.

PM. 5:2. Mr. 25, '45. Mexico City adds up to this.

Reader's Digest. 43:1-14. D. '43. American internationalism: America should join the world and be more American than ever. William Hard.

Rotarian. 65:12-14. D. '44. Dumbarton Oaks and after. V. M. Dean.

Scholastic. 45:12. O. 30, '44. Dumbarton Oaks finals.

Survey Graphic. 34:5. Ja. '45. Dumbarton hopes. E. A. Mowrer.

Talks. 9:3-6. Ap. '44. World federation. Ely Culbertson.

Talks. 9:28-9. Ap. '44. United in war and peace. H. J. Van Mook.

Thought. 17:211. Je. '42. The strategy of the coming peace. F. Baerwald.

Time. 43:11-12. Je. 12, '44. Great blueprint: world organization to keep the peace.

Time. 44:19. O. 16, '44. Warning; Dumbarton Oaks proposals. J. F. Dulles.

*United Nations Review. 5:4-6. Ja. 15, '45. Excerpts from a statement by Australian Minister for External Affairs, Herbert V. Evatt.
Issued monthly by the United Nations Information Office. New York. Contains official statements by leaders of United Nations (chiefly European) on current international developments; texts of all important agreements and other documents.

*United States News. p. 24-6. O. 20, '44. Plan for world security.

Vital Speeches. 10:370-2. Ap. 1, '44. Sovereignty not impaired by world federation. F. G. Tyrrell.

Vital Speeches. 10:492-5. Je. 1, '44. Post-war peace organization of nations; are administrative foreign policies making formation difficult? R. A. Taft.

Vital Speeches. 10:495-9. Je. 1, '44. How much international government do we want? A. J. Peaslee.

Vital Speeches. 10:593-601. Jl. 15, '44. We are losing the battle for collective security; power politics emerging as American foreign policy. W. G. Carleton.

Vital Speeches. 11:106-8. D. 1, '44. Dumbarton Oaks proposals. E. C. Wilson.

Vital Speeches. 11:205-9. Ja. 15, '45. Maintaining world peace and security; methods available to security council. J. C. Grew.

Vital Speeches. 11:230-9. F. 1, '45. Solidarity of three great powers; the war and foreign policies; address to House of Commons, Ja. 18, '45. Winston Churchill.

Vital Speeches. 11:246-9. F. 1, '45. Collaboration must be practical; American generalities no advance over isolationism. J. F. Dulles.

World Affairs. 107:78. 1944. French colonial policy. Raoul Aglion.
Issued monthly by the American Peace Society, Washington, D.C. Contains articles on nearly every phase of peace organization and international relations.

World Affairs. 107:100. 1944. Anglo-American cooperation in the Caribbean. Sir Frank Stockdale.

World Affairs. 107:107. 1944. Collaboration by the U.S. with the British Commonwealth. Charles L. Wheeler.

*World Affairs. 107:237-51. D. '44. The Dumbarton Oaks proposals.

*World Federation Now. 6:2. N. '44. Dumbarton Oaks.

Date Due

SPEECH AND DEBATING

Anthology of Public Speeches. Mabel Platz, comp. 895p. 1940. $3.75.

Selections from speeches representing all cultures from Pericles and Cicero to Chiang Kai-shek and Neville Chamberlain.

Competitive Debate: Rules and Strategy. By George McCoy Musgrave. 128p. 1945. $1.25.

Debate Coaching. By Carroll P. Lahman. (Handbook Series. Ser IV, Vol. 1) 2d rev. ed. 428p. 1936. $2.40.

A manual for teachers and coaches. Especially helpful to the inexperienced coach.

Discussion Methods: Explained and Illustrated. By J. V. Garland and C. F. Phillips (Reference Shelf. Vol. XII, No. 2) 2d ed. rev. 378p. 1940. $1.25.

High School Forensics: An Integrated Program. By Arnold E. Melzer. 153p. 1940. 90c.

How to Debate: A Textbook for Beginners. By H. B. Summers and F. L. Whan. 336p. 1940. $1.25.

Modern Group Discussion: Public and Private. By Lyman and Ellen Judson. (Reference Shelf. Vol. XI, No. 6) 1937. 90c.

Oral Interpretation of Literature in American Colleges and Universities. By Mary Margaret Robb. 242p. 1941. $2.75.

Representative American Speeches. By A. Craig Baird, comp. Published annually in The Reference Shelf. Seven volumes now available from 1937-1938 to 1943-1944 inclusive. Price $1.25 a volume, except that for 1939-1940 which is $1.50.

Each volume contains representative speeches by eminent men and women on public occasions during the year. Each speech is prefaced by a short sketch of the speaker and the occasion.

Selected Readings in Rhetoric and Public Speaking. By Lester Thonssen. comp. 324p. 1942. $3.